DHARMAKĪRTI'S *RŪPĀVATĀRA* — A CRITICAL STUDY

Bibliotheca Indo - Buddhica Series No. 153

DHARMAKĪRTI'S *RŪPĀVATĀRA* — A CRITICAL STUDY

DR. K.S. LALITHAMBAL

Sri Satguru Publications
A Division of
Indian Books Centre
Delhi - India

Published by :
SRI SATGURU PUBLICATIONS
Indological and Oriental Publishers
A Division of
INDIAN BOOKS CENTRE
40/5, Shakti Nagar,
Delhi-110007
(INDIA)

First Edition : Delhi, 1995

ISBN 81-7030-437-7

PRINTED IN INDIA

Dedicated

To the sacred memory of

my beloved parents

Pandit. Sri. K.N. Subrahmania Sastry

and

Smt. N.S. Meenakshi Ammal

Contents

Foreword

Of recent Pāṇini's grammar has evoked a fresh interest in the minds not only of linguists but also of scientists in different areas such as the natural sciences and the computer science, mainly because of his refined methodology. His derivational approach to Sanskrit language is one of the prominent aspects of his descriptive technique. However, his grammar, formulated in a pithy *sūtra*-style governed by the dictates of Anuvṛtti remained beyond the reach of common students of grammar even in the past. Its study received a flow because of its concise character. It lost its position and popular school grammars which could cater to the needs of different groups of students arose in the course of time. In the 10/11th century a Buddhist Pandit, Dharmakīrti undertook the task of remoulding Pāṇini's grammar as a reply to the classroom needs and presented it in the form of a series of formations of words entitled Rupāvatāra. This new appearance of Pāṇini succeeded in popularizing and establishing, once again, the Pāṇinian tradition in the Indian system of education. The emergence of the Rupāvatāra lay foundation of a new teaching methodology in Pāṇinian School which culminated in the Vaiyākaraṇa Siddhāntakaumudi of Bhattoji Dīkṣita. The method popularly known as the Prakriyā method has been the popular method of studying Pāṇini since its emergence. Since the reestablishment of Pāṇinian tradition in the history of the study of Sanskrit grammar is due to the introduction of the *prakriyā* method. Rupāvatāra which serves as a gate-way to this method occupies an important position in the study of Pāṇinian grammatical tradition.

The present work, which is a critical study of this important text, fulfils the longfelt desideratum for a good, complete work dealing with Rupāvatāra, with all its aspects. The author deserves compliments for her comprehensive approach. Her study of the text reflected in this book has a wider significance than it appears to have. For instance, the variant readings in the *sūtrapāṭha* as well as the *Vārttikapāṭha* recorded by her as well as the comparison of the text with other important Pāṇinian grammatical texts like the *Kāśikā* and the *Siddhāntakaumudī* are very important contributions of the author which are useful for the historical study of Pāṇini's grammar. The scholarly and thorough approach to the text with critical acumen is reflected in the book. I strongly believe, the book will be a welcome addition to the shelf of Pāṇinian studies.

(Dr. Saroja Bhate)

Pune,
7-1-1995.

Head of the Dept. of Sanskrit,
University of Poona.

Preface

Rūpāvatāra is the first work composed in the *prakriyā* style of treatment of the sutras of *Aṣṭādhyāyī* and is written by Dharmakīrti, a Buddhist philosopher. The work aims to bring within the easy grasp of the students of grammar, the accomplishment of the vocabulary of Sanskrit language by means of the *Aṣṭādhyāyī* of Pāṇini. To secure this purpose, the method adopted by the author shows his originality and this is well acknowledged by the fact that his successors in the field of grammar began to copy his method of forming recasts of *Aṣṭādhyāyī* for the easy understanding of the *pariniṣṭhitarūpa* (fully furnished form). As one, who invented for the first time a new style of treatment of *Aṣṭādhyāyī*, Dharmakīrti no doubt occupies an enviable status among the Sanskrit grammarians and his work too, stands as a torch beconing a new path of approach in the study of the sutras of *Aṣṭādhyāyī*.

The present book is the printed form of my Doctoral thesis 'Rūpāvatāra—A Critical Study'. The study of Rūpāvatāra was undertaken by me in 1980 at the instance of late Dr. S. Venkitasubramonia Iyer who had been the Professor and Head of the Department of Sanskrit, University of Kerala and was executed under the guidance of Dr. E. Easwaran Nampoothiry who was then the Reader in Sanskrit, in the University of Kerala. I am thankful to the authorities of the University of Kerala for granting me the permission to publish my doctoral thesis. I also express my sincere thanks to Dr. (Mrs.) Saroja Bhate, Professor and Head of the Department of Sanskrit, University of Poona, Pune for contributing a foreword for the book.

In this book I have given the results of my close study of Rūpāvatāra. The study has made me to go into the depth of this work and has led me to the conclusion that the study of Rūpāvatāra is essential for a beginner of Pāninian grammar and

My obligations are due to Indian Books Centre, for the neat and quick printing of the book.

Ernakulam,
14th January, 1995.

Dr. (Miss) K.S. Lalithambal

Abbreviations

Ast	Aṣṭādhyāyī of Pāṇini
BD	Bhaṭṭoji Dīkṣita
DK	Dharmakīrti
Dpp	Dhātupratyayapañcikā
K	Kāśikāvṛtti of Jayāditya and Vāmana
KAT	Kātyāyana
K.S.C.	Kerala Sahitya Caritram of Ullur S. Parameswara Iyer
K.S.S.C	Kerala Samskrta Sahitya Caritram of Rajarajavarma, Vatakkumkur
Mbh	Mahābhāsya of Patañjali
PAN	Pāṇini
PAT	Patañjali
PK	Prakriyākaumudī of Rāmachandra
PS	Prakriyāsarvasva of Nārāyaṇa Bhaṭṭa
Rep	Repetition
Rup P-I,	Rūpāvatāra Part-I,
P-II	Part-II
Rang	Rangacharya
SK	Siddhāntakaumudī of Bhaṭṭoji Dīkṣita
T.C.	A Descriptive Catalogue of the Sanskrit Manuscripts in the Curator's Office Library, Trivandrum.
T.P.	A Descriptive Catalogue of the Sanskrit Manuscripts in H.H. The Maharaja's Palace Library, Trivandrum.
VAK	Vākyapadīya of Bhartṛhari
Var, Vars	Vārtika, Vartikas

Introduction

Vyākaraṇa, the most prominent of the six vedangas has been studied with great zeal in ancient India. Among the different systems of Sanskrit grammar that arose in India, the school of Pāṇini is the most outstanding and the most popular. Pāṇini (c. 600 B.C.) the author of *Aṣṭādhyāyī*, Kātyāyāna (c. 500 to 350 B.C.) the author of the vartikas and Patañjali (c. 150 B.C.) the author of *Mahābhāṣya* are traditionally known as *'munitraya'* who gave the law to the science of grammar.

The *Kāśikā* of Jayāditya and Vāmana of the 7th century A.D. is the fullest commentary on *Aṣṭādhyāyī*. The rules of *Aṣṭādhyāyī* are arranged in such a manner that only after a careful study of *Aṣṭādhyāyī*, one acquires knowledge of the various topics of grammar and hence the students of Pāṇini were not satisfied with the exhaustive commentaries like *Kāśikā* which explained the rules in the order of *Aṣṭādhyāyī* itself. An attempt was therefore made to recast the sutras of Pāṇini according to the subjects treated therein. The works, which are the outcome of this subject-wise treatment of *Aṣṭādhyāyī*, are better known as *Prakriyā* works and proved most suitable to the changing needs of the hour because Sanskrit was no longer a spoken language. *Rūpāvatāra* is the earliest work of this type. It is followed by later works like *Prakriyāratna* of unknown authorship (c. 13th century A.D.), Rūpamālā of Vimalasarasvati (c. 13th Century A.D.), *Prakriyākaumudī* of Rāmacandra (15th century A.D.), Prakriyāsarvasva of Nārāyaṇa Bhaṭṭa (16th-17th century A.D.) and *Siddhāntakaumudī* of Bhaṭṭoji Dīkṣita (16th-17th century A.D.).

The present study is divided into three parts. Part I 'GENERAL,' consisting of three chapters, aims at introducing the author and his work. Chapter I is concerned with Dharmakīrti with particular reference to his authorship, identity and date. Chapter II gives a description of the work with main reference to its origin, title, contents, sources and commentaries. The characteristic features of the work as well as its defects and drawbacks are elaborated in chapter III. PART II is termed 'ANALYTICAL STUDY' and contains chapters IV to VII. The text is analysed in all its details in this part. Chapters IV and V are meant for examining the treatment of the science of grammar by Dharmakīrti with particular regard to the interpretation, illustration of sutras and the like. Chapter VI examines the readings of the sutras and discusses the vartikas while Chapter VII is concerned with the verses of *Rūpāvatāra*, a meritorious feature of the work. Part III 'OBSERVATIONS' comprehends Chapters VIII and IX. A comparative study of *Rūpāvatāra* with *Kāśikā* and later recasts like *Siddhāntakaumudī* is attempted in Chapter VIII and Chapter IX sums up the results of this critical study and concludes with an attempt to evaluate the work. The appendix, comprehending 1. List of rules of *Aṣṭādhyāyī* interpreted in *Rūpāvatāra*, and 2. List of rules of *Aṣṭādhyāyī* referred to in *Rūpāvatāra*, has got great bearing on this thesis since it gives an analytical outline of this recast of *Aṣṭādhyāyī*.

In this book, an attempt has been made to bring out all the meritorious as well as defective aspects of the work which is the first outcome of *prakriyā* style of treatment of the rules of *Aṣṭādhyāyī* and consequently it has been established that Dharmakīrti deserves high esteem for the creation of this recast ad that, to a beginner of Sanskrit grammar expounded by Pāṇini, this work is a better asset than any other one in the field.

PART I
GENERAL

Chapter 1

Dharmakīrti - The Author

Dharmakīrti, the well-known Buddhist philosopher is the author of *Rūpāvatāra.* He is accredited with the initiation of a new style of treatment of the sutras of *Aṣṭādhyāyī* of Pāṇini, viz. the *prakriyā* style. It was Dharmakīrti who framed the first recast of *Aṣṭādhyāyī* which played no less an important role in the study of *Aṣṭādhyāyī* afterwards. He is followed in this task by later authors, like Vimalasarasvati of the 13th century A.D., Rāmacandra of the 15th century A.D. and Nārāyaṇa Bhaṭṭa and Bhaṭṭoji Dīkṣita of the 17th century A.D. in whose hands the recasts of *Aṣṭādhyayī* got more and more modification and perfection. But, the credit for having first conceived the idea of such a recast of *Aṣṭādhyāyī* and carried it into execution, certainly goes to Dharmakīrti, the author of *Rūpāvatāra.* However, there is a controversy regarding the authorship of the work as well as the identity and date of the author with which we are now concerned.

Authorship of the work

There is difference of opinion regarding the authorship of the work. According to A.C. Burnell, a great scholar, one Kṛṣṇadīkṣita is the author of *Rūpāvatāra.*[1] The famous scholar Gustav Opert also refers to this Kṛṣṇadīkṣita as the author of *Rup.*[2] Professor Rangacharya who has made an excellent edition of *Rup,* has established in his introduction that DK himself is the author of *Rup.*[3] He says that DK's authorship of the work is known in many ways. He points out that the verse,

kṛtā sukṛitinā ceyam prakriyā dharmakīrtinā
potānām potavat kṣipram sabdābdhau pāragāminām //

seen in the beginning of the work printed in the Durbar Library, Nepal makes clear that DK is the author of *Rup.*[4] So also in the commentary of the work in Trivandrum Manuscripts Library, the commentator praises the author thus :[5]

abhigataṣaḍabhi jñaprakriyopi svayam yaḥ
prathamasamayasajjadvāsanāvāsitātmā /
akalayadatihṛdyam śabdavidyānumodam
sa jayati navakīrtiḥ sanmato dharmakīrtiḥ / /

In the Mss. which Rang got from Kṛṣṇa Śāstrī, Head of the Dept. of Sanskrit in the Pachayappa College, also, DK is said to be the author of *Rup*, in the line *'iti dharmakīrtiviracite rūpāvatāre kṛdantakhaṇḍam samāptam.'*[6] By giving ample evidence Rang also confirms that *Dhātupratyayapañcikā* is the second part of *Rup*. *Dpp* contains the introductory verse,

praṇamya śirasā devīm bālānām hitakāriṇīm /
yathāsāram pravakṣyāmi dhātupratyayapañcikām / /

and has the colophon *'iti rūpāvatāraḥ samaptaḥ.'*[7] Moreover, in one of the Mss. of *Dpp* the name *'Rūpāvatāra'* is given in the beginning.[8] DK's authorship of *Dpp* also, is known from the colophon *'ityācāryamiśradharmakīrtiviracite tiṅantakhaṇḍe saptamaḥ paricchedaḥ samāptaḥ.'*[9] From these evidences it is clear that DK himself is the author of *Rup*.

Identity of the author

DK, the author of *Rup* was a Buddhist. But, we find that K.V. Abhyankar in his *'Dictionary of Sanskrit Grammar'* refers to him as a Jain scholar.[10] That DK was a Buddhist, is known from the second introductory verse in which he pays homage to *sarvajña* i.e. Buddha.[11] Now, we have to determine which DK was the author of *Rup* as there are several Buddhist monks known by the name DK. Rang elaborately deals with this topic in his introduction to the edition of the work. He comes to the conclusion that the author of *Rup*, is different from the famous logician DK and also another DK who is referred to by Ānandavardhana in his *Dhvanyāloka.*[12] He further points out that there are no ample evidences to prove that the DK referred to by the author of *Dhvanyāloka*, is different from the famous logician DK. Even if we do not accept their identity, we cannot attribute the authorship of *Rup* to them since it is sure that they lived much earlier than the author of *Rup*. Among these the name of DK who was a logician is quoted by Mādhavācārya in his *Sarvadarśanasaṅgraha* while describing the *Yogācāramata* of Buddhism.[13] Scholars are of opinion that it is this DK who is referred to as the *pūrvapakṣin* by Śankarācārya while explaining the rule *'nābhāva upalabdheḥ.'*[14] Hence, this DK (logician) must have lived much earlier than Śankarācārya. Many modern scholars also are of opinion that the DK lived much earlier. The great scholar Satish Chandra Vidyabhusan states that this DK flourished during the time of Diṅnāga. He also points out that the Chinese traveller I-sing also is of opinion that this DK lived before the 7th century.[15]

DK quoted by Dhvanikāra, was a poet and rhetorician. Many verses written by this Bhadanta DK are seen in the *Subhāṣitāvalī.*[16] The name Bhadanta shows that he was treated with great respect. Rang turns our attention to an indirect reference to this DK in the *Vāsavadattā* of Subandhu. In that work we get the description of *Vāsavadattā* as *'Baudhasaṅgatimivālaṅkarabhūṣitām.'* The great scholar Durgaprasāda states that this is explained as *'Baudhasaṅgatirnāma Dharmakīrtikṛto granthaviśeṣaḥ'* by Sivarāma, the ṭikākāra of the work. From this it is clear that according to Subandhu the work was well-knitted with the alankaras. Since Subandhu's name has been mentioned by Baṇa in the beginning of *Harṣacarita,* he must have lived before the 7th century and the Bhadanta DK must have lived even before that. Thus we see that both of these (DK, the logician and DK, the rhetorician) lived before the 7th century A.D. Rang opines that as both of them thus belong to the same period, their identity can also be well determined. Pointing out the great scholar Diṅnāga as an example, Rang confirms the probability of one having the same qualities of logician, rhetorician and poet. Thus the author of *Rup* who is assigned to a later priod than 7th century A.D. is a Buddhist different from the logician and rhetorician by name DK, whether these latter two, who lived before the 7th century A.D., be identical or not.[17]

Rang identifies the author of *Rup* with the DK who was a contemporary of the Ceylonese King Prathamaparākramabāhu. From the *'Mahāvamśa'* a work which deals with the life of the Ceylonese kings, we know that this king was an ardent Buddhist and he appointed a great Buddhist saint by name Mahākāśyapa, the *Saṅghasthavira.*[18] This Mahākāśyapa was a great grammarian and the work *Bālāvabodhana* written by him following the *Cāndravyākaraṇa* is even now studied in Ceylon. It is held that a scholar by name Saṅgharājadharmakirti, a student of the disciple of Mahākāśyapa has written a work by name *Bālāvatāra*, a grammar of the Pali Language.[19] Moreover, it is known from '*Mahāvamśa*' itself that there was a scholar by name DK in the assembly of Prathamaparākramabāhu.[20] Rang opines that this DK may be the same one known by the name Saṅgharāja, who is the author of *Bālāvatāra* and attributes the authorship of *Rup* to this Dharmakīrti.

The view of Rang that DK, the author of *Rup*, is identical with DK the author of *Bālāvatāra* can be clearly refuted on the basis of the facts brought to light by the famous scholar Wikremsinghe. While preparing the catalogues of Sinhalese books and Mss. in the British Museum, Wikremsinghe says that he had come across the name Dharmakīrti Thera as the author of several ancient works in the Bali and Sinhalese languages.[21] In his opinion there are no less than five Buddhist monks, bearing this name, who distinguished themselves as authors and held att different times high positions in the Buddhist order. The fifth one among these Dharmakirtis is the author of *Bālāvatāra*. The earliest of these five, was Dharmakīrti Thera a pupil of Śārīputta of Polonnarura who was a great scholar of many works in Pali and who lived at Polonnarura during the reign of King Parākramabāhu, the Great (1164-97 A.D.). "This Dharmakirti" says Wikremsinghe, "whom we call 'the first' was the composer of the well-known Pali poem, *Dāthāvamśa* on the tooth-relic of Buddha." He wrote it at the request of the minister Parākrama, who restored Līlāvati the widow of Parākramabāhu, the Great, to the throne in 1211 A.D. Since this DK of the 12th century A.D. who comes first in the list is not the author of *Bālāvatāra* and if he be the author of *Rup* as pointed out by Rang, we can well assume that DK the author of *Rup* is different from DK the author of *Bālāvatāra*.

Again, the fifth DK mentioned by Wikremsinghe, is said to be the author of about six important works including *Bālāvatāra*.[22] He was also called Devarakṣita or Jayabahu Maha Thera who lived during the reign of Bhuvanekabāhu and Vīrabāhu III (1372-1410).

If it is this DK the author of *Bālāvatāra* whom Rang refers to as the author of *Rup* the same also can be refuted since according to Rang, DK, the author of *Rup* lived in the latter half of the 12th century A.D. and this DK the author of *Bālāvatāra*, lived in the 14th century A.D. Hence it is clear that DK the author of *Rup* is not identical with DK, the author of *Bālāvatāra*. Though Rang identifies the author of *Rup* with the author of *Bālāvatāra*, he admits the absence of a more reliable authority for the same.[23]

Rang says that, from the former part of the introductory verse,

'abhigataṣaḍabhijñaprakriyopi svayam yaḥ

prathamasamayasajjadvāsanāvāsitatmā . . . .'

of the commentary of *Rup*, it seems that the author was at first a Brahmin, well-versed in the Vedas, who later on became a Buddhist.[24] Further he adds that the wide popularity of the work in Kerala and Tamil Nadu gives a Ceylonese origin for the work.[25] The fact, that DK was at first a Brahmin who later on became a Buddhist, also leads one to think that the name *Kṛṣṇadīkṣita* mentioned in some of the Mss. may be perhaps the author's name when he was at first a Brahmin who might have later assumed the title DK when he became a Buddhist. That he salutes Goddess in the introductory verse, 'praṇamya śirasā devīm . . . *pañeikām*,' found in *Dpp*, also favours the view that he was originally a Brahmin.[26] If this view be correct, DK can be treated as one whose native land was India. Venkatesha Sastri Joshi refers to DK as one who flourished in the region of Bengal.[27] In the absence of more reliable sources it is not possible to give more specific details about his nativity, life etc.

Date of the author

There is a great controversy regarding the date of DK. Scholars assign different dates to him. Rang accepts the possibility of a period ranging from the 9th to the 13th century A.D. and assigns him to the latter half of the 12th century A.D. According to Srish Chandra Chakravarty, DK lived in the beginning of the 11th century A.D. whereas Yudhisthira Mimamsaka is of the view that DK belongs to the latter half of the 11th century A.D., the lower limit being 1083/4 A.D. Nīlakaṇṭha Śāstri takes 7th and 10th century A.D. as the upper and lower limit to fix the date of DK and favours the view that he belongs to the 10th century A.D. George Cardona holds a similar opinion in as much as he assigns DK to the 10th century A.D. Now we are to discuss the views of these scholars.

Rang assigns DK to a period between 9th and 13th century A.D. He has arrived at this conclusion on the basis of the following reasons. DK, the author of *Rup* follows *Kāśikā* very much and hence he must have lived after Jayāditya and Vāmana, the authors of K.[28] According to I-tsing, Jayāditya and Vāmana lived in the second half of the 7th century A.D.[29] The exact date of the completion of the work by Vāmana is indefinite. Modern scholars are of opinion that *K* might have been probably completed in the 8th or 9th century A.D. In the *Dpp*, the second part of *Rup*, also we get the names of Haradatta and Jinendrabuddhi, the commentators on the *K*.[30] Hence DK must have lived after the 9th century A.D. Gauraṇārya, the author of *Lakṣaṇadīpikā* quotes *Rup* while dealing with the *sthāna* of letters :

> 'atha varṇasthānāni rūpāvatāre :
> aṣṭau sthānāni varṇānāmuraḥ kaṇṭhaḥ śirastathā /
> jihvāmūlaśca dantāśca nāsikoṣṭhau ca tālu ca / /

Rang points out that Gauraṇārya can be assigned to the first half of the 14th century A.D. and since *Rup* has been mentioned by Gauraṇārya the date of DK must be earlier than that of Gauraṇārya.[31] Moreover Maitreyarakṣita mentions the name of *Rup* in his *Tantrapradīpa*.[32] We get a reference to Maitreyarakṣita in the *Mādhavīyadhātuvṛtti* of Sāyaṇa.[33] Hence Maitreyarakṣita might have lived before Sāyaṇa who has been assigned to the middle of the 14th century A.D. As *Rup* has been quoted by Maitreyarakṣita DK must have lived before the 13th century A.D.

Thus after fixing the upper and lower age limit of DK as the 9th and 13th century A.D., Rang puts the author of *Rup* in the latter half of the 12th century A.D. There was a Buddhist scholar by name DK who was a contemporary of the Ceylonese king Prathamaparākramabāhu and this DK is regarded as the author of *Rup* by Rang. From the *Mahāvamśa* a work which deals with the life of the Ceylonese kings it is understood the Prathamaparākramabāhu lived in the latter half of the 12th century A.D. and that there was a scholar by name DK in the assembly of this king Prathamaparākramabāhu. Attributing the authorship of *Rup* to this DK, Rang fixes his date as the latter half of the 12th century A.D.

K.V. Abhyankar mentions DK, *Dpp* and *Rup* in three places (according to their alphabetical order) in his *Dictionary of Sanskrit Grammar*. While dealing with DK, he says that DK is a Jain scholar called by the name Kīrti also who was the author of *Dpp* and *Rup*, but he does not mention anything about the date of DK in that context.[34] However he makes a contradictory statement about the date of DK while dealing with *Dpp* and *Rup*. For, while referring to *Dpp*, he states that it is a work dealing with verbal forms written by DK, a Jain grammarian of the 8th century A.D.; but while referring to *Rup* he says that it is a well-known work on word formation written by DK a Jain grammarian of the 12th century A.D.[35]

Srish Chandra Chakravarti who has edited the *Dhātupradīpa* of Maitreyarakṣita assigns DK to the beginning of the 11th century A.D.[36] He points out that Maitreya who is the author of *Dhātupradīpa* and *Tantrapradīpa* refers to *Rup* in both of them. Since Maitreyarakṣita refers to the *Bhāsyaṭīkā* of Kaiyaṭa also in his *Tantrapradīpa* S.C. Chakravarti comes to the conclusion that the date of Maitreyarakṣita cannot be earlier than that of Kaiyaṭa or of DK. As it is said that Kaiyaṭa was a kinsman or pupil of Mammaṭabhaṭṭa, S.C. Chakravarti states that he lived at about 1050 A.D. and opines that DK too flourished at the beginning of the 11th century A.D.

Yudhisthira Mimamsaka says that a Buddhist scholar by name DK is the author of *Rup*.[37] He also states that this DK, is different from the famous DK who is the author of *Nyāyabindu*. He fixes the date of DK at about 1083/4 A.D. on the basis of the following reasons :

1. Śaraṇadeva in his *Durghaṭavṛtti* has mentioned both *Rup* and DK. *Durghaṭavṛtti* is written in Śaka Year 1095 and Samvat 1230.[38]
2. Hemacandra in his *Svopajñavivarana* of *Liṅgānuśāsana* has mentioned *Rup* and DK.[39] The date of Hemacandra's work is intermediate between Samvat 1193-1200.[40]
3. The name *Rup* has been mentioned in the *Dhātupradīpa* of Maitreyarakṣita.[41] The date of Maitreya is at about Samvat 1165. Yudhisthira Mimamsaka says that this is the lower age limit of DK.
4. DK in his *Rup* has cited the name of Haradatta, the author of *Padamañjarī*.[42] The date of Haradatta is at about Samvat 1115. This has been taken as the upper age limit of DK by Yudhisthira. Thus he puts DK approximately at Samvat 1140 i.e., 1083/84 A.D. But, he

states that the date of Haradatta is only inferred and if his date is earlier, then the date of DK will also be earlier.

Nīlakaṇṭha Śāstri says that the place of Rup as the beginner's manual of Sanskrit Grammar had become well established much earlier than the 14th century.[43] He points out many Cola inscriptions mentioning the study of *Rup*, as part of the curriculum of higher Sanskrit schools. The ennayiram inscriptions of the reign of Rajendra (1012-1044) makes provision for feeding forty pupils who learn Rup "rūpāvatāram kētpār naṟpadiṉmar" and for the maintenance of one teacher (rūpāvatāram vakkāṇippāṉ oruvaṉ) on a salary of three 'kuṟuṇis' of paddy per diem and one half of a 'kaḻañju' of gold per annum. A similar provision is made at Tribhuvaṇi for the maintenance of a teacher of *Rup* in a College during the reign of Rājādhirāja I, the successor of Rājēndra I : "rūpāvatāraṅ-kēṭpippāṉ oruvaṉukku nel tūṇip-padakkum", a wage twice as much as in the record cited above, the same inscription provided again for the feeding of thirty pupils studying this work - "rūpāvatāraṅkēṭpār muppadiṉmar." It is worth mentioning that both these inscriptions state that there were other students and teachers in each of these colleges pursuing the study of advanced grammar (*Vyākaraṇa*). Yet another record dated A.D. 1067 gives details relating to a third educational institution at Tirumukkūḍal. Here both *Vyākaraṇa* and *Rup* were taught by a single teacher who was paid a daily wage of one 'tūṇi' and ten 'kāśus' apparently in the year : "vyākaraṇam rūpāvatāram vakkāṇikkum bhaṭṭaṉ oruvaṉukku nāḷonrukku nel tūṇiyum kāśu pattum." His pupils numbered twenty in all. "Vyākaraṇamum rūpāvatāramum kēṭkum brāhmaṇac-cāttirar irupadiṇmarum." Pointing out these instances Nīlakaṇṭha Śāstri says that the popularity of *Rup* dates back at least to the 11th century. Hence he says that the Ceylonese monk DK who was the contemporary of Parākramabāhu I (latter half of the 12th century A.D.) could not have been the author of *Rup* as held by Rang.

Rang in his introduction to *Rup* mentions a reference to this work of DK, in the commentary written by Guṇasāgara to the "*yāpparuṅgala-k-kārikai*" of Amitasāgara. Commenting on this Nīlakaṇṭha Śāstri says "it is noteworthy that Rang also noticed another reference to *Rup* though he missed its significance."[44] He quotes the whole passage in the commentary of Guṇasāgara, where we get the reference to *Rup* and gives its translation. The passage contains many reasons for having given the title "*Yāpparuṅgala-k-kārikai*" for the work. One of the reasons, is that it contains 'leading stanzas' (nītaka-śloka) just as those in *Rup* (urūpāvatārattiṟku nītakacculōkamē).[45] Nīlakaṇṭha Śāstri continues, "Now, the date of Guṇasagara, the disciple and younger contemporary of Amitasāgara, has been settled with great probability to be the early part of the eleventh century, (4. Journal of Indian History, Vol. v, pp. 204-9), that is about the same time as the inscriptions cited above. It should be noted that Dhammakitti (Dharmakīrti) is a very common name among Buddhist monks, and without more specific details about the author of the *Rūpāvatāra* than we seem to have now, it will not be possible to determine his exact date."[46] Thus Nīlakaṇṭha Śāstri points out that DK must be earlier than the 11th century A.D. He also states that the "*Rūpāvatāra*" mentioned in the "*yāpparuṅgala-k-kārikai*" and *Cola inscriptions,* is the work of Dharmakīrti on Sanskrit Grammar and not the *Prākṛtarūpāvatāra* of Simharāja. The absence of any verses in the *Prākṛtarūpāvatāra* which could be referred to as '*nītaka* slokas', and the citation by Siṃharāja of Kṣīrasvāmin, an eleventh century writer, convert the presumption into a certainty.[47] It is possible that the *Prākṛtarūpāvatāra,* as its name implies, had the work of DK for its model. Thus Nīlakaṇṭha Śāstri puts back the lower limit, for the date of *Rūpāvatāra* from the twelfth to the tenth century. He also says that the upper limit is also much earlier than the 9th century, for *K* appears to have been completed not in the 9th century as Rang held, but sometimes in the 7th century, a commentary on that work having been composed at about 700 A.D.[48]

George Cardona in his *Panini — A Survey of Research* refers to DK, the author of *Rup* as a Ceylonese Buddhist.[49] He says that *Rup* is quoted by the Jain grammarian Hemacandra (1088-1172) and by Maitreya Rakṣita as well as by Śaraṇadeva. These facts support a date of about 1100. He adds, however there is some inscriptional evidence which would indicate that the *Rup* was included in the grammatical curriculum of schools established by the king Rājendra Cola in the 11th century and on the basis of this evidence *Rup* could be placed in the 10th century.

Thus we can see that the famous scholars, Srish Chandra Chakravarti, Yudhisthira Mimamsaka, Nīlakaṇṭha Śāstri and George Cardona assign DK to a period much earlier than Rang's conclusion which takes DK to the latter half of the 12th century A.D. The inscriptional evidence pointed out by Nīlakaṇṭha Śāstri which throws light on the fact, that *Rup* was included in the grammatical curriculum of schools established by the King Rājendra Cola in the eleventh century, is of great importance in fixing the date of DK. On the basis of this information DK can be assigned to the 10th century A.D.

Notes and References

1. Vide Classified Index to the Sanskrit Mss. in the Palace at Tanjore, p. 41b.
2. Vide The List of Sanskrit Mss. in the Private Libraries of Southern India, Vol. I, Nos. 2991, 5152 & 5826.
3. *Rup* Part I, pp. i to xix.
4. Vide Catalogue of Palmleaf and Selected Paper Mss. belonging to the Durbar Library, Nepal, p. 60 under No. 1475.
5. Vide infra pp. 7 & 8.
6. *Rup* Part 1, p. ii.
7. Vide Mss. No. 1332, Descriptive Catalogue of the Sanskrit Mss. Government Oriental Mss. Library, Madras.
8. Ibid, Mss. No. 1335.
9. Vide Rajendralala Mitra Notices of the Sanskrit Mss. 1882-83, Vol. VII, Part I, *Dpp*, No. 2390.
10. Vide infra p. 8.
11. Sarvajñamanantaguṇam praṇamya bālaprabodhanārthamidam /
    rūpāvatāramalpam sukalāpamṛjum kariṣyāmi / /
12. *Rup* Part I, pp. iv to vi.
13. eṣā hi teṣām paribhāṣā—svayamvedanam tāvadaṅgīkāryam anyathā jagadāndhyam prasajyeta / tat kīrtitam dharmakirtinā "apratyakṣopalambhasya nārthadṛṣṭiḥ prasidhyati' iti" (p. 32)
14. Vedantasutras II - 2-28.
15. Vide 'The Buddhist Version of the Nyaya Philosophy,' *Journal of the Buddhist Text and Research Society*, Vol. VII, Part IV, March 1906, p. 6.

16. Vide *Rup* Part I footnote (p.v.) : - "In the introduction to his edition of the *Subhāṣitāvalī*, Peterson, in remarking about Bhadanta-Dharmakīrti, quotes Aufrecht thus : 'Dharmakīrti is one of the older writers on Alaṅkāra. His work *'Baudhasaṅgati'* is mentioned by Subandhu in the *Vāsavadattā*. In all probability he is identical with the Buddhist philosopher of the same name, who, according to Wasiljew, wrote a commentary to Diṅnaga's *Pramāṇa-samaccaya*.... A half verse by the philosophical writer is mentioned in the Bauddha chapter of the *Sarvadarśanasaṅgraha*.' "
17. Vide infra pp. 7 & 8.
18. Vide L.C. Wijesimha Mudaliar, Translation of the Second part of *Mahāvamśa*, Chapter LXXVIII.
19. Vide Rambukpota Pannasara, Introduction to the *Bālāvabodhana* of Mahākāśyapa, p. ii last para.
20. Vide L.C. Wijesimha Mudaliar, Translation of the Second Part of *Mahāvamsa*, Chapter LXXVI.
21. Vide 'The Several Pali and Sinhalese authors known as Dharmakirti,' J.R.A.S., 1896, p. 200.
22. The other works are *Sabdhammālaṅkāra, Bala Samkhepa, Nikāya-Saṅgaha, Gaduladeni-Sama* and *Saddhammasaṅgaha.*
23. *Rup* Part I, p. xv.
24. Vide Supra p. 4.
25. 'keraleṣu drāviḍeṣu cāsya rūpāvatārasya yat kādācitkam pracārabāhulyam dṛśyate tadapi tadgranthakartuḥ dharmakirteḥ simhalasthatvam sthāpayitumarhati' (*Rup* Part I, p. xv).
26. Vide Supra p. 6.
27. Vide *'Problems in Sanskrit Grammar,'* p. 82.
28. *Rup* Part I, pp. vii & viii, footnote — h.
29. *Rup* Part I, p. vii.
30. "Dīrghānta evāyam haradattābhimataḥ, tadā seṭtvāt 'akuviṣṭa' ityapi bhavati, jinendrastu hrasvāntamevāpāṭhit, tattadā 'akuta' iti bhavati." (*Rup* Part II, p. 157).
31. Rang establishes the date of Gauraṇārya as the first half of the 14th century A.D. in the following manner :

Gauraṇārya in the beginning of *Lakṣaṇadīpikā* gives a description of his own family. In it we get a reference to one Siṅgayamādhavendra as the king of Recallavamśa. From the description of Recallavamśa in the *Rasārṇavasudhākara* of Singabhūpala otherwise known as Sarvajñasimha, we know that Singayamādhavendra was the father of Singabhūpala. That this Singabhūpala was a contemporary of Venkaṭanātha who was well-known by the name Vedāntadeśika is known from the information we get from the *Sāratatvasandeśa* of Vedāntadeśika. It is also said that the Vedāntadeśika by name Nāyiñarya made discussions with the scholars who were contemporaries of Singabhūpala. On the basis of this information and certain other facts Singabhūpala is assigned to the first half of the 14th century A.D. Hence Rang points out that Gauraṇārya can also be assigned to the 14th century A.D.

32. *Rup* Part I, p. x.
33. Vide *Dhātuvṛtti*, Vol. I, Part I, p. 229 published under the authority of the Government of H.H. the Maharaja of Mysore.
34. K.V. Abhyankar cites the following verse to point out that DK is referred to by the name Kīrti :
bopadevamahāgrāhagrasto vāmanadiggajaḥ /
kīrtereva prasaṅgena mādhavena samuddhṛtaḥ / /
(pp. 192 & 193).
35. Op. cit., pp. 194 & 303.
36. Vide Introduction to *Dhātupradīpa*, p. 1.
37. Vide *Vyākaran Śāstr kā itihās*, Part I, pp. 481 & 482.
38. Śaraṇadeva in his *Durghaṭavṛtti* gives the date of composition of the work in the introductory verse :
śākamahīpativatsaramāne ekanabhonavapañcavimāne /
durghaṭavṛttirakārimudeva kaṇṭhavibhūṣaṇahāralateva /
39. "vāḥ vāri rūpāvatāre tu dharmakīrtināsya napumsakatvamuktam," p. 71.
40. Vide *Vyakaraṇ śāstr kā itihās*, Part I, p. 481.
41. "rūpāvatāre tu ṇilope pratyayotpatteḥ prāgeva kṛte satyekāctvād yaṅudāhṛtaścocūryate iti," p. 131.
42. "dīrghānta evāyam haradattābhimataḥ," (Part II, p. 157)

43. Vide "A Note on Rūpāvatāra," *Journal of Oriental Research Institute,* Madras, July-September 1934, pp. 277 to 280.
44. Ibid, p. 278.
45. Vide infra p. 229.
46. Vide 'A Note on Rūpāvātāra,' *Journal of Oriental Research Institute,* Madras July-September 1934, p. 280.
47. Ibid, p. 280, footnote No. 1 :
"*Prākṛtarūpāvatāra*" ed. Hultzseh, viii, ii, p. 37.
48. Vide A.B. Keith — '*Sanskrit Literature,*' p. 430.
49. Ibid, p. 285.

Chapter II

Rūpāvatāra - The Work

Rup, the prototype of the works in the *prakriyā* style of treatment of *Ast*, is noteworthy for the convenience it provides in the study of the Sanskrit language with main reference to the *Ast* of PAN. In this chapter we are to discuss the origin, significance of the title and contents of the work. The aim and scope of the work, its sources and the commentaries on it are also dealt with here.

Origin

A brief survey of the different phases of study in the Paninian school upto the time of *Rup* is relevant here for tracing the origin of this *prakriyā* work.

We know that the study of *Ast* was prevalent in India during the time of I-tsing, a Chinese Traveller of the 7th century A.D., for he says that the Chinese students who came to learn Sanskrit were first made to study *Ast* and then only they were given tuition in other subjects.[1]

PAN composed his rules in the *sūtra* style which is defined as one which brief but unambiguous, concise but comprehensive, impersonal and objective. This style was the fashion of his age and was used for the doctrination of various philosophical and liturgical texts. PAN's style is more specialised than that of the other treatises by its peculiarities like the process of *anuvṛtti*, *adhikāra*, technical terms, paribhasas, the phenomenon of *asidhatva* etc. The *Ast* of PAN has been rightly referred to by L. Bloomfield as 'a monumental work of human intelligence.'[2]

Sanskrit has undergone tremendous changes in the intervals which might have been sufficiently long, between the composition of *Ast* and of the vartikas. For, we know that language always tend to change. Even languages fortified by the most scopeful grammar cannot escape this inexorable process. And when numerous phonetic, semantic and syntactic changes carried the language beyond the reaches of PAN, KĀTYĀYANA of the 2nd century B.C. set himself to writing the vars to the rules of PAN. The vars of KAT are meant to correct, modify or supplement the rules of PAN wherever they were or had become partially or totally inapplicable. S.K. Belvalkar says that, of the nearly 4000 sutras of *Ast*, KAT noticed over 1500 in about 4000 vars.[3] KAT's purpose was not only to doubt the validity of the rules of PAN with reference to the language in use in his time and area but to give alternative modifications to the rules of PAN wherever necessary.

KAT was followed in his task by a vast number of writers but none of these successors are known to us otherwise than through quotations made by PATAÑJALI in his *MAHĀBHĀṢYA*. The *Mbh* is written in a language which is rendered almost unique by the combination of simplicity and vigour, and consisting mainly of dialogues which impart to it an absorbing interest, saving it from the dryness that usually characterises a sastraic commentary. The stand-points, of these two commentators KAT and PAT, are quite different. KAT, as a rule, introduces a modification whenever he finds a *sūtra* insufficient. But, PAT's view of approach is entirely different. PAT first sees whether the *Ast* can be so construed as to yield the requisite meaning and proceeds to supplement or amend it only after being convinced that it cannot. Another important feature of the work is that it contains many maxims derived from day-to-day life in order to tackle problems relating to rules. PAN, KAT and PAT are considered to be the three sages of grammar (*munitrayam*) and the tradition has nicknamed the system as *trimunivyākaraṇam*. With PAT the first period in the development of Sanskrit grammar comes to an end.

The *K* of Jayāditya and Vāmana of the 7th century A.D. marks the peak of the second phase in the development of the Paninian school. *K* is the fullest commentary available on the *Ast* in the same order, explaining every rule and clearly indicating all the anuvrttis and giving numerous illustrations for each rule. It also often gives the vars while discussing the rules. We get two commentaries on *K*, one *Nyāsa* of Jinendrabudhi of the 8th century A.D. and other *Padamañjarī* or Haradatta of the 9th century A.D. To this stage also belongs the *Vākyapadīya* of Bhartṛhari of the 7th century A.D. in which an attempt is made to set up grammar as a system of philosophy. Kaiyaṭa of the 10th century A.D. has written a commentary on *Mbh,* by name *Pradīpa* and with it the second phase in the development of Paninian school comes to an end.

The third phase begins with the *prakriyā* works in Sanskrit grammar. The main problem confronting the authors of the first and second phases was to explain threadbare the rules of *Ast,* to supplement shortcomings and to do away with its superfluousness. In other words their main objective was to bring about perfection of the *Ast* which they fully achieved. Nothing had been left untouched by the writers of grammar and hence there was no occasion for any creative work. Early in the first century A.D. we find in the *Kātantra* grammar of Sarvavarman a subjectwise arrangement of rules. It will not be improper to say that the subjectwise treatment of the *Kātantra* grammar to some extent, influenced the students of grammar which paved the way to the development of *prakriyā* works in the Paninian school. The rules of *Ast* are arranged in such a manner that only after a careful study of *Ast,* one acquires knowledge of the various topics of grammar like *sandhi, samāsa* etc. Those who study a part of it, does not become proficient even in a single topic. For instance, the rules ordaining the various samasas are given in the second chapter while the rules governing the *samāsānta* pratyayas are given in the fifth chapter and the rules dealing with the conditions of *purvanipāta* in samasas are given in the third *pāda* of the sixth chapter. Thus we see that various problems relating to samasas are dealt with in different places. One should study at least six chapters to become proficient in samasas. With the coming of *Kātantra* grammar there arose a trend among the students to turn towards it which enabled a subjectwise study. Hence in order to prevent these, the system of subjectwise treatment was later adopted by the followers of the Paninian school. The students of PAN, not satisfied with the exhaustive commentary of *K* which explained the rules in the order of *Ast* itself, made an attempt to recast the sutras of PAN according to subjects treated therein to facilitate the study of the learner. The works of this phase, better known as *prakriyā* works, proved most suitable to the changing needs of the hour, because Sanskrit was no longer a spoken language and had long left its claim as such. These works distinguish themselves by changing the order of the sutras of *Ast*. The underlying motive of this change, is to secure convenience in word formation as the ultimate purpose of grammar. PAN followed the technique of composing the general (*utsarga*) sutras followed by exceptional (*apavāda*) sutras to them, with many other techniques adopted therein. To the authors of the third phase, on the other hand, the formation of words was the primary consideration and they rearranged the rules of *Ast* under the grammatical topics like *sandhi*, karakas, samasas etc. The *Rup* of DK is the earliest work of this type. It is followed by later works like *Rūpamālā* of Vimalasarasvaty, *Prakriyāratna* of unknown authorship, *PK* of Rāmacandra, *PS* of Nārāyana Bhaṭṭa and *SK* of BD. The *SK* of BD is the best work of this type which became the most popular of all the works of the Paniniam system. But, at the same time it cannot be forgotten that it is the *Rup* of DK that laid the foundation-stone for the latter.

Aim and scope of the work

The aim and scope of the work is explicitly mentioned by the author himself in the second one among the two introductory verses of the work. The verse runs as follows :

> sarvajnamanantaguṇam praṇamya bālaprabodhanārthamidam /
> rūpāvatāramalpam sukalāpamṛjum kariṣyāmi //

In *K* though we get a detailed description of the rules of *Ast*, we find that these rules are dealt with in the order of *Ast* itself. Hence it was not an easy method, especially for the beginners of Sanskrit grammar, to arrive at the rupas or accomplished forms and to understand their *prakriyā*, since the sutras needed to get a particular form (*rūpa*), are scattered in the different chapters of *Ast*. Hence for the beginners of Sanskrit grammar (*bālānām*) the author aims to bring within the limit of this work a concise, well-framed and straight-forward exposition of rupas or accomplished forms, which is achieved as we see, by the rearrangement of the Paninian rules. We thus find that *Rup* is the first attempt in this field and as such, it has succeeded well by making the study of the Paninian grammar easier.

The title of the work

DK has given a significant title to his work. Unlike his illustrious predecessors in the grammatical field, DK was able to cut a profile of his own by viewing the Paninian rules from a quite different angle. In order to make the accomplished forms within the easy reach of the reader, he gave a new frame to the Paninian rules in which they are arranged to introduce the *rūpa* or accomplished form as easy as possible. Thus he gives more stress to the forms (rupas) than to the rules which help to arrive at them. It may be this factor which prompted him to give the title, '*Rūpāvatāra*' to his work. The compound word, '*Rūpāvatāra*' can be explained as : *rūpāṇām avatāraḥ rūpāvatāraḥ. Upacārād rūpāvatāramadhikṛtya kṛto granthopi Rūpāvatāraḥ.*[4] However, it cannot be ignored that the rupas are presented on the basis of the Paninian rules which also have no less an important role in his work. The different sections of *Rup* have got the sub-titles *samjnāvatāra, samhitāvatāra, kṛdantāvatāra,* etc. which also have the same significance.

The second part of *Rup* has got a sub-title as '*Dhātupratyayapañcikā*. According to the sense of the word, the title can mean a part or section in which the five groups of suffixes that are added to roots are dealt with. Hence it can be said that the second part is termed as '*Dhātupratyayapañcikā*' as it deals with the five suffixes *tiṅ, san, ṇic, yaṅ* and *kṛt* which are added to roots. A similar interpretation is given by Adyaprasadamisra.[5] Rang makes a remark : "It goes by the name of *Dhātupratyayapañcikā*, which means that it is a well-ordered exposition of the roots of the language along with their formative and inflectional suffixes as are found in the structure of finite verbs and other primary derivatives."[6]

It seems that *Dpp* has got another title *Tiṅataśiromaṇi*, for, at the end of the *yaṅlukpariccheda* of the second part of *Rup*, we get the colophon 'iti tiṅantaśiromaṇau yaṅlukparicchedaḥ.'[7] '*Tiṅantaśiromaṇi*' means 'that which has got *tiṅanta* as the head-decorating gem' and this title is quite befitting to the second part of *Rup* i.e., *Dpp*, in as-much as all the various sections of the same except the tenth one (*kṛdantāvatāra*), cite tinantarupas. Yudhisthira Mimamsaka points out that in the index kept in the Adayar Sanskrit Library, a manuscript of *dhātupāṭha* is mentioned wherein we get a reference to a work by name *Tiṅantaśiromaṇi* : "tiṅantaśiromaṇirityā dhātavo likhyante."[8] Since in the second part of *Rup*, DK does not mention all the roots, but only a select few of them coming under the ten ganas, this reference can, in all probability, be to the second part of *Rup*.

Contents

The work is divided into two sections *pūrvabhāga* and *uttarabhāga*. The first part (*pūrvabhāga*) contains eight sections which are termed as avataras. They are *samjnāvatāra, samhitāvatāra, vibhaktyavatāra, avyayāvatāra, strīpratyayāvatāra, kārakāvatāra, samāsāvātāra,* and *taddhitāvatāra.* The second part named '*Dhātupratyayapañcika*' opens with a very brief introductory section in which the purpose of the various anubandhas in roots, lakaras and *tiṅ* suffixes, as well as the division of roots, into sakarmakas and akarmakas as also into *parasmaipadin, atmanepadin* and *ubhayapadin,* are given mention. Then follows the ten sections *sārvadhātukapariccheda, ārdhadhātukapariccheda, sannantapariccheda, yaṅantapariccheda, yaṅlukpariccheda, hetumaṇṇic (ṇijanta) pratyayamālāpariccheda, subdhātupariccheda, tiṅvibhaktyartha* and *kṛdantāvatāra.*[9]

Pūrvabhāga

1. **Samjñāvatāra** : After the two introductory verses the work rightly opens with the Mahesvarasutras which are inevitable for the understanding of pratyaharas. The different pratyaharas and a few samjnas are dealt with citing the relevant rules of PAN. Contextually phonetic matters like the various places of articulation and different modes of articulation of phonemes are also explained.

2. **Samhitāvatāra** : This deals with euphonic combination. The six types of sandhis viz. *tuksandhi, svarasandhi, prakṛtisandhi, vyanjañasandhi* and *visargasandhi* are dealt with here.

3. **Vibhaktyavatāra** : This *avatāra* deals with declensions classed into *ajanta* and *halanta* under which the masculine, feminine and neuter are given in order. A fourth variety, viz. '*aliṅga*' is dealt with, separately, under the *halanta* section.

4. **Avyayāvatāra** : The indeclinables are dealt with here. The avyayas coming under ganas like *cādi, svarādi* etc. and the avyayas pertaining to the addition of certain *kṛt* and *taddhita* suffixes are enumerated.

5. **Strīpratyayāvatāra** : Here the rules of *Ast* governing the stripratyayas like *ṭāp, ḍāp, cāp, ṅīp, ṅīṣ, ṅīn, ūṅ, ti* are dealt with. Wherever necessary, rules other than those governing stripratyayas, are also explained for the sake of word formation.

6. **Kārakāvatāra** : This deals with the meaning of the case suffixes (*subvibhakti*) which convey *kāraka* relation. Though the *avatāra* is termed *kārakavatāra,* it is also concerned with the sense

of *prathamāvibhakti* and *ṣaṣṭhīvibhakti* which do not convey any *kāraka* relation.

7. **Samāsāvatāra** : This *avatāra* deals with the compounds. There are six sections dealing with *avyayībhāva, tatpuruṣa* (including *dvigu, karmadhāraya* and *nañsamāsa*), *bahuvarīhi, dvandva* (including *ekaśeṣa*) *samāsānta* and *alug̃adisamāsāśrayavidhi*.

8. **Taddhitāvatāra** : Here the derivation of the nominal bases derived by the addition of secondary suffixes like *aṇ, añ, ḍhak* etc., to words in different cases in construction, to certain verbs and indeclinables, are dealt with. The rules relating to the *taddhita* suffixes are given in a sequence following their order in *Ast*.

Dhātupratyayapañcikā

The ten sections of *Dpp* are :

1. **Sārvadhātukapariccheda** : This is concerned with the conjugation in the four lakaras *laṭ, laṅ, loṭ* and *vidhiliṅ*. He illustrates each of these lakaras with certain roots selected from the ten ganas. The passives occurring in the above said four lakaras, are also dealt with here.

2. **Ārdhadhātukapariccheda** : This deals with the conjugation in the six lakaras *āśīrliṅ, liṭ, luṅ, luṭ, lṛṅ* and *lṛṭ*. Here also each *lakāra* is dealt with reference to certain roots selected from the ten ganas. The passives occurring in the said six lakaras are also explained here.

3. **Sannantapariccheda** : Here the desiderative forms of roots by the addition of the suffix *'san'* are dealt with.

4. **Yaṅpariccheda** : This deals with the formation of the *parasmaipada* intensives and frequentatives by the application of the suffix *yaṅ*.

5. **Yaṅlukpariccheda** : This is on the formation of the *ātmanepada* intensives and frequentatives where the suffix yaṅ gets elided.

6. **Hetumaṇṇic** : This section deals with the causatives formed from the roots by adding the suffix *ṇic* taught by the rule *'hetumati ca'* (3-1-26).

7. **Pratyayamālāpariccheda** : This deals with the rosary of suffixes that comes after the root by which we get forms like *bubhūṣayati, bibhāvayiṣati, bibhāvayiṣayiṣati*, etc.

8. **Subdhātuparicccheda :** Here the denominative verbs i.e. the verbs formed from nominal bases by adding suffixes like *kyac, kyaṣ kyaṅ* etc. are given.

9. **Tiṅvibhaktyartha :** This deals with the sense of the moods and tenses.

10. **Kṛdantāvatāra :** The primary suffixes like *śatṛ, ṇvul, tṛc, aṅ, kta, kvip* etc. added to roots giving rise to the primary nominal bases comprising the participles and verbal nouns, form the subject of this final section.

Sources

Among the most important sources of the work, the *Ast* of PAN, the *Pāṇinīyaśikṣā*, the *Mbh* of PAT, the *VAK* of Bhartṛhari, the *K* of Jayāditya and Vāmana, the *Nyāsa* of Jinendrabuddhi, the *Pradīpa* of Kaiyaṭa and the *Padamañjarī* of Haradatta deserve special mention.

Aṣṭādhyāyi of Pāṇini

Ast of *PAN* is the main source of *Rup* from which rules are selected and reshuffled for adopting the *prakriyā* method. Out of the 4000 rules of *Ast* about 2381 rules are taken for interpretation by DK. Almost all the Vedic rules and the rules relating to *svara* are omitted in the work.

Pāṇinīyaśikṣā

Two verses from the *Paṇinīyaśikṣā* are quoted in *Rup* :[10] These two verses 'hakāram . . . ' and 'aṣṭau . . . ' deal with the places of articulation of sounds.[11] In this respect we find that DK closely follows the *Paṇinīyaśikṣā* whereas later grammarians do not adhere to what is said in *Pāṇinīyaśikṣā.*[12]

Mahābhāṣya of Patañjali

It is clear that DK has made a thorough study of *Mbh* for compiling his work. He has drawn a number of vars, verses, nyayas and istis from it. All these are dealt with in the ensuing chapters.[13]

Vākyapadīya of Bhartṛhari

While interpreting the rules of PAN, DK rarely resorts to *VAK*. We find that the verse : 'vastūpalakṣaṇam . . . ' of VAK, which deals with the nature of *dravya* is quoted in *Rup.*[14] So also the former half of the verse : 'nirvartyañca . . . ' dealing with the three varieties of *karma* is also adopted from *VAK.*[15]

Kāśikā of Jayāditya and Vāmana

It is worthy of mention that *K* is the foundation on which *Rup* is laid up. Thereby itself the study of *Rup* means the examination of its relation with *K*. No study of *Rup* can be possible without examining its relation with *K*. The present study itself makes this point clear.[16]

Nyāsa of Jinendrabudhi

Nyāsa has also its influence on *Rup*. While dealing with the aorist forms of the root *kuṅ*, DK cites the view of Jinendra, the author of *Nyāsa.*[17] The verse : "praparāsam . . . " mentioned in *Nyāsa* under rule 1-1-14 is quoted in *Rup.*[18] So also the verse : "kvacit pravṛttiḥ . . . " found quoted in *Nyāsa* under the rule 3-3-1 is also given in *Rup.*[19]

Pradīpa of Kaiyaṭa

The verse : "guṇo vṛdhirguṇo . . . " of Kaiyaṭa seen in his *Pradīpa* is quoted in *Rup* while dealing with the rule *'jāgroviciṇṇalṅitsu'* (7-3-85).[20]

Padamañjarī of Haradatta

We know that DK was familiar with the *Padamañjarī* of Haradatta from his statement in *Rup.*[21] Moreover, the verse : 'radhirnaśi . . . 'quoted in *Padamañjarī* under rule 7-2-45, is also adopted in *Rup.*[22]

Commentaries

The study of *Rup* was prevalent in Kerala. From ancient times itself this work was adopted in Kerala as a basic text for the study of Sanskrit grammar. It was the advent of the *SK* of BD that put an end to the study of *Rup*.

We get three commentaries on the *Rup* from Kerala. They are 1. the *Nīvī* of Śaṅkara Vāriyar, 2. the *Tattvārthadīpikā* of a disciple of Nārāyaṇa Bhaṭṭa, the author of *PS*, and 3. a Malayalam commentary of unknown authorship. These commentaries themselves will suffice to prove the popularity of the work which it, once, enjoyed in Kerala.

Nīvī

We know that the author of this commentary is Śaṅkara Vāriyar from the colophon : 'iti pāraśavakulatilakena śaṅkarāryeṇa viracite nīvīsamjñake rūpāvatāravyākhyāne aṣṭamaḥ paricchedaḥ.'[23] Ullur S. Parameśwara Iyer assigns this work to the 16th century A.D.[24] Though it is said that Śekhara Vāriyar of Deśamaṅgalattu Vāriyam who was a friend of King Mañaveda of Calicut the commentator of Śukasandeśa, is the author of the work, Ullur S. Parameswara Iyer denies the same. He argues that there are no evidences to prove that Śaṅkara Vāriyar belonged to Deśamaṅgalattu Vāriyam. He points out that Srīkaṇṭha Vāriyar, the commentator of *Māgha,* who belonged to Deśamaṅgalaṭṭu Vāriyam does not refer to this Śaṅkara Vāriyar while mentioning his predecessors. Hence he says that the author of *Nīvī* cannot be assigned to a period before the commentator of *Māgha.* According to him the author of *Nīvī* might have lived in the 16th century A.D.

Yudhisthira Mimamsaka refers to the author of *Nīvī* as Śaṅkararāma.[25] He says that the name Śaṅkara has been several times quoted by Nārāyaṇa Bhaṭṭa in his *PS* and if this reference is to the author of *Nīvī* then he must have lived before the 17th century A.D.

We get six Mss. of this commentary from Kerala. Three of these Mss. deal with the first part of *Rup.*[26] This commentary dealing with the first part of *Rup,* is accepted as *Nīvī,* though the name *Nīvī* is not mentioned in the following introductory verses found in these three Mss.[27]

> "śrīgaṇapataye namaḥ / avighnamastu/
> abhitrilokīnālīkamāmnāyatanavanti ye/
> tebhyaḥ kalyāṇahetubhyo bhūdevebhyo namo namaḥ//
>
> abhigataṣaḍabhijñaprakriyopi svayam yaḥ
> prathamasamayasajjadvāsanāvāsitātmā /
> akalayadatihṛdyam śabdavidyānumodam
> sa jayati navakīrtiḥ sanmato dharmakīrtiḥ / /[28]
>
> amuṣya hṛdi vāridhipratinidheḥ kṛtervyākṛtau
> katham bhavati yogyatā laghurapīdṛśām mādṛśām /

cirānmahadanugrahādiha tu labdhavāṇilavā-
danusmaraṇahetave likhitayāmyaham kevalam / /
atra rūpāvatārasya pāṭheṣu vividheṣvapi
ekasyaiva prayatnoyamanuvṛttyai vitanyate
granthārambhe maṅgalārtham granthakṛt
prasidharasikatvāllaukikasmṛtyā paramācāryam
namasyati yenākṣarasamāmnāyamiti :

In these verses the commentator first salutes Brahmins and then pays tribute to DK whom he refers to as a Buddhist who was originally a Brahmin. The commentator also expresses here his intention to write a commentary on *Rup.*

All these three Mss. are incomplete. In two of these Mss. we get the colophon 'iti samāsāntāḥ' and 'iti vyañjanasandhiḥ' respectively and the other ends with the part 'tathā coktam :

ātmā buddhyā sametyārthānmano yuṅkte vivakṣayā /
manaḥ kāyāgnimāhanti sa prerayati mārutam / /

iti, tacca jñānam drividham, samyaṅ mithyā ca / ubhayamapyetat brāhmaṇaśabdam pravartayati tatra samyagjñānam'[29]

We also get a similar Mss. from the Oriental Manuscripts Library of Madras University.[30] It begins with the same verses seen in the above Mss. and breaks off in the middle.

Among the six Mss. of the commentary *Nīvī*, mentioned already, we find that three of them deal with the second part of *Rup.*[31] In one of these manuscripts we get the colophon : 'iti pāraśavakulatilakena saṅkarāryeṇa viracite nīvīsamjñake rūpāvatāravyākhyāne aṣṭamaḥ paricchedaḥ' wherein the name of the commentator as well as the commentary is mentioned.[32]

Tattvārthadīpikā

We get another commentary on *Rup* by name *Tattvārthadīpikā.* We get two Mss. of the work.[33] Here we get the beginning as :

hariḥ / sriganạpataye namaḥ / avighnamastu /
avighnamastu śivayoḥ sucaritrāṅguram mahaḥ
bandhujīvacchavinibham bandhurānanam
natvā sarvasvakṛtam nārāyaṇamamalacaritamācāryam
rūpāvatāraṭīkām tattvārthadīpikām karoti kaścit
prāripsitasya granthasyāvighnaparisamāptyādyartham

samuciteṣṭadevatārūpamācāryam praṇamatiyenetyādinā

One of these Mss. breaks off in the middle of *ajantapulliṅgaprakaraṇa.*[34] In the other Mss. we get the colophon :[35]

'iti rūpāvatāraṭikāyām tattvārthadīpikāyāmaṣṭamaḥ paricchedaḥ

srīnārāyaṇakāruṇyāttikā tattvārthadīpikā

samāptā parigṛhṇantu sajjanāḥ vītamatsarāḥ / /

harīharahiraṇyagarbhebhyo namaḥ / /

We know that the author of this commentary is a student of Nārāyaṇa Bhaṭṭa from the two verses 'natvā sarvasvakṛtam . . .' 'śrīnārāyaṇakāruṇyāt . . .' seen at the beginning and end respectively, of the work.[36] Vadakkumkur identifies the author of this work with Nārāyaṇan Nampūtiri of Velānallur also known as Madhom Namputiri.[37] But Ullur doubts the probability of this identification.[38]

Malayalam commentary

We also get an anonymous Malayalam commentary on *Rup.* There are two Mss. which give the text of *Rup* along with this Malayalam Commentary.[39] One of these Mss. begin with the *svarasandhi* and breaks off in the middle of the *taddhita* section.[40]

The other Mss. starts from the beginning of *Rup* and ends somewhere in the middle of the second part of *Rup.*[41]

Notes and References

1. Vide *Bharatayatra*, p. 268.
2. Vide *Language*, p. 11.
3. Vide *Systems of Sanskrit Grammar*, p. 24.
4. *'rūpāvatāra'* means presentation of rupas. In a secondary sense, the work which deals with *'rūpāvatāra'* (i.e. presentation of rupas) can be designated as *'Rūpāvatāra'*.
5. Vide *Prakriyākaumudīvimarśaḥ* : 'tatra pañcikāśabdaprayogena mayaivamanumīyate yat tasmin prakaraṇe pañcadhā pratyayā vihitāḥ vartante/ tadyathā śudhadhātubhyo tiṅkṛdbhedena pratyayānām prakāradvayam / evam sapratyayadhātubhyo tiṅ nyantasannantayaṅantab-

hedena ca traidhamityevamrītyā pañcānām pratyayānām nirdeśena dhātupratyayapañciketyuktam' (p. 12).

6. Vide Preface to *Rup*, Part II.
7. *Rup* Part II, p. 211.
8. Vide *Vyakaran Sastr Ka Ithihas*, Part II, p. 116.
9. The sections dealing with *hetumaṇṇic* (*ṇijanta*) and tiṅvibhaktyartha are not designated by him either as paricheda or *avatāra* and he concludes these sections saying : "iti ṇijantāḥ" and "iti tiṅvibhaktyarthāḥ" (*Rup* Part. II, pp. 227 & 241).
10. Vide *Pāṇinīyaśikṣā*, p. 2 & *Rup* Part I, pp. 4 & 5.
11. Vide Infra, p. 117.
12. In *SK* while enumerating the places of articulation, BD speaks of only seven among those eight mentioned in *Pāṇinīyaśikṣā*. He does not mention *uras* as one among the places of articulation.
13. Vide Infra chapters V, VI & VII.
14. Vide *VAK* 'bhūyodravyasamuddeśa' 3-4-3 (p. 75) & *Rup* Part I, p. 14.
15. Vide *VAK* 'Sādhanasamuddeśa' 3-7-45 (p. 82) & *Rup* Part I, p. 146.
16. Vide Infra chapters VI, VII & VIII.
17. Vide Supra, p. 8.
18. Vide Infra, p. 128.
19. Vide Infra, p. 128.
20. Vide *Pradīpa* of *Mbh* under rule neḍvaśi kṛti (7-2-8) & *Rup* Part II, p. 165.
21. Vide Supra, p. 8.
22. *Rup* Part II, p. 145.
23. Vide the Mss. No. 730, T.P., Vol. III.
24. Vide *K.S.C.*, Vol. II, pp. 409 & 410.
25. Vide *Vyakaran Sastr Ka Itihas*, Part I pp. 482 & 483
26. Vide Mss. Nos. 526A & 527 of T.C. Vol. III and 726 of TP. Vol. III. It deserves mention that under the said Mss. Nos. seen in the T.C. and T.P. catalogues, the name of this commentary is wrongly given as *Tattvārthadīpikā*. For, in the introductory verses (quoted above) found in these Mss. we do not get the name '*Tattvārthadīpikā*' whereas the name '*Tattvārthadīpikā*' is mentioned in the entirely different introductory verses :

'...
rūpāvatāraṭīkām karoti tattvārthadīpikām...' found in the Mss. of *Tattvārthadīpikā* (No. 802 T.P. & 525 T.C.)

27. Ullur gives the verses seen in the beginning of these three Mss. as the opening verses of *Nīvī* (Vide *K.S.C.*, Vol. II, pp 409 & 410).
28. Vide Supra, p. 7.
29. Mss. No. 526 A.T.C. Vol. III, No. 726, T.P. Vol. III and No. 527, T.C. Vol. III.
30. Vide Mss. No. 15713 M.C. Vol. XXVIII.
31. Vide Mss. Nos. 528 & 529 T.C. Vol. III and 730 T.P. Vol. III.
32. Vide Supra, p. 26.
33. Vide Mss. No. 802, T.P. Vol. III & No. 525, T.C. Vol. III.
34. Vide Mss. No. 802, T.P. Vol. III.
35. Vide Mss. No. 525, T.C. Vol. III.
36. Vide Supra, p. 48 & vide Kunjunni Raja, *'Contribution of Kerala to Sanskrit Literature*, p. 152.
37. Vide *K.S.S.C.*, Vol. III, pp. 187 to 189 & 196.
38. Vide *K.S.C.*, Vol. II, pp. 401 & 402.
39. Vide Mss. Nos. 523 & 524 A, T.C. Vol. III.
40. Vide Mss. No. 523, T.C. Vol. III.
41. Vide Mss. No. 524 A, T.C. Vol. III.

Chapter III

Characteristics of the Work

Rup is a unique attempt in the history of Sanskrit grammar by its novel treatment of *Ast*, quite different from the style existent upto that time. It is the first remodelling of *Ast*. Though not the most prominent among the various recasts of *Ast*, which in course of time came into existence, it is DK's *Rup* that gave the start to a new treatment of *Ast*. It is this unique feature of *Rup*, which makes it a notable one from the earlier and later works of even illustrious authors in the field. Hence, in this chapter, we are concerned with the characteristic features of this work. The defects and draw-backs of the work, are also viewed here.

Among the two introductory verses in *Rup*, the second one is noteworthy while examining the characteristic features of this work.[1] In these verses DK pays homage to PAN and then refers to Buddha for purpose of salutation and states that his work is meant to give aid to the beginners of grammar by providing them with a concise, well-framed and straight forward exposition, of rupas or accomplished forms, which is achieved, as we see, by reshuffling the sutras of *Ast* and excluding grammatical intricacies. Thus it can be seen that the foremost characteristic feature of the work is that it is a remodelling of *Ast*, to be more correct, the first of the kind. Certain characteristic features of the work are, in one way or other, related to this fact. Hence we are to discuss the characteristic features of the work in a two-fold manner viz. (1) Characteristics of the work as a recast of *Ast* and (2) Salient features of the work in particular.

Characteristics of the work as a recast

Among the general characteristic features of the work as a recast, we first notice that it is the first remodelling of *Ast*. Secondly, we find that in it we get a subjectwise grouping of the sutras of *Ast*. Lastly we find that this rearrangement of the *Ast*, is meant for the purpose of the accomplishment of *pariniṣṭhitarūpa* or the final level of utterance and hence the work is characterised by the method of illustration found in it.

1. The first remodelling of Ast

The first notable feature of *Rup* is that it is in this work that we get for the first time in the history of Sanskrit grammar, a rearrangement of the sutras of PAN. This is secured by giving readily and regularly all the sutras that help to arrive at the accomplished form. It is, hence, quite evident that the order of the sutras of *Ast*, cannot be maintained in this work. This must naturally block the easy understanding of the meanings of the sutras of *Ast*, since a Paninian rule is not self-sufficient by containing in itself all the words essential for the conveyance of its idea and moreover, many of the words for a rule are to be got mainly by *anuvṛtti* from previous rules and rarely by *apakarṣa* from the succeeding rules.[2] To a person who follows the order of the sutras in *Ast*, this difficulty will not hence arise. This unavoidable defect thus caused by changing the order of the rules of *Ast*, is wonderfully and cleverly rectified in *Rup* by giving first, the sutras that are necessary for the *anuvṛtti* of words for a sutra before interpreting the same. For example, before interpreting the rule *'svaujasamauṭ . . . '* (4-1-2) DK gives the rules *'pratyayaḥ'* (3-1-1) *'paraśca'* (3-1-2), *ṅyāpprātipadikāt* (4-1-1), and says, *'ityanuvartamāne, svaujasamauṭ . . . '* (4-1-2) and then only gives the meaning.[3] The work abounds in such similar examples. Thus it can be seen that even by tilting the table of *Ast*, DK has succeeded in keeping in tact, the contents placed over there. The other characteristic features of this work owe their origin in one way or other to this wonderful treatment of *Ast* by DK.

2. Subjectwise grouping of the rules of Ast

This is the foremost characteristic feature of a recast of *Ast* since, it is the subjectwise grouping of the sutras of *Ast* that resulted in modelling them. It is worthy of mention here that the effort of the author in this regard is praiseworthy. That he was to divide his work into two major parts and to subdivide them into different avataras and paricchedas, is, itself, the outcome of this subjectwise grouping. In *samjñāvatāra* we get samjnasutras and vidhisutras which in *Ast* are scattered in the first three padas. Thus the sutras scattered in the three padas of *Ast* are grouped in this avatāra, so as to teach the student the operation of *pratyāhāra* and *savarṇagrahaṇa.* So also in *samhitāvatāra,* we get six types of sandhis viz. *tuksandhi, svarasandhi, prakṛtisandhi, vyañjanasandhi, visarjanīyasandhi* and *svādisandhi.* From *Ast* or *K,* one cannot easily gather the sandhis because the rules of *tuksandhi* are scattered in the first *pāda* of the sixth chapter and the third *pāda* of the 8th chapter, the rules of *svarasandhi* in the first *pāda* of the 6th chapter, some of the rules of both the *halsandhi* and *visarjanīyasandhi* in the third *pāda* of the 8th chapter, those of the *svādisandhi* in the second and third *pāda* of the 8th chapter and in the first *pāda* of the 6th chapter. Thus it may be said that the subjectwise treatment of the rules of *sandhi* into six divisions by DK makes the study of these easier. This subjectwise grouping of rules is likewise evident in all the successive avataras and paricchedas.

3. Method of illustration

Another striking feature of *Rup* is seen in the mode of illustration of sutras. The accomplished forms are the main tenets of the work and it is in order to illustrate and point out a particular form that rules are introduced and interpreted in this work. Wc thus find that rules are given secondary importance as it were in this recast. To begin with the first *avatāra,* it is to illustrate the *aṇpratyāhāra* that the rules *'halantyam'* (1-3-3) and *'ādirantyenasahetā'* (1-1-71) etc. are taken by him for interpretation.[4] Thus it is well evident that when *Ast* gives its stress on the grammatical rules which consequently make us aware of the rupas, in *Rup* the situation is vice-versa. The reader is first informed of a particular *rūpa* or form and the author turns his attention to narrate the process of formation of the same for which he has, accidentally and unavoidably to resort to the interpretation of the rules of *Ast.* This is indicated in the naming itself of the work as *'Rūpāvatāra.'* The originality of the work owes much to this factor.

Salient features of the work in particular

Among the salient features of the work, when viewed particularly, the following are noteworthy. The fact that it is an abridgement of *Ast,* deserves mention first of all. The others viz. the emphasis it lays on the *rūpa* of classical Sanskrit alone, the motive force of the work to educate a beginner, coherence of the work, the systematic classification of the subject matter noticed in it, the superb style of interpretation found in it, a mere reference made to certain rules of *Ast* and the citation of verses meant for the explanation and illustration of rules; all these give to *Rup* a place of its own, not only among the different recasts of *Ast,* but also in the realm of the study of Sanskrit grammar itself.

1. An abridgement of Ast

Rūp is characterised from the earlier works on *Ast* like K etc. in the fact that it is an abridgement of *Ast.* While remodelling *Ast,* DK has achieved the purpose of an abridgement of it also which is calculated for the benefit of the beginners of grammar. The fact that DK has made a selection of Paninian rules for his work has resulted in making an abridged recast of it. After selecting the Paninian rules, he himself has grouped them under different headings to suit his purpose of the easy understanding of the *parinișṭhitarūpa* or the final level of utterance. It can also be seen that the selection and omission of the rules of *Ast* in *Rup,* is justifiable to a great extent since it paves the way for the novel treatment of the science of grammar. It is thus very clear that the selection and omission of the rules of *Ast* is a unique feature, which resulted in its abridgement as well as paved the way for its simplicity as opposed to the grammatical engrossment and enrichment of the work.

2. Emphasis laid on the rūpa of Classical Sanskrit alone

Another characterizing feature of *Rup* among the recasts of *Ast* is the emphasis it lays on classical Sanskrit alone and it is that which actually resulted in the abridgement of *Ast.* DK's intention was to deal with the vocabulary of Classical Sanskrit. Therefore he deals with the rules concerned with Classical Sanskrit alone and in his work rules dealing with Vedic Sanskrit (except in certain rare instances) are omitted.[5] The rules of the second *pāda* of the first chapter, relating to *svara* except the three rules *uccairudāttaḥ* (1-1-29), *'nīcairanudāttaḥ'* (1-1-30) and *'samāhāraḥ svaritaḥ* (1-1-31) which define *udātta, anudātta* and *svarita* respectively, have been omitted. So also the second *pāda* of the 6th chapter of *Ast* which deals with *svara* has been completely omitted.

3. Motivated to educate the beginner

The fact that the work is designed with the purpose of educating a beginner strikes one, as one of the characteristic featurēs of this work. The access for a beginner to the realm of Sanskrit grammar is made easy all through the composition of the work. In order to point out as to how, long and prolate vowels are enunciated, even though not enumerated in the Sivasutras, he introduces the rules *'aṇudit . . . '* (1-1-69), *'taparas'. . . '* (1-1-70) and *'tulyāsyaprayatnam savarṇam'* (1-1-9).[6] He then enumerates the varieties of each and every vowel and consonant and then states that these varieties are comprehended by the letters enumerated in the fourteen Sivasutras. Contextually he enumerates the sthanas and prayatnas also. Such is the simplicity of his narration that a beginner does never find any difficulty in understanding him.

Again while explaining the procedure of *sandhi* for the first time, he points out as to how the vowel *'a'* in *deva* in the proximity of the word *chatram,* gets *tugāgama* and the like, and how the combined form *devacchatram* is got. Then he makes a statement *'śliṣṭoccāraṇam kartavyam, devacchatram iti siddham bhavati.'*[7] It means that sandhi operations occur only when there is *samhitā* and hence one has to utter the letters of the combined form in their maximum proximity. Such a statement is in reminder of this fact already indicated by the name *'Samhitāvatārā'* and it is well evident that the same is exclusively meant for a beginner.

4. Coherence of the work

Another notable feature of the work, is its coherence which is maintained throughout the work and *DK* deserves special appreciation for it. Since the work is intended to give a readymade knowledge of grammatical formations and not the exposition of PAN's *Ast,* DK gives individual introduction for almost all the sutras before interpreting the same. Never does he directly take a rule for interpretation without an introduction which is sometimes in the form of a question. Whatever the mode of introduction be, he never refrains from giving it. The work therefore begins with the sentence *'tatrādau tāvat pratyāhāraśśāstre samvyavahārajñāpanārtham anuvarṇyate.'*[8] He points out that it is the *pratyāhāra* that is taken by him first for explanation since it makes us familiar with the treatment of the subject matter in this science of grammar. Thus after introducing the *pratyāhāra,* he says that *aṇ* is the first one among the pratyaharas. Arousing the anxiety of the student as to how it is obtained he brings the rule *'halantyam'* (1-3-3) to the stage with the rule *'upadeśejanunāsika it'* (1-3-2) as its predecessor which is necessary for the *anuvŕtti* of the word *upadeśe* and *'it'* in *'halantyam.'* Thus the work from the beginning to the end, seems to be a continuous narration of relevant facts and ideas and we find that DK aims at the coherence of the work by means of this introductive style of interpretation.

5. Systematic classification of the subject matter

Rup is remarkable for its systematic classification of the subject matter. The contents of *Ast* are dealt with in two major sections, the latter being named by him as *'dhātupratyayapañcikā.*[9] The principle underlying this two-fold division is the two-fold classification of padas into *subanta* and *tiṅanta* which have got *prātipadika* and *dhātu* as their bases respectively. It can be seen that the former part of the work is concerned with *prātipadika* and the latter is concerned with *dhātu*. In the first part of the work, immediately after dealing with the preliminary details of letters and their combination he deals with the operation that are related to *prātipadika* viz. the *sup* suffixes and feminine suffixes that are added to it, the *taddhita* suffixes that are added to the sup-inflected *prātipadika* and the composition of the sup-inflected pratipadikas to form different kinds of samasas. In the latter part the addition of the different suffixes like *tiṅ*, *kṛt* etc. to *dhātu* are dealt with. It can also be sen that the further subdivision of these parts into different avataras and paricchedas, is also based on certain principles with which we are to deal with in the following chapter.[10]

6. Superb style of interpretation

Rup is endowed with a superb style of interpretation which adheres to the need of the *'bāla,'* the beginner. The sutras are provided with a *vṛtti* which is very simple and straight-forward. DK while interpreting a rule, does not always care for brevity nor does he attempt to introduce grammatical controversies. Hence he does not purplex the reader or demand strenuous effort from him to understand his work. Even, rules are repeatedly interpreted with a view to the easy understanding of the context.[11] We are to dwell on his style of interpretation as well as the interpretation of various rules in the following chapter.[12]

7. Mere reference to certain rules of Ast

Another distinguishing feature of *Rup*, is that in it we meet with the novelty of the mere mention of sutras without their interpretation by the author. Many a rule of *Ast*, is mentioned in this work for the single purpose of the *anuvṛtti* of words contained in it. So also certain sutras of *Ast* are referred to here to justify certain usages on the basis of similar usages found in the sutras.

A detailed study of both kinds of these rules, is attempted in the following chapter.[13]

8. Citation of verses

The citation of verses is a meritorious feature of *Rup*. DK has cited wherever he deems necessary, verses of his own as well as of others which help to illustrate and explain the sutras of PAN. This has won applause from later authors. In Gunasagara's commentary to *yāpparuṅgala-k-kārikai*, a Tamil work by Amitasāgara, we find that the verses in *Rup* are referred to as a complementary feature of this work.[14] A brief survey of the verses cited in *Rup* is made in the coming chapter.[15]

Finally, it may be pointed out here that the author has indicated almost all the characteristic features of this work in the introductory verses :

yenākṣarasamāmnāyamadhigamya maheśvarāt /
kṛtsnam vyākaraṇam proktam tasmai pāṇinaye namaḥ / /
sarvajnamanantaguṇam praṇamya bālaprabodhanārthamidam /
rūpāvatāramalpam sukalāpamṛjum kariṣyāmi / /

The mention of the name of the work, *'Rūpāvatāra,'* in the verse shows that it is a remodelling of *Ast* in order to cater to the rupas and hence the main stress is laid here on rupas and not on the Paninian rules. The author has kept in his work, the grammatical spirit of *Ast*, to a great extent and it is indicated by saluting PAN as one who enunciated the science of grammar. The adjective *'alpam'* to *rūpāvatāram* in the verse, shows that the work is an abridged recast. The adjective *sukalāpam* hints at the coherence of the work as well as the systematic classification of the subject matter whereas the adjective *ṛjum* shows the simplicity and lucidity which characterises the interpretation of the rules. The part *'bālaprabodhanārtham'* marks it as one meant for a beginner, original in presentation, profuse in incorporating everything useful to the context and introducing all relevant details. All these characterise the work as one having a superb style of interpretation.

Defects and drawbacks

As common to any form of new invention or creation, *Rup*, the first recast of *Ast*, is also wanting in certain respects and it is not at all flawless. This imperfection is discernable most clearly when viewing the work as a source for getting the knowledge of the contents of *Ast*. Secondly, one is inclined to charge him of over-enthusiasm while executing the purpose of the accomplishment of the rupas and one may find in his work a less meritorious method of re-arrangement of rules. Since the avowed aim of the author, is not the exposition of *Ast*, only those defects, noted secondly, are more prominent. It can thus be pointed out that *Rup* is not free from defects and drawbacks which are being discussed now.

1. Omission of necessary rules

It is only natural that *Rup* cannot comprehend all the rules of *Ast* since it is envisaged as an abridged recast of the same, by the author as stated in the latter part of the second introductory verse.[16] The author has omitted almost all the rules relating to Vedic language and many other rules relating to Classical Sanskrit.[17] Such kind of omission of rules cannot be regarded as defective since the same is a must for executing the purpose of the abridgement of *Ast*, even though Nārāyaṇa Bhaṭṭa in his introductory verse to *PS* points out the omission itself of the rules of *Ast* as a major defect of *Rup*.[18] Here, we are therefore, concerned with the omission of only such rules of *Ast* which must have never been excluded from *Rup* so as to suit the purpose of creating even a simplified or abridged recast of *Ast*. It can be pointed out that the omission of such rules is really defective. For example, he has omitted the two *paribhāṣā* rules *'tasminniti . . .'* (1-1-66) and *'tasmādityuttarasya'* (1-1-67). These two rules deal with the sense of the locative and ablative cases used in sutras and generally these cases are not used in the Sanskrit language in the sense taught by these rules. Therefore, while dealing with the rule *'che ca'* (6-1-73) in the *ṣamhitāvatāra*, where he first interprets this rule, he ought to have mentioned the *paribhāṣā* rule *'tasminniti . . . '* to explain the locative case used in the word *'che.'* But without giving any interpretation or reference to this rule he gives the meaning of the word *'che'* as *chakāre parataḥ.*[19]

So also while interpreting the rule *'anaci ca'* (8-4-47) where the word *'acaḥ'* in the ablative case, is got by *anuvṛtti*, he gives the meaning of the word *'acaḥ'* as *aca uttarasya* without making any reference to the *paribhāṣa* rule *'tasmād . . . .'*[20] Hence the reader may naturally find it difficult to know as to how the words *'che'* and *'acaḥ'* could mean *che parataḥ* and *aca uttarasya* respectively.

2. Shortcomings in the re-arrangement of the rules of Ast

One major defect of the re-arrangement of the sutras, is that the process of *adhikāra, anuvṛtti* and the technique of *pūrvatrāsiddham* in *Ast,* are disturbed. Though the author has tried his maximum to avert this by readily giving the rules necessary for *anuvṛtti* and giving reference to *asiddhatva,* this defect is unavoidably seen in his work as well as in all other recasts, as a must since the process of *adhikāra, anuvṛtti* and the technique of *pūrvatrāsiddham* could be readily understood from the order of *Ast* alone. In addition to this, certain inaccuracies have crept in the rearrangements of the rules of *Ast.* They are pointed out now.

While dealing with *tatpuruṣasamāsa,* he mentions the *adhikāra* rule *'vibhāṣā'* (2-1-11) before the rule *'tatpuruṣaḥ'* (2-1-22) which is made optional on account of this *adhikāra* rule.[21] It is noteworthy here that by this *adhikāra* rule, *'vibhāṣā,'* the two rules *'apapari . . .* (2-1-12) and *'āṅ . . . '* (2-1-13) are also made optional. But he does not mention this *adhikāra* rule *'vibhāṣā'* while dealing with these two rules in the *avyayībhāva* section which comes before the *tatpuruṣa* section in his work.[22] Eventhough this rule *'vibhāṣā'* is not mentioned there, he interprets the said two rules (*apapari . . .* & *āṅ . . .*) to be optional. Hence one may naturally entertain a doubt as to how the function of these two rules becomes optional. Therefore he could have better mentioned the rule *'vibhāṣā'* before the said two rules *'apapari . . . '* and *'āṅ . . .'* which come in the *avyayībhāva* section, than, before the rule *'tatpuruṣaḥ'* in the *tatpuruṣa* section. Or he could have at least made mention of the rule *'vibhāṣā'* in both the places since he always makes repetition of one and the same rule on several occasions.[23]

So also in the *vibhaktyāvatāra* he speaks of the contingency of the function of the *paribhāṣā* rule *'ādeḥ parasya'* (1-1-54) while dealing with the rule *'ato bhisa ais'* (7-1-9) and points out that the *paribhāṣā* rule *'anekālśitsarvasya'* (1-1-55) operates in the said rule defeating the function of the *paribhāṣā* rule *'ādeḥ parasya.'*[24] To the reader of *Rup,* there is no possibility of a doubt regarding the contingency of the function of the rule *'ādeḥ parasya'* in the rule *'ato bhisa ais'* since the author has not made mention of the rule *'ādeḥ parasya'* earlier. Therefore, strictly speaking, this is not the proper context to present the rule *'adeḥ parasya.'* Moreover quite early in the *vyañjanasandhi* of *samhitāvatāra* itself, there was the context, for mention of the rule *'ādeḥ parasya,'* i.e., while dealing with the rule *'udaḥ sthāsthambhoḥ . . .'* (8-4-61).[25] It is by the function of the *paribhāṣā* rule *'ādeḥ . . . '* in the rule *'udaḥ sthā . . . '* that the *pūrvasavarṇa* taught by it, substitutes the initial letter *'s'* of the roots *sthā* and *sthambh* which occur after the *upasarga 'ud'*. But without mentioning the rule *'ādeḥ parasya'* in this context, he simply incorporates its meaning in the interpretation given to the rule *'udaḥ . . . '* And the reader is sure to find himself at a dismay, as to how such an idea is derived.

Again it is in the *vibhaktyavatāra* that he includes the rules *'bhūvādayo dhātavaḥ'* (1-3-1) and *'upasargāḥ kriyāyoge'* (1-4-59) which teach the term *dhātu* and *upasarga*, whereas quite early in the *samhitāvatāra* itself, he had dealt with the rules which are concerned with *dhātu* and *upasarga.*[26] Hence, in *samhitāvatāra* itself, he could have rearranged these two *samjñā* rules before the rule *'eṅipararūpam'* (6-1-94) which is concerned with the euphonic combination of *dhātu* and *upasarga.*[27] These inaccuracies in the rearrangement of the rules of *Ast*, are definite to strike one while going through the work.

3. Drawbacks in the presentation of rupas

It has already been stated that the conception itself of the work by the author, was to present the rupas readily and regularly to the beginner of Sanskrit grammar and hence the author has tried his best and succeeded to a great extent in the task of presenting the rupas in their maximum number and in the easiest method of presentation. Yet the same too, cannot be pointed out to be free from fault. For example while dealing with the conjugation, he presents the tiṅantarupas in the two categories of *sārvadhātukalakāra* and *ārdhadhātukalakāra*. He selects certain roots from the ten *gaṇas* and cites their rupas in the *lakāra laṭ* first, then in *laṅ, next in loṭ* and finally in *vidhiliṅ*. Then he passes on to the ardhadhatukalakaras where also the rupas of roots selected from the ten ganas are given in the *lakāra, āśīrlin* first. Then the rupas in the other *lakāras* are given in the order of *liṭ, luṅ, luṭ, lṛṅ* and *lṛṭ*. Therefore, to a student who tries to study the different rupas of the root *bhū*, it is the forms of other roots in the *lakāra laṭ* that follow the rupas of the root *bhū* in the *laṭprakaraṇa.*[28] Therefore he has to make a leap to the *laṅprakaraṇa* wherein also he can get the forms of the root *bhū* in the *lakāra laṅ only.*[29] Thus he has to master the whole ten prakaranas in order to understand the different conjugational forms of a single root bhū.[30] Hence, the difficulty in this kind of citation, is that the student gets puzzled with regard to the rupas of one and the same root in all the lakaras as the same cannot be understood readily at one time from the work.

4. Lack of explanation

Before interpreting a rule DK generally cites rules from which words are got by *anuvṛtti* in that particular rule. It is in this respect that we find lack of explanation. He gives the same remark *'iti vartamāne'* in both circumstances where a rule is to be completely got by *anuvṛtti* as well as where one or two words of a particular rule is to be partially got by *anuvṛtti.* For example the rule *'ato dīrgho yañi'* (7-3-101) is completely got by *anuvṛtti* in the rule *supi ca* (7-3-102). Here he says *'ato dīrgho yañi iti vartamāne, supi ca . . ''.*[31] But the word *śī* alone of the rule *'jasaḥ śī,* (7-1-17) is got by *anuvṛtti* in the rule *'auṅ ā paḥ'* (7-1-18). Here too he says *'jasaḥ śī iti vartamāne au a āpaḥ ' . . . '.*[32] Hence the student cannot understand at a glance when a rule is to be completely or partially got by *anuvṛtti.*

So also he does not specify clearly as to whether a word is got by *anuvṛtti* or *adhikāra* making a synonimous usage of the expressions *'ityanuvartamāne, iti vartamāne* and *ityadhikṛtya* though technically there is difference between *anuvṛtti* and *adhikāra.* For example, before interpreting the rule *'che ca'* (6-1-73) he says *'hrasvasya piti kṛti tuk'* (6-1-71) *samhitāyām* (6-1-72), *'ityanuvartamāne . . . '*[33] Here it is to be noted that the rule *'hrasvasya piti . . . '* has got a specific meaning of its own and the word *hrasvasya* is taken from it for the rule *'che ca'* by the technical process known as *anuvṛtti* as expressed in the traditional maxim *'sūtreṣvadṛṣṭam padam sutrāntarādanuvartanīyam sarvatra.'* But the rule *'samhitāyām,'* being an *adhikāra* rule, has no specific meaning of its own, and simply provides the word *samhitāyām* to many a latter rule among which the rule *'che ca'* is also the one to be benefitted by the word. This kind of availability of a word in a rule is what is known by the technical process *'adhikāra.'*[34] Therefore, he could have stated clearly 'samhitāyām ityadhikāre hrasvasya ityanuvartamāne.' Hence the common usage 'ityanuvartamāne' points out lack of specification.

Moreover, when a change is to be effected in regard to the case or number of a word got by anuvṛtti (i.e. *anuvṛtti* along with *vacanavipariṇāma* or *vibhaktivipariṇāma*) DK does not specifically mention the same, but gives the usual vague remark *'ityanuvartamāne.'* For example the word *'pratyayādīnām'* of the rule *'āyaneyī*

. . . ' (7-1-2) is to be got by *anuvṛtti,* with the change of the plural number into singular as *'pratyayādeḥ,'* in the rule *'jhontaḥ'* (7-1-3) so as to qualify the word *jhaḥ.* But he does not speak of this *vacanavipariṇāma* and merely says : "āyaneyīnīyiyaḥ phaḍhakhachaghām pratyayādīnām ityanuvartamāne jhontaḥ' . . . '[35]

5. Unnecessary explanation

Quite different from the above, one meets with certain instances in *Rup* where explanations, which are not relevant or strictly essential, are given. For example, in the *Vibhaktyavatāra,* after dealing with the declensional forms of the masculine stems ending in the vowel *'a,'* he draws our attention to the base *'somapa'* which is a masculine stem ending in *'a.'* Before giving its declensional forms he elaborates the derivation of the base *somapā* pointing out that the root *pā* with the *upapada soma* gets the *kṛt* suffix, *vic* and to explain the same he deals with ten rules.[36] Among these ten rules cited, some do not have their function in the base *somapā;* even then he deals with the contingency of their function in the base. Thus only after dwelling too much on the derivation of the base *somapā* at the expense of the patience of the reader, he turns to give its declensional forms. One is naturally prone to feel tiresome here. Instead of going into the details of the derivation of the base, he could have directly declined the rupas of the stem *somapā* simply stating, 'ākārāntaḥ pulliṅgassomapāśabdaḥ / sa ca somaśabdopapadāt pibatidhātoḥ vijantaḥ / tasmāt svādyutpattiḥ *i.e.* sup suffixes come after the base *somapā* which is a masculine stem derived by the addition of the suffix *vic* to the root *pā* with the *upapada soma.* This would have been more intelligible and relevant to the context. Here he may be charged of over enthusiasm in his endeavour.

Similarly in order to deal with the declensional forms of the feminine stems ending in *'ī'* he first narrates the declensional forms of the stem kartrī, then he turns to deal with the feminine stems *bhavatī, yāntī yātī* and *bhavantī,* all of which have forms alike those of *kartrī.* He narrates the different rules by which the feminine suffix *nīp* occurs in these bases; so also he discusses whether *numāgama* is to operate in these bases or not.[37] It is to be opined here that in a context, when the declensional forms of feminine stems ending in *'ī'* are to be narrated, the narration of the derivation of these *'ī'* stems does not seem necessary since the variant derivation of each of these stems does not in any way influence their declensional forms unfavourably so that they cannot be modelled like those of *kartrī*. Hence instead of going into the details of the process of formation of these bases he could have made a statement like 'evam bhavatīyātīyāntībhavantītyādayaḥ,' after dealing with the declensional forms of the base *kartrī*.

It is to be remarked here that in a critical study the defects and drawbacks also deserve attention so as to make the criticism complete. Therefore though these defects are pointed out from the critical point of view, it has also to be admitted without any doubt that in the light of the merits of *Rup*, these defects can be simply ignored.

Notes and References

1. yenākṣarasamāmnāyamadhigamya maheśvarāt / kṛtsnam vyākaraṇam proktam tasmai pāṇinaye namaḥ // sarvajñamanantaguṇam praṇamya bālaprabodhanārthamidam / rūpāvatāramalpam sukalāpamṛjum kariṣyāmi // (p. 1).
2. DK mentions the *apakarṣa* of the word *vā* for the rule *kimot* (5-3-12) from the succeeding rule *vā ha ca cchandasi* (5-3-13) *Rup* Part I, p. 290.
3. Vide Part I, p. 23.
4. Ibid, pp. 1 & 2.
5. The sutras dealing with Vedic Sanskrit and selected by DK are :
    1. *'ṅyāpossamjñā . . .'* (6-3-63) Part I, p. 209.
    2. *'nonayati . . .'* (3-1-51) Part II, p. 165.
    3. *'chandasi saha'* (3-2-63) Part II, p. 221.
6. 'katham punaranupadiṣṭā dīrghādayo gṛhyante? savarṇagrahaṇāt katham . . .' (*Rup*, p. 3.)
7. *Rup* Part I, p. 7.
8. *Rup* Part I, p. 1.
9. Vide Supra, p. 21.
10. Vide Infra, pp. 54 to 60.
11. Vide Infra, pp. 65 & 155.
12. Vide Infra, pp. 62 to 70.
13. Vide Infra, pp. 61 & 62.
14. Vide Infra, p. 117.

15. Vide Infra, pp. 117 to 136.
16. 'rupavatāramalpam sukalāpamṛjum kariṣyāmi' (Part I, p. 1).
17. Vide Infra, p. 61.
18. '. . . rūpāvatāre punaḥ kaumudyādiṣu cātra sūtramakhilam nāstyeva . . . ' (*PS*. Part I, p. 2).
19. *Rup* Part I, p. 6.
20. Ibid, p. 8.
21. Ibid, p. 171.
22. Ibid, p. 169.
23. Vide Infra, pp. 65 & 155.
24. *Rup* Part I, p. 33.
25. Ibid, p. 18.
26. Ibid, pp. 42 & 51.
27. Ibid, p. 10.
28. *Rup* Part II, p. 8.
29. Ibid, p. 51.
30. Ibid, pp. 74, 92, 108, 119, 142, 168, 172 & 174.
31. Ibid, p. 33.
32. Ibid, p. 61.
33. Ibid, p. 6.
34. Grammarians say : "adhikāro nāma uttaratra sambandhaḥ."
35. *Rup* Part II, p. 7.
36. ākārāntaḥ pulliṅgassomapāśabdaḥ sa ca somaśabdopapadāt pibatidhātoḥ vijantaḥ / katham?.. evam niṣpannāt somapāśabdāt svādyutpattiḥ / (*Rup* Part I, p. 42).
37. *Rup* Part I, pp. 67 & 68.

PART II
ANALYTICAL STUDY

Chapter IV

Dharmakīrti's Treatment of the Science of Grammar

The realm of DK's work *Rup*, is the science of grammar expounded in *Ast* and the treatment of the same by the author is remarkable and praiseworthy when viewed from the point of view of the purpose of the text. The novelty of the work is that it does neither deny one the knowledge of the Paninian rules nor does it offer one the knowledge of all the rules of *Ast*. This apparent anomaly is calculated to execute the main purpose of the author to create a work with its main stress on the accomplished forms. DK's method of treatment of the subject matter dealt with in *Ast*, is therefore distinguished by the selection and omission of the Paninian rules, by the mere reference to them and by the result-oriented grouping of the selected rules into avataras and paricchedas based on certain principles. In this chapter we are therefore to examine how far this method has succeeded in achieving his purpose of modelling the first recast of *Ast* aimed to impart an easy knowledge of accomplished forms. We are hence concerned with the propriety and the significance of the selection, omission, the mere mention of the sutras of *Ast* and the subjectwise grouping of them for this novel attempt. Also we are to discuss his style of interpretation and deal with the interpretation given by him to certain sutras of *Ast*.

Selection and rearrangement of the sutras of Ast

The first noteworthy point in DK's treatment of the Paninian grammar is the selection of rules from *Ast* and their rearrangement to form avataras and paricchedas. While making a rearrangement of the rules of *Ast* calculated to suit his purpose, he has not made an attempt to comprehend in it all the rules of *Ast*. His discerning eye was keen enough to cite the most necessary and useful sutras for his work. Hence of the nearly 4000 rules of *Ast*, 2381 sutras alone have been selected by DK for his work.[1] Now follows the systematic analysis of each and every *avatāra* with particular bearing to the selection and arrangement of rules therein from *Ast*.

Samjñā rules : *Samjñāvatāra* begins with the 14 Sivasutras and consists of 14 sutras out of which 13 are selected from the first three padas of the first chapter and one from the fourth *pāda* of the eighth chapter of *Ast.*[2] Of these 14 rules, 10 are *samjñā* rules.[3] Here it is to be noted that though the *avatāra* is termed *samjñāvatāra*, all the *samjñā* rules of *Ast* do not find their place therein. Only 11 samjnas viz. *it, pratyāhāra, lopa, savarṇa, hrasva, dīrgha, pluta, udātta, anudātta, svarita* and *anunāsika* are dealt with. This is because by the term *'samjñāvatāra'* what he means is that, this particular *avatāra* is meant to make the student aware of certain samjnas which is necessary for the initial study of the science of grammar dealt with by him. Moreover to his work which has a particular network quite different from *Ast*, these particular samjnas alone need be mentioned at the outset. This is borne out by the fact that in the following avataras and paricchedas also he includes certain *samjñā* rules when the context demands the same.[4]

Again though the *avatāra* is termed *samjñāvatāra*, four rules which do not teach any *samjñā*, are also selected here. They are 1. the rule *'tasya lopaḥ'* (1-3-39) which deals with the elision of the anubandhas, 2. the rule *'aṇudit . . . '* (1-1-69), 3. the rule *'taparas . . . '* (1-1-70) both of which do not directly teach any *samjñā* but only mean that *aṇ udit* and *tapara* are indicative of certain distinct group of letters, and 4. *'a a'* (8-4-68) which deals with the *ābhyantaraprayatna* of the short vowel *'a.'*[5] Such is the style of his selection of rules for an *avatāra* that they must all help to execute the purpose of creating a new outlook in the study of *Ast* and facilitate the easier study of accomplished forms.

Sandhi rules : Under *Samhitāvatāra* which is divided into six sections, DK has selected 113 rules.[6] In the first sub-section named *tuksandhi* we get totally 10 rules which are selected from the first sixth and eighth chapters of *Ast.*[7] Of these ten, four *vidhi* rules deal with *tuksandhi*, three are *paribhāṣā* rules, one is an *adhikāra* rule, one is a *samjñā* rule enjoining the term *samhitā* and the remaining one deals with *vyañjanasandhi*. The fact, that *sandhi* operations occur only when there is *samhitā*, is mentioned at the outset by giving the *adhikāra* rule *'samhitāyām'* (6-1-72) and the rule enjoining the term *'samhitā'* is interpreted for the same. So also three *paribhāṣā* rules which supplement the *vidhi* rules enjoining *tuksandhi* are dealt with here. In his eagerness to illustrate *tuksandhi,* he selects for this section the rule *stoḥ* . . . (8-4-40) dealing with *vyañjanasandhi* since the latter is to function in the instance selected by him to illustrate *tuksandhi.*[8]

For the next section named *svarasandhi,* DK has selected 29 rules from the first sixth and eighth chapters of *Ast.*[9] Among these, 13 rules deal with *acsandhi. Paribhāṣā* rules selected for this section number five. Three *samjñā* rules enjoining terms like *samyoga, guṇa, vṛddhi* and one rule prohibiting *savarṇasamjñā* find their place here. Of these the terms *guṇa* and *vṛddhi* are necessary for the rules *ādguṇaḥ* (6-1-87) and *vṛddhireci* (6-1-88) whereas *samyogasamjñā* is introduced to interpret the *vidhi* rule *'samyogāntasya lopaḥ'* (8-2-23) which has its place here to explain its probable contingency in the instance *'sudhyupāsyaḥ'* illustrating the rule *'iko yaṇaci'* (6-1-77). Four *vidhi* rules dealing with *sandhi* operations of consonants also find their place here in view of the instances cited to illustrate *acsandhi.* The *atideśa* rule *'pūrvatrā . . .'* (8-2-1) and the *adhikāra* rule *'ekaḥ . . .'* (6-1-84) are also included in this section.

Among the rules of *Ast* dealing with *'acsandhi,'* DK has selected some of them in such a way that all the *sandhi* operations of *ac* are comprehended in them, though all the rules relating to each and every *sandhi* operation are not dealt with. For example while dealing with *vṛddhi* operation, DK has not selected the rule *'vā supyā . . .'* (6-1-92) though he has taken the three previous rules dealing with the same viz. *'vṛddhireci* (6-1-88) *etyedhat . . .'* (6-1-89) and *upasargād . . .* (6-1-91).

The *vidhi* rule *'pluta . . .'* (6-1-125) dealing with the unchanged aspect of vowels, is given place under the section named *prakṛtisandhi* consisting of 13 rules which are selected from the first, sixth and eighth chapters of *Ast.*[10] Among these, six deal with *pluta* and *pragṛhya,* three deal with the samjnas *ṭi* and *nipāta,* two are *paribhāṣā* rules and the rest two are *adhikāra* rules.

21 rules dealing with the *sandhi* operation of consonants, come under the section *vyañjanasandhi* which totally consists of 23 rules selected from the eighth chapter of *Ast.*[11] Among these two rules, in addition to the 21 mentioned above in the beginning, one is an *adhikāra* rule and the other one relates to the change of *visarga.*

The rule *stoḥ* . . . (8-4-40) though dealt with in *tuksandhi*, is selected first here for illustration since it deals with *vyañjanasandhi*.[12]

Five rules dealing with *visargasandhi* are selected from the third *pāda* of the 8th chapter of *Ast* and are grouped under the section titled *visargasandhi*.[13] The rule *visarjanīyasya saḥ* (8-3-34) though already dealt with in the previous section is mentioned here first, to point out its grouping under the section *visargasandhi*.[14]

For *svādisandhi*, DK selects rules from all the chapters of *Ast* except from the fifth. Among the 33 rules grouped under *svādisandhi*, 16 rules deal directly with *svadisandhi*.[15] Among the rest 17 rules, five are *adhikāra* rules, six rules deal with samjnas like *prātipadika pada, gha, nipāta, ekavacana, dvivacana, luk ślu*, and *lup*, five rules are *vidhi* rules and the remaining one is a *paribhāṣā* rule *'vipratiṣedhe . . .'* (1-4-2). The *paribhāṣā* rule *'alontyasya'* (1-1-52) though dealt with in the previous section is selected here also to supplement the rule *sasajuṣo ruḥ* (8-2-66).[16]

Rules of Declension : Rules of declension are dealt with in the section entitled *vibhaktyavatāra* which totally consists of 289 rules selected from all the chapters of *Ast* and are distributed among seven sections viz. *ajantapulliṅga, ajantastrīliṅga, ajantanapuṃsakaliṅga, halantapulliṅga, halantastrīliṅga, halantanapuṃsakaliṅga* and *aliṅga*.[17] The first section *ajantapulliṅgaprakaraṇa* is formed of 130 rules of which 33 are *saṃjñā* rules, 6 are *adhikāra* rules, 4 are *atideśa* rules, two are *paribhāṣā* rules and the rest[85] are *vidhi* rules which relate mostly to the declension of masculine bases ending in vowels.[18] 32 rules are grouped under the next section *ajantastrīliṅgaprakaraṇa* wherein we get 26 *vidhi* rules mostly relating to the declension of feminine bases ending in vowels, two *saṃjñā* rules enjoining the optional function of the term *nadī*, two *atideśa* rules, an *adhikāra* rule *'striyām'* (4-1-3) and lastly one *paribhāṣā* rule, *'midacontyāt . . .'* (1-1-47) also.[19] Among the 16 rules which form the third section *ajantanapuṃsakaliṅgaprakaraṇa'* one deals with the term *sarvanāmasthāna*, one is an atideśa rule, *'tṛitīyādiṣu*, (7-1-74) and the rest 14 are *vidhi* rules mostly relating to the declension of neuter bases ending in vowels.[20]

The *halanta* section dealing with masculine bases ending in consonants consists of 75 rules of which 71 are *vidhi* rules relating mainly to the declension, three are *saṃjñā* rules teaching the technical terms *pada* and *ṣat*, and the remaining one, *hanteratpūr-*

vasya (8-4-22) is a *niyama* rule.[21] The *halantastrīliṅgaprakaraṅa* consists of four *vidhi* rules and three *vidhi* rules come under *'halantanapumsakaliṅgaprakaraṇa.'*[22] The last section dealing with the alingas are formed of 29 rules of which one is an *adhikāra* rule, *'maparyantasya'* (7-2-91), one is an *atideśa* rule, *'āmantritam pūrvam . . .'* (8-1-72) and the rest 27 are *vidhi* rules.[23]

The indeclinables wherein the *sup* suffixes get elided and which have hence no different declensional forms are dealt with in the section *avyayāvatāra* consisting of three rules which are already included in the previous prakaranas contexually.[24] Two *vidhi* rules *upasargād . . .* (8-4-14) and *aca . . .* (7-4-47) which are interpreted in the second part of the work are given here a passing reference with regard to their meaning.[25]

Rules dealing with feminine suffixes : 48 rules dealing with feminine suffixes are selected for the next section entitled *strīpratyayāvatāra* which totally consists of 64 rules selected from the third, fourth, fifth, sixth and the eighth chapters of *Ast.*[26] 16 rules in addition to the 48 rules mentioned above, deal with certain *kṛt* and *taddhita* suffixes, the substitute *ānan* and *lopa* of the letter *'y.'* Rules dealing with *kṛt* and *taddhita* suffixes, are selected for this section because these suffixes are referred to in the rules enjoining the feminine suffixes, viz. *'ṭiṭḍhāṇañ . . .'* (4-1-15), *'yāñaśca'* (4-1-16) and *'ṣidgaurā . . .'* (4-1-41). So also rules like *'ajādyataṣṭāp'* (4-1-4), *ṛennebhyo . . .* (4-1-5), *'ugitaśca'* (4-1-6) etc. though mentioned contextually in previous avataras, are interpreted and illustrated in detail here for the reason that they suit this section most.[27]

Rules dealing with the meaning of case-suffixes

For the section *Kārakāvatāra* in which he deals with case relationship, DK has selected 81 rules from the 1st, 2nd, 4th and 8th chapters of Ast.[28] Of these, 32 rules deal with samjnas like *kartṛ, karman, karaṇa, sampradāna, apādāna, adhikaraṇa, hetu* and *karmapravacanīya,* three rules deal with *dvitva,* the taddhita suffix *aṇ* and its elision, one is an *adhikāra* rule *karmapravacanīyāḥ* (1-4-83) and the remaining 45 deal with the conditions and varieties of meaning in which the different case suffixes are to be used.

Rules of composition

286 are comprehended in *Samāsāvatāra* dealing with the composition of subantas.[29] This *avatāra* is divided into six sections of which the first deals with the *avyayībhāvasamāsa.* It is composed

of 31 rules selected from the 1st, 2nd, 5th, 6th and 8th chapters of *Ast.*[30] Of these one is a *samjñā* rule enjoining *upasarjanasamjñā*, one is a *paribhāṣā* rule, *'samarthaḥ padavidhiḥ'* (2-1-1), three are *adhikāra* rules and the remaining 25 deal with *avyayībhāvasamāsa,* its gender, the suffixes, that come at the end of the same and such other related matters.

The section titled *tatpuruṣa* consists of 54 rules of which four are *samjñā* rules enjoining the terms *tatpuruṣa, dvigu, karmadhāraya* and *upasarjana,* two are *adhikāra* rules and the rest 48 rules deal with *tatpuruṣasamāsa* and the operations connected with it.[31] The rules of this section are selected from the 1st, 2nd and 6th chapters of *Ast.*

The next section dealing with *bahuvrīhisamāsa* consists of 15 rules selected from the 2nd and 6th chapters of *Ast* and these rules deal with *bahuvrīhisamāsa* and the operations connected with it.[32] The succeeding section dealing with *dvandvasamāsa* is formed of 23 rules selected from the 1st, 2nd and 6th chapters of *Ast.*[33] Of these one is the rule enjoining the *dvandvasamāsa i.e. 'cārthe dvandvaḥ* (2-2-29) and the rest deal with the *purvanipāta* and other peculiarities in *dvandva* compound, its gender and *ekaśeṣa.* The last two sections of *samāsāvatāra* are named as *samāsānta* and *alugādisamāsāśrayavidhi.* Of these the former section is formed of 67 rules selected from the 5th, 6th, 7th, and 8th chapters of *Ast.*[34] These rules deal with the suffixes like *'a,' 'ac'* etc. that occur at the end of the various compounds.[35] The last section named *alugādisamāsāśrayavidhi* consists of 97 rules taken from the 2nd, 6th and 8th chapters of *Ast.*[36] Among these, one is an *adhikāra* rule *'sarvasya dve'* (8-1-1) and the rest 96 rules deal, as the title suggests, with the operations like *alug, ānaṅ,* etc. that are seen in the various compounds.

Rules dealing with taddhita suffixes

The *taddhitāvatāra* is the largest section in *pūrvārdha* and consists of 554 rules.[37] This section is not divided into any sub-section and consists of rules almost all of which are selected from the 4th and 5th chapters and arranged more or less in the same order in which they are found in *Ast.* Among the 554 rules of this major section, 5 are *adhikāra* rules, 7 are *samjñā* rules and three are niyamasutras. The rest deal with *taddhita* suffixes.

Rules showing the purpose of anubandhas in roots

The second part of *Rup* begins with a brief introductory section enumerating 32 rules which are selected from the 1st, 2nd, 3rd and 7th chapters of *Ast* which show the purpose served by the various anubandhas in roots and suffixes.[38] DK simply quotes these rules and does not take pains to interpret them here. For example he mentions the rule *'irito vā'* (3-1-57) only to point out the fact that the part *'ir'* in roots help the same to be comprehended by the rule *'irito vā'* and does not interpret this rule here.[39] Contextually he interprets four rules in this section.[40] Of these four, two rules deal with the term *ātmanepada* and *parasmaipada* and the other two rules enjoin *tiṇ* suffixes and lakaras.

Rules dealing with sarvadhatukalakaras

Rules dealing with the sarvadhatukalakaras come under the section viz. *sārvadhātukapariccheda* which is comprised of 263 rules selected from all the chapters of *Ast* except the fourth and fifth and distributed in the five sub-section in *Dpp* i.e., *laṭprakaraṇa, loṭprakaraṇa, liṅprakaraṇa* and *yakprakaraṇa.*[41] *Laṭprakaraṇa* consists of 167 rules, *liṅprakaraṅa* 29 rules, *loṭprakaraṇa*[39] rules, *vidhililiṅprakaraṇa,* 10 rules and the *yakprakaraṇa,* the last section of *Sar̄vadhātukapariccheda* contains 18 rules.[42]

Rules dealing with ārdhadhātukalakaras

194 rules dealing with the ārdhadhātukalakaras are dealt with in the *Ārdhadhātukapariccheda* which is divided into six prakaranas of *āśīnliṅ, liṭ, luṅ, luṭ, lṛṅ* and *lṛṭ.*[43] These prakaranas are dealt with twice on the basis of the ideas conveyed viz. 1. *kartṛ,* 2. *bhāva* & *karman.* DK makes use of 180 rules for dealing with these lakaras occurring in the sense of *kartṛ* and 14 rules for dealing with the same occurring in the sense of *bhāva* and *karman.* In all these prakaranas, certain rules which are already interpreted in previous prakaranas are also included, considering their relevance to these prakaranas also. These rules of the *Ārdhadhātukapariccheda* also, are selected from all the chapters of *Ast* except the 4th and 5th.

Rules related to the different varieties of roots

DK selects 34 rules for the *Sannantapariccheda* dealing with *sannanta* roots, 22 rules for *yaṅpariccheda* dealing with *yaṅanta* roots, 4 rules for *yaṅlukpariccheda* dealing with *yaṅluganta* roots, 39 rules for the section dealing with *ṇijanta* roots and 21 rules for

Subdhātupariccheda dealing with nominal roots.[44] All the rules grouped under the *Pratyayamālāpariccheda* which come before the Subdhātupariccheda in *Rup*, are already interpreted previously.[45]

Rules concerned with the sense conveyed by the tiṅ suffixes

The section named, *'Tiṅvibhaktyartha'* is constituted of 22 rules taken from *Ast* and they deal with the sense conveyed by the *tiṅ* suffixes.[46] Besides these, rules, which deal with the sense of *tiṅ* suffixes and which are already interpreted in the previous prakaranas, are also included here.

Rules enjoining the kṛt suffixes

Rules dealing with the *kṛt* suffixes are included in the *kṛdantāvatara* wherein DK selects 375 rules from 1st, 3rd, 6th, 7th and 8th chapters of *Ast.*[47] The majority of the rules of this section are selected from the third chapter and they deal with *kṛt* suffixes.

Principles underlying the formation of avataras and paricchedas

Another most important feature in the mode of treatment of the science of grammar by DK in this work is the grouping of the Paninian rules into avataras and paricchedas. It goes to the credit of DK that this grouping, of the Paninian rules into avataras and paricchedas, is based on certain principles and now we are to examine them.

The two-fold classification of padas

Panini's rule *'suptiṅantam padam'* (1-4-14) classify the vocabulary of Sanskrit language into two groups viz. *subanta* and *tiṅanta* which comprehend the four-fold classification of them (*nāman, ākhyāta, upasarga* and *nipāta*) by others.[48] It seems that this two-fold classification of padas, has struck the author very much and influenced him to divide his work into two major parts, dealing with the bases of these two respectively, viz. *prātipadika* and *dhātu*. The first part of *Rup* deals with the pratipadikas by dealing with the *sup* suffixes and feminine suffixes that are added to it, the case relationship of the sup-suffixes when added to the same, so also the addition of the *taddhita* suffixes to the sup-inflected pratipadikas and the composition of the sup-inflectd pratipadikas to form different kinds of samasas. The latter part viz. *Dpp* deals with the *dhātu* with reference to the addition of the five types of suffixes *tiṅ, san, ṇic, yaṅ* and *kṛt* to *Dhātu.*[49]

Preliminary details

Narration of preliminary details is unavoidable in any work on the science of grammar. This is the criterion which underlies the formation of *Samjñāvatāra* given at the outset of the first part. The title *Samjñāvatāra* means 'that which introduces technical terms.' That he termed the first section of his work as *Samjñāvatāra* may be due to the fact that, among the preliminary details which he intends to give at the outset, *samjñā* rules form the majority. Therefore in *samjñāvatāra,* the author makes one aware of certain technical terms which he deems necessary for understanding his new type of attempt on *Ast.* That he includes in this section certain *vidhi* rules also, is because that he treats those rules as giving preliminary details.[50]

Again we see that in the arrangement of the rules in this section termed '*Samjñāvatāra,*' the author has followed the pattern of explanation accepted by PAT i.e. letters are to be taught first, next the *itsamjñā,* after that, the *pratyāhārasamjñā,* then the *savarṇasamjñā* and the rule dealing with the *savarnagrahaṇa* (1-1-69) is to be taught only after the awareness of *savarṇasamjñā.*[51] However a slight deviation from the above is made by DK who explains the rule *tulyāsya . . .* (1-1-9) governing *savarṇasamjñā* only after interpreting the rule '*aṇudit . . .*' (1-1-69) describing *savarṇagrahaṇa.*[52]

Juxtaposition of letters

Juxtaposition of letters is the next concern of DK, in the structural development of his work. Hence he envisages the next section as *Samhitāvatāra* which deals with the *sandhi* operations that letters undergo when they are given maximum juxtaposition.

Also a question may arise as to the particular one which among the numerous *sandhi* operations, is to be selected first. The architect of Rup finds no hesitation in selecting *tuksandhi* first of all, for elucidation, since the same is an operation caused by the juxtaposition of letters of both *ac* and *hal.* It can be seen that the four rules beginning with '*che ca*' (6-1-73 to 76) enjoin *tuk* in the proximity of vowels and consonants. So as a general operation dealing with the letters of both *ac* and *hal,* he deals with *tuksandhi* mentioned in the said four rules.[53] This is borne out by the fact that the rule '*śi tuk*' (8-3-31) dealing with the *tuksandhi* caused by the proximity of consonants alone, is not included here and dealt with in *halsandhi* alone.[54]

The criterion underlying the formation of the section '*svarasandhi*' (combination of vowels) before the section '*vyañjanasandhi*' (combination of consonants) is that vowels occur before consonants in the Mahesvarasutras as well as in the alphabet of the language.

Prakṛtibhāva, the special characteristic feature of vowels dealt with in the rule '*plutapragṛhyā aci nityam*' (6-1-125) is given prominence by forming a separate section named *Prakṛtisandhi.*[55] The conditions, under which vowels remain unchanged, is pointed out by the said rule and hence this section is formed of the rules dealing with plutas and *pragṛhya* referred to, in the said rule.

Now comes the turn for the section *vyañjanasandhi* in which all the rules relating to the combination of consonants are dealt with. In his eagerness for bringing out a specific classification, he begins this section with the rule '*stoḥ* . . .' (8-4-40) and illustrates the same though it has already been dealt with in *tuksandhi.*[56]

The followers of PAN read *visarjanīya* after '*a*' and have also included it in the '*śarpratyāhāra*' whereby the same can be characterised as *ac* as well as *hal.*[57] Eventhough there is no need to give a separate division for *visargasandhi,* as it can be included either in *svarasandhi* or *vyañjanasandhi,* the author has made a separate section giving prominence to *visarjanīya* which occupies an important position in the Sanskrit speech and also in view of its peculiar nature of not being *ac* alone or *hal* alone, but of being both *ac* and *hal.*

So also, though the *svādisandhi* comes within the scope of *vyañjanasandhi,* the author has formed a separate division for it, considering its use in the following *subanta* section (*vibhaktyavatāra*).

Declension

Pratipadikas are the main concern of DK in the first part of his work.[58] Hence having dealt with the preliminary details and juxtaposition of letters he turns his attention to the declensions i.e. pratipadikas with the *sup* suffixes added to them. Pratipadikas ending in vowels, are given priority here and there too, he deals with them in a three-fold manner based on their gender viz. masculine, feminine and neuter. Next the pratipadikas ending in consonants, are dealt with based on a four-fold division of them, the *aliṅga* forming the fourth one, in addition to the three genders mentioned. In each of these categories except the *aliṅga,* pratipadikas ending in consonants are dealt with in the order in which their final consonants occur in Mahesvarasutras. But the pratipadikas *yuṣmad* and *asmad* though ending in the consonant *'d'* are not included among them and are grouped separately under the section *aliṅga* since their declensional forms are uniform in the three genders. It is on the basis of this fact that he treats them as *alingas.*[59] The *sup* suffixes being termed *vibhakti*, this section dealing with the declension is termed *vibhaktyavatāra*.

Contextually the indeclinables which also are subantas, wherein the *sup* suffixes enjoy elision, and hence have no varied declensional forms, are dealt with under the section *Avyayāvatāra.*[60]

Gender

DK next passes on to deal with another set of suffixes which also are added to the pratipadikas in view of the feminine gender conveyed by them.[61] These are the feminine suffixes and hence the section dealing with them, is designated as *Strīpratyayāvatāra*.

Meaning of the declensional suffixes

Now follows the section termed *kārakāvatāra* which deals with the meaning of the *sup* suffixes. The *sup* suffixes are added to mere pratipadikas as well as pratipadikas with feminine suffixes. Hence only after dealing with the pratipadikas and feminine suffixes, he turns his attention to narrate the meaning of *sup* suffixes (*vibhakti*) in the section *Kārakāvatāra* which comes next to *Strīpratyayāvatāra.*[62]

Formation of compound and its accessories

DK himself points out the criterion which was responsible for forming the next section named *Samāsāvatāra*. After dealing with the subantas in the previous section, he passes on to deal with *samāsa* because it is an operation involving the subantas which are related in meaning, moreover, the form resulting from the composition (*samāsa*) of the same, is also a *subanta* and finally this compound form (*samastarūpa*) has subantas as its component parts. He adds that he is to deal with the same in a concise manner.[63]

That the arrangement of *Samāsāvatāra* is also principled is clearly discernable. Among the two component parts of a compound form, the meaning conveyed by either of them has got a prominent role to play. Hence based on the importance given to it in the compound expression, he deals with them in a four-fold manner. At first, he deals with the *avyayībhāva* compounds wherein the meaning conveyed by the former part (*pūrvapada*) prevails over the other, secondly with the *tatpuruṣa* compounds wherein the meaning of the latter part (*uttarapada*) of the compound is prevalent over the other, thirdly with the *bahuvrīhi* compounds wherein *anyapadārtha*, a meaning quite different from that conveyed by the former and latter parts prevails over these two and lastly with the *dvandva* compounds wherein the meanings conveyed by both of the component parts are given equal importance.[64] While enumerating the *tatpuruṣa*, he gives a systematic arrangement of them by beginning with *dvitīyātatpuruṣa* and continues to deal with *tatpuruṣa* in the order of *tṛtiyā, caturthī, pañcami, ṣaṣṭhī* and *saptamī* and then deals with *dvigu, karmadhāraya, nañsamāsa* and *gatisamāsa* all of which also come under *tatpuruṣa.*

After dealing with *bahuvrīhi* and *dvandva*, DK turns his attention to the accessories of *samāsa.* Among them, the *samāsānta* suffixes are taken first. They are dealt with under a sub-section entitled *Samāsānta.* Then he passes on to deal with other accessories of samasas viz. *aluk, ānaṅ* etc. The reason for dealing with them at this juncture is that in certain compound expressions like *kaṇṭhekālaḥ,* the *sup* suffixes of the component parts do not get elision which they generally undergo in compound expressions, by the force of the rule '*supo dhātu . . .*' (2-4-71). Hence there is every chance of them being doubted to be separate words. So also in compounds like '*mātāpitarau*' to be two words as '*mātā*' and *pitarau* whereas actually it is a compound expression. It is on account of the operation of *ānaṅ* taught by the rule '*ānaṅṛto . . .*' (6-3-25) on the part *mātṛ,* that the compound expression becomes *mātāpitarau.* Therefore to give clarification in that regard, he deals with the operations like *aluk, ānaṅ* etc. in the following sub-section entitled *Alugādisamāsāśrayavidhi.*[65]

Taddhita derivatives

In accordance with the fact that the *taddhita* derivatives are formed by the addition of *taddhita* suffixes to the sup-inflected *prātipadika* (*subanta*), DK next turns his attention to the *taddhita* suffixes and the varieties of the meaning conveyed by them when added to the subantas. According to him, the most suitable opportunity to deal with the same comes at present, since he has only just now dealt with the subantas.[66] However while dealing with the *taddhita* suffixes, he strictly adheres to the order of those rules in the 4th and 5th chapters of *Ast* and does not attempt to group them in a different manner.

Roots

As told previously roots are the main concern of DK in the second part of his work.[67] Hence at the outset, he briefly narrates the manifold purposes served by the various anubandhas in the roots.[68] In this brief section beginning with the statement *"atha anubandhādayaḥ,'* he also gives certain introductory details regarding roots viz. the ten lakaras, the varieties of sense i.e. *kartṛ*, *karman* and *bhāva* in which these lakaras occur, the ten ganas of roots like *bhavādi adādi* etc. along with the ten vikaranas like *śabvikaraṇa*, *lugvikaraṇa* etc. and the eighteen *tiṅ* suffixes which replace the lakaras whereby the roots are termed as *parasmaipadin* or *ātmanepadin.*[69]

The Sarvadhatukalakaras

The ten lakaras, which are added to roots, are replaced by *tiṅ* suffixes termed *sārvadhātuka* or *ārdhadhātuka*. Hence DK deals with the lakaras in a two-fold manner i.e. *sārvadhātukalakāra* and *ardhadhātukalakāra*. He, first of all, deals with the sarvadhatukalakaras under the section titled *'Sārvadhātukapariccheda.'*[70] It is worthy of mention that while dealing with these sarvadhatukalakaras viz. *laṭ*, *laṅ*, *loṭ* and *liṅ* he gives priority to sequence. For example among the ten ganas of roots he takes the *bhvādigaṇa* first for illustration and there too he deals with the first *lakāra laṭ* with reference to the root *bhū* which is the first one in the *bhvādigana.*[71] He then passes on to deal with certain roots in the *bhvādigaṇa* that end in vowels and states that conjugational forms of the roots ending in vowels and coming under *bhvādigaṇa* are to be understood likewise.[72] With regard to the roots ending in consonants in the *bhvādigana*, we find that they are dealt with on the basis of their penultimate vowel.[73] In this way he deals with the other three sarvadhatukalakaras like *laṅ*, *loṭ* and *vidhiliṅ*.

Again it is to be noted that these sarvadhatukalakaras occur in three varieties of sense i.e. *kartṛ*, *bhāva*, and *karman*. So after dealing with the four sarvadhatukalakaras in the sense of *kartṛ*, with regard to the ten ganas, he also deals with the same in the sense of *bhāva* and *karman.*[74]

Ardhadhatukalakaras

DK now passes on to deal with ardhadhatukalakaras like *āśīrliṅ, liṭ, luṅ, luṭ, lṛṅ and lṛṭ* which also occur in the three varieties of sense *kartṛ, karman* and *bhāva.*[75] It is to be noted that for each *lakāra*, he illustrates the roots from the ten ganas in order to make the relevant section more comprehensive and pervading.

Different varieties of roots

Since there are different varieties of roots in addition to the roots comprehended in the ten ganas, DK next draws our attention to them after making us aware of the lakaras that are added to roots. They are the *sannantadhātu, yaṅantadhātu, yaṅlugantadhātu, ṇijantadhātu* and *subdhātu* which are termed so by the rule '*sanādyantā dhātavaḥ*' (3-1-32). Hence these are dealt with by him in the subsequent sections titled *sannantapariccheda, yaṅpariccheda, yaṅlukpaariccheda, hetumaṇṇic* and *yaṅpariccheda.*[76] Before the section *subdhātupariccheda*, a section titled *pratyayamālāpariccheda* (*uparyuparivihitapratyayamālāpariccheda*), is also formed in order to point out the fact that the different suffixes like *san, ṇic* etc. can be added to one and the same root one over the other as in instances like *bubhūṣayati, edidhiṣayati* etc.[77]

The varieties of sense conveyed by the tiṅ suffixes

The varieties of sense conveyed by the *tiṅ* suffixes are dealt with next by DK in the section '*tiṅvibhaktyartha*' since he has dispensed with the varieties of roots and the lakaras which are added to roots and which are being replaced by *tiṅ suffixes.*[78]

The numerous kṛt suffixes and their sense

DK now, passes on to deal with another set of suffixes which are added to roots and yet are quite different from the *tiṅ* suffixes. They are named '*kṛt*' by the rule '*kṛdatiṅ*' (3-1-93) by PAN. After dealing with the *tiṅ* suffixes and their sense, DK feels that it is quite appropriate to deal with *kṛt* suffixes.[79] He names this major section as *Kṛdantāvatāra.* In this section he deals first with the two suffixes *śatṛ* and *śānac which* replace lakaras like *laṭ* and *lṛṭ*, next with a subdivision of *kṛṭ* suffixes named '*kṛtya*' suffixes and lastly deals with the rest manifold varieties of *kṛt* suffixes and their sense.

Rules of Ast omitted or merely referred to in Rup

DK while framing his work by selecting rules from *Ast*, has omitted many a rule incorporated in it. In *Ast* PAN has given rules not only dealing with classical Sanskrit but also with Vedic Sanskrit whereas in *Rup*, DK has omitted almost all the rules relating to Vedic Sanskrit and accent, since his idea was to deal with the vocabulary of Classical Sanskrit alone.[80] Again in view of his work being an abridged recast, he has omitted a number of rules relating to Classical Sanskrit also. Totally the rules of *Ast* omitted in *Rup* number about 1600.

With regard to the significance of the omission of the rules of *Ast* in *Rup*, it can be pointed out that it is the omission of certain rules of *Ast* that served his purpose of bringing out an abridged recast. The factors which helped him to omit the rules of *Ast* may be pointed out as 1. stress on Classical Sanskrit alone, 2. exclusion of elaboration of *facts*, and. 3. the refutation of certain rules of *Ast* by PAT. The first important factor which was responsible for the omission of numerous rules of *Ast*, is that the same deal with Vedic Sanskrit and accent. Thus we find that nine rules in the second *pāda* of the first chapter (1-2-32 to 40), 225 rules of the 1st and 2nd padas of the sixth chapter (6-1-158 to 6-2-199), as well as many other rules scattered in the other chapters of *Ast*, are omitted by him for the single reason that the same deal with Vedic Sanskrit and accent. It is in order to avoid elaboration of facts on one and the same point that sometimes the author omits certain rules of *Ast*. For example when PAN deals with *gatisamjñā* in 20 rules, DK selects only one of them viz. *'gatiśca'* (1-4-60) and omits the rest 19 rules (1-4-61 to 99) which elaborate the *gatisamjñā*.[81] Finally we find that PAT has refuted certain rules like *'na bahuvrīhau'* (1-1-29), *'na veti vibhāṣā'* (1-1-44) and following him DK also omits those rules in the work.[82]

Besides the omission of certain rules of *Ast*, DK has given mere reference only, to certain other rules of *Ast*. This kind of mere mention of the rules of *Ast* is mainly made for the purpose of the *anuvṛtti* of their words for the succeeding rules and rarely for justifying certain usages or for citing the purpose served by anubandhas. For example he mentions the rule *'vibhāṣā jasi'* (1-1-32) simply to point out the *anuvṛtti* of its words *vibhāṣā* and *jasi* for the succeeding rules (1-1-33 & 34).[83] The rule *'vṛddho yūnā, . . .'* (1-2-65) is merely referred to in *Rup*, to justify the usage of the instrumental case where the idea of the indeclinable *saha* is conveyed without its usage.[84] The rule *'sahayuktepradhāne'* (2-3-19) enjoins the instrumental case to a word used with the indeclinable *saha*. But in the rule *'vṛddho yūnā . . .'* the instrumental case is used in the word *yūnā* though the indeclinable *saha* is not used in the rule. Therefore on the authority of this instrumental case employed in the word *yūnā* of this rule, DK points out that the instrumental case taught by the rule *sahayukte*. . . can be employed even in instances wherein the idea of the indeclinable *saha* is intended without its usage. Thus it is in order to explain the instrumental case in the absence of the indeclinable *saha*, that he makes a mere reference to the rule *'vṛddho yūnā, . . .'* and never does he interpret nor give the idea of this rule in his work. Again we find that the rule *'anudāttau . . .'* (3-1-4) is merely taken to point out the fact that the *anubandha* 'p' in the suffix *tip* helps the same to be comprehended as *pit* and hence benefited by the said rule and the same rule is not interpreted in *Rup*.[85] Finally it deserves mention here that the rules of *Ast* which get accidental reference in *Rup* as pointed out just now, can rightly be grouped under the omitted rules since they are not interpreted or taken here in view of the idea conveyed by them and such rules amount to 49 in number.[86]

Style of interpretation

The style of interpretation adopted in *Rup* by DK, is distinguished by its simplicity and lucidity which is indicated by the author himself by referring to his work as *'ṛju.'*[87] Also the author claims his work to be well knit (*sukalapam*). We are convinced of the propriety of this statement when we examine his work and we can also gather that it is his style of interpretation that made his work *ṛju* and *sukalāpa*. Hence we now turn our attention to certain noteworthy features in his style of interpretation.

Clarity of expression

Clarity of expression is the foremost factor which characterises the method of interpretation adopted by DK for his work. The work is written in such a lucid style that nowhere one needs to have a pause for getting the clarity of idea of the context. His language is very simple, straightforward, and conversational in style. For example before explaining the meaning of the *sup* suffixes termed *vibhakti*, he says "atha vibhaktyarthāḥ pradarśyante/kā punarvibhaktyaḥ? su au jas iti prathamā — ityevamādayaḥ/kasminnarthe prathamā? prātipadikārthaliṅgaparimāṇavacanamātre prathamā (2-3-46)/kim prātipadikam? arthavadadhāturapratyayaḥ prātipadikam (1-2-45).[88] As a result of this conversational style one is apt to feel, while going through the work, that a teacher orally teaches the same.

So also absence of long and thread-bearing discussions on technical matters, paves the way for the clarity of expression. For example while dealing with the rule '*taparastaṭkālasya*' (1-1-70), he does not lead the reader to a debate as to whether the rule is a *niyamasūtra* on *vidhisūtra*.[89] Further with regard to some rules he gives certain remarks or hints which make his work more and more simple and clear. For example after giving the meaning of the rule '*ādyantau ṭakitau* (1-1-46) he makes the remark "ādyantau ṭakitau iti deśavidhiḥ" meaning that the rule '*ādyantau . . .*' points out the place of occurrence of the augments which are *ṭit* and *kit*.[90] So also after giving the meaning of the rule '*vā padāntasya*' he gives the following hints with regard to the outcome of the rule teaching *parasavarṇa*, "iti sparśeṣu vargapañcamāḥ yavaleṣu sānunāsikā yavalā bhavanti."[91] He also gives explanations of certain usages. For example in *Dpp*, in order to point out the gender in which krdantarupas are used he says, "apica kṛdantāḥ prāyeṇa vācyaliṅgāḥ."[92] So also, while dealing with certain rules he gives the meaning of their words. For example he gives the meaning of the word *saṅkhyā* in the rule '*yathāsaṅkhyamanu . . .*' (1-3-10), as "saṅkhyāśabdena kramo lakṣyate."[93] Similarly he gives the relevant meaning of numerous words like *viṣaya, para, sannikarṣa, śeṣa, artha, sambodhana* etc. occurring in various rules.[94] So also while dealing with *adhikāra* rules, he gives the limit upto which these *adhikāra* rules extend.[95] Sometimes, he points out the place where the power of jurisdiction of an *adhikāra* rule is terminated.[96] All these factors combinedly render his style of interpretation characterised by lucidity and simplicity of expression.

Scientific discussions

Rup also comprises in its scientific discussions necessary for the context and which in no way mar its lucidity or simplicity of expression. For example while dealing with the declensional form of the neuter stem '*trapu*,' he points out that the same has two forms in the vocative singular viz. '*he trapo*' and '*he trapu*' and continues that the same is due to the fact that the rule 'na lumatāṅgasya' (1-1-63) pertaining to the prohibition of *pratyayalakṣaṇa* is to be understood as *anitya*.[97] He establishes the same on the basis of the word *aci* included in the rule *'ikoci . . .'* (7-1-73) and discusses the same scientifically, thus throwing light on the scientific matters related to the way of interpretation of rules. So also we get scientific discussions relating to the process of formation of the nominative dual form *'arvantau'* or *arvan* as well as of the accusative plural form *'seduṣaḥ'* of the base *sedivas*.[98] So also in the second part of the work, he gives a discussion as to how one get the usages like *somam pavamānaḥ* etc.[99] He also speaks of the *yogavibhāga* of certain rules which is a scientific device used to interpret the rules.[100] For example, he speaks of the *yogavibhāga* of the rules *'saptamī śauṇḍaiḥ'* (2-1-40) and *'ānmahataḥ . . .'* (6-3-46) in order to justify the *tatpuruṣa* compound *madhyeguruḥ* and the lengthening of the *dvandva* compound, *'ekādaśa'* respectively.[100]

Relevance to the context

The method of interpretation adopted by DK, is result-oriented and hence relevance to context is the deciding factor as to whether a rule is to be interpreted or not. Certain rules are therefore given detailed interpretation in accordance with the context, while, with regard to some others, only a passing reference to their contents is given. For example, while dealing with the possessive singular form *vṛkṣasya* of the base *vṛkṣa*, he deals with the relevant rule *'ṣaṣṭhī śeṣe* (2-3-50) which enjoins the possessive case in the said instance.[101] We find that a detailed interpretation of the rule is given here. The meaning of the word *śeṣa* is given first, then the meaning of the rule is given; then follows a clarification of the usage of the possessive case enjoined by this rule. A relevant verse 'bhedya . . .' is also cited here.[102] In contrast, we find that the idea of the rule *'bahugaṇavatuḍati saṅkhyā'* (1-1-23) is given a passing reference only, while dealing with the nominative plural form *'kati'* of the *'i'* stem *kati*.[103] After stating the fact that *'kati'* is formed by the addition of the suffix *ḍati* to the stem *kim*, he passes on to state that it has the term *"saṅkhyā"* by the said rule, *"bahugaṇavatuḍati* (1-1-23) *iti saṅkhyātvam."* He gives no interpretation of this rule since the context does not demand the same.

Again while interpreting a rule, he sometimes narrates the purpose of each and every one of its words, cites the positive and negative instances of application of the rule, but with a sense of propriety avoids these items severally or wholly in accordance with the context. For example while interpreting the rule *'halṅyābhyo . . .'* (6-1-68) he cites the form *sakhā* as a positive example for the function of the elision of the suffix *'su'* taught by the rule.[104] He also cites forms like *grāmaṇīḥ, niṣkauśāmbiḥ*, etc. as counter examples (*pratyudāharaṇa*) since in these instances the elision of the suffix taught by the rule, does not function owing to the absence of the conditions for the operation of the rule prescribed by the parts *ṅī, hal*, etc. of it. He also cites the verse, *'saṃyogāntasya . . . '* to confirm his interpretation.[105] Quite in contrast to this, we find that he does not attempt to deal with the interpretation nor give the examples of each and every word of the rule *'aniditām . . .'* (6-4-24) enjoining *nalopa*, since he cites the rule only to introduce its prohibition by the rule *'nañjeḥ pūjāyām'* (6-4-30) in the context of explaining the nominative singular form *'prāṅ'* of the base *'prāñc.'*[106] Since the rule does not operate in the said instance, he merely says 'aniditām hala upadhāyāḥ k ṅiti *(6-4-24) iti nalope prāpte, nāñjeḥ pūjāyām (6-4-30).*

Moreover, when the context demands, DK does not have any hesitation to deal with the interpretation of the rules repeatedly. Thus many rules like *'dīrghājjasi ca'* (6-1-105), *'ambārthanadyorhrasvaḥ'* (7-3-107) etc. are repeatedly interpreted by him.[107] Rarely we find that DK does not attempt to give the meaning of rules which are clear by themselves. For example he does not give any interpretation to the rule *'hrasvam laghu'* (1-4-10) since its idea is clear by the rule itself.[108]

Originality of presentation

While recasting the rules of *Ast* in his work, DK has shown his originality of presentation which is well-evident in the introduction of apavāda rules as well as optional rules. An *apavāda* rule is not brought before the reader all on a sudden. Before introducing the same, he makes the reader aware of the general rule (*utsarga*) which is contingent, in the particular instance, cited in the context and then says that in the event of the contingency of the *utsarga*, it is the *apavāda* rule of the same that is to operate there and then only interprets the *apavāda* rule. By this method, the reader is made familiar with the relationship of the *utsarga* and *apavāda* rules. For example, he says "*padāntādvā* (6-1-76) iti vikalpena tuki prāpte tadapavādaḥ āṅmaṅośca (6-1-74) iti" in order to introduce the rule *'āṅmāṅośca'* which is the *apavāda* of the rule *'padāntādvā'* and then only interprets the *apavāda* rule *'āṅmāṅośca.'*[109] The same method of presentation is observed while introducing the optional rules also. He first makes us aware of the rules which operate invariably and then only introduces the optional rule of the same and then proceeds to give its interpretation. For example he at first says, "vadhū+ chāyā, kumārī + chāyā, iti sthite, dīrghāt iti nityam tuki prāpte, dīrghāt ityanuvartamāne, padāntādvā (6-1-76) for introducing the optional rule *'padāntādvā'* and then only the interpretation of the optional rule is given.[110]

Introduction of other relevant details

The style of interpretation adopted by DK in *Rup*, is distinguished by the introduction of relevant details necessary for the interpretation of the rules of *Ast*, or for the citation of rupas or for narrating the process of formation of the same. He therefore lavishly introduces in his work the vars of KAT, *istis* of PAT, verses of his own as well as of other grammarians like Bhartṛhari, paribhasas or maxims, unadisutras and ganapathas with which we are to deal with in detail in the following chapters.[111]

Sutras interpreted

Now we pass on to deal with a few sutras among the many interpreted by DK, so as to have an idea of his method of interpretation.

Halantyam (1-3-3) : This rule enjoins the term *'it'* to the final consonants in *'upadeśa.'*[112] In Mbh under rule 1-3-2 we get a detailed discussion with regard to the meaning of the term *upadeśa* as well as its derivation. DK who is intent on writing a simplified grammatical treatise, does not lead the reader to the different derivations of the technical term as to whether it is *bhāvaghañanta*, *karaṇaghañanta* or *karmaghañanta*. He simply states that the term *upadeśa* comprehends *āgama*, *ādeśa* etc. saying "āgamādeśadhātugaṇapāṭhapratyayapratyāhārasutrāṇyupadeśāh" and also cites the verse :[113]

dhātusūtragaṇoṇādivākyali ḡanuśāsanam /
āgamapratyayādeśā upadeśāḥ prakīrtitāḥ / /

This kind of interpretation well suits his work meant for simplicity and thus facilitate the easier study of the science of grammar.

Sarūpaṇāmekaśeṣa ekavibhaktau (1-2-64) : This rule enjoining *ekaśeṣa*, is dealt in all its details by DK.[114] He points out that the word *sarūpa* in the rule, means 'those sounds which have a common *rūpa* and *'rūpa'* denotes both the letters and sense, by virtue of its connotation as "rūpyate bodhyate aneneti rūpaḥ, artho varṇaśca."[115] Therefore he points out that according to this rule which enjoin the survival of only one, among the similar forms, when followed by one and the same *vibhakti*, *ekaśeṣa* can occur not only in the case of forms which are similar in regard to their component letters but also in the case of those which, though dissimilar in regard to their component letters, are similar in regard to the sense conveyed by them. Hence just the *ekaśeṣa* can be illustrated in the instance *rāmaśca rāmaśca* as *rāmau*, the same can be also be illustrated, in the instance *vakradaṇḍaśca kuṭiladaṇḍaśca* from which one can derive the *ekaśeṣa* as either *vakradaṇḍau* or *kuṭiladaṇḍau*.[116]

Sthānivadādeśonalvidhau (1-1-56)

DK points out that according to this rule a substitute i.e. *ādeśa* is to be treated just like its original i.e. *sthānin* except in cases which involve the operations based on the component letter of the original.[117] He therefore comes to the conclusion that this rule is beneficient, only to the substitutes of groups of letters like *dhātu, aṅga, kṛt, taddhita, avyaya, sup, tiṅ* and *pada* and makes the remark "dhātvaṅgakṛttaddhitāvyayasuptiṅpadādeśāḥ samudāyagatā eva atra prayojanam."

Kṛttaddhitasamāsāśca (1-2-46) : DK deals with this rule twice in his work. He first deals with the same in order to point out the *prātipadikasamjñā* to the *kṛdanta* stem *somapā*.[118] While dealing with the sense of *prathamāvibhakti* in *kārakāvatāra*, he draws our attention to the term *prātipadika*, so as to explain the rule '*prātipadikārtha* . . .' (2-3-46). Here again, he deals with this rule since it deals with the *prātipadikasamjña* and gives a clear interpretation of the rule.[119] He points out that the previous rule 'athavad . . . ' (1-2-4-5) does not enjoin the pratipadikasamjñā to those which end in *kṛt* or *taddhita* suffixes, this rule provides the same. Again this rule, by virtue of its part '*samāsa*' makes a restriction (*niyama*) of the application of *prātipadikasamjñā* enjoined already to sounds having a sense, by the previous rule (1-2-45). The previous rule (1-2-45) enjoin *prātipadikasamjñā* to sounds having sense, and hence the term may relate to *samāsa* and *vākya* both of which are *arthavat*. This rule which gives the term *prātipadika* to *samāsa* is thus making a repetition in that regard. And this repeated statement makes a restriction as stated in the maxim" siddhe satyārambho niyamāya." Hence, among the *samāsa* and *vākya* both of which are groups of words, the term is restricted only to *samāsa* and the rule prevents the same applying to *vākya*. Therefore DK points out that the sentences like "devadatta gāmānaya śuklām daṇḍena" cannot be designated as *prātipadika*.

Sa napumsakam (2-4-17) : This rule enjoins neuter gender to the *dvigu* compound and *dvandva* compound to which *ekavadbhāva* is enjoined by the rules *dvigurekavacanam* (2-4-1) to *vibhāṣā samīpe* (2-4-16) and is interpreted twice in *Rup* i.e. in the *tatpuruṣa* and *dvandva* sections of *Samāsāvatāra*. While dealing with *dvigu* compounds in the *tatpuruṣa* section of *Samāsāvatāra*, the author gives the interpretation of the rule as follows "yasyāyamekavadbhāvo vihitaḥ as napumsako bhavati" meaning 'that *samāsa* to which *ekavadbhāva* is enjoined is to be used in neuter gender.[120] In the *dvandva* section of the *Samāsāvatāra* he interprets the same as "sa dvando napumsakaliṅgo bhavati/ekavadbhāvadekavacanameva bhavati" meaning *dvandva* is to be understood as neuter in gender and has got *ekavacana* owing to *ekavadbhāva*.[121] Though the meaning given to the rule in these two instances may seem apparently different it can be seen that there is no contradiction since, he gives only that part, of the meaning of the rule, which is relevant to the context and does not give the meaning of the rule as a whole in either of these instances. Hence while dealing with *dvigu*, he narrates that neuter gender is assigned to *dvigu* compound to which *ekavadbhāva* is enjoined and while dealing with *dvandva*, he says that the *dvandva* compound to which *ekavadbhāva* is assigned, is to be sued in neuter gender and gets *ekavacana* owing to *ekavadbhāva*.

Śeṣe (4-2-92) : This rule is given a systematic analysis by DK while interpreting the same.[122] First of all he points out the meaning of the word *śeṣa* as "kaśca śeṣa iti cet, apatyādibhyascaturarthaparyantebhyo yonyorthaḥ sa śesaḥ." He opines that the word *'seṣe'* means *'śeṣe arthe'* and since the varieties of sense like *apatya* upto *caturārtha* are already dealt with in rules beginning from *'tasyāpatyam'* (4-1-92) to *'adūrabhavaśca'* (4-2-70), the same denotes the sense other than those mentioned in the said rules. He continues to state that this rule is an *adhikāra* rule as well as a *vidhi* rule. It is an *adhikāra* rule extending from the rule *'tatra jātaḥ'* (4-3-25) to *'tasya vikāraḥ'* (4-3-134). It is also a *vidhisūtra* and hence the suffixes which are taught previously and those to be taught later should be understood in the sense also which is other than those already mentioned. Hence one gets the *aṇ* suffix in the instance *cākṣuṣam* meaning *cakṣuṣā gṛhyate iti*.

Tuhyostātaṅṅāśiṣyanyatarasyām (7-1-35) : This rule is interpreted by DK laying stress on the purpose of the anubandha *'ṅ'* in the substitute *'tātaṅ.'*[123] As per this rule, *'tātaṅ' replaces tu* and *hi* which themselves are the substitutes of the suffixes *tip* and *sip*, the third person singular and second person singular of *loṭ*, when used in the benedictory sense. The *anubandha 'ṅ'* in a substitute, is to make the same an *antyādeśa* by the rule *'ṅicca'* (1-1-53). But the *anubandha 'ṅ'* in the substitute *tātaṅ* which also happens to be a suffix by means of *sthānivadbhāva*, has got other purposes like bringing out *guṇavṛddhipratiṣedha, samprasāraṇa* etc. and hence being satisfied with these purposes, it *('ṅ') does not bring forth the purpose of antyādeśatva* in this particular instance *tātaṅ* unlike in the substitutes like *anaṅ. Tātaṅ* therefore becomes the *sarvādeśa* i.e. the substitute of the whole of *tu* or *hi* as opposed to that of the final letter of *tu* or *hi*.

DK also points out that *tātaṅ* by means of its ṇitv a wards off the pitva of its original (*sthānin*), *tu* or *hi* which is *pit* by means of the *sthānivadbhāva* of its original *tip* or *sip*. Therefore in the instance *brūtāt* where *tātan* has replaced either *tu* or *hi*, the part *tāt* (or *tātaṅ*) is not provided with *iḍāgama* which is contingent there by the rule *'bruva īṭ'* (7-3-93) if *tātaṅ* does not ward off *pitva*. DK quotes the statement of PAT "" *ṅicca pinna bhavati.'*[124]

He also quotes two verses 'tātaṅi ṅitvam...' and 'tātaṅo ṅitva ...' from *K*, to point out that the purpose of *guṇavṛddhipratiṣedha* and the like are served by the *'ṅ'* of *tātaṅ* and that it does not bring *antyādeśatva* unlike the *anubandha 'ṅ'* in other substitutes like *'anaṅ' etc.*[125] He also gives a detailed discussion of these verses here.

Vyaktavācām samuccāraṇe : This rule teaches the *ātmanepada* terminations to the root *'vad'* when it denotes the combined talk of human beings. Here DK points out the purpose of the part *vyaktavācām* which literally means, 'of those who speak clearly.'[126] He states that the root *'vad'* itself means 'to speak clearly' since it is read as 'vada vyaktāyām vāci' in *dhātupāṭha*. Hence one may doubt the necessity of the word *vyaktavācām* in this rule. DK raises this doubt in these words "nanu ca vada vyaktāyām vācīti paṭhyate ; tatra kim vyaktavācāmiti viśeṣaṇena ?" and gives the answer, "prasiddhyupasaṅgrahārthamidam vacanam, vyaktavāca iti hi manuṣyāh prasiddhāḥ, teṣām samuccāraṇe - yathā sampravadantām brāhmaṇāh." DK means that human beings are well-known as *vyaktavācaḥ* and it is because of this popular reference to human beings, that in this rule they are referred to by the word *vyaktavācām*. Hence he justifies the *ātmanepada* terminations in the usage *sampravadantām brāhmaṇāḥ* whereas in the instance "varatanu! sampravadanti kukkuṭāḥ" the root *vad* does not get the *ātmanepada* termination since it denotes the utterances of cocks there. DK also continues to state that since in the combined talk alone, the *ātmanepada* termination is ordained to the root *'vad,'* this root does not get the *atmanepada* termination in the instance *'brāhmaṇo vadatu'* wherein the talk of a single person is referred to.

Notes and References

1. Vide Appendix, pp. 169 to 211.
2. Vide Appendix, p. 169.
3. The six-fold division of the rules of *Ast* into *samjñā, paribhāṣā vidhi, niyama, atideśa* and *adhikāra* deserves mention here. The same is given in the verse :

   samjñā ca paribhāṣā ca vidhirniyama eva ca /
   atideśodhikāraśca ṣadvidham sūtramucyate / /
4. Vide Infra, pp. 49 to 53.
5. Vide Infra, p. 55.
6. Vide Appendix, pp. 169 to 171.
7. Vide Appendix, p. 169.
8. Vide *Rup* Part I, p. 6.
9. Vide Appendix, pp. 169 & 170.
10. Vide Appendix, p. 170.
11. Vide Appendix, pp. 170.
12. *Rup* Part I, pp. 6 & 15.
13. Vide Appendix, p. 170.
14. *Rup* Part I, pp. 19 & 21.
15. Vide Appendix, pp. 170 & 171.
16. *Rup* Part I, pp. 12 & 24.
17. Vide Appendix, pp. 171 & 176.
18. Ibid, pp. 336 to 339.
19. Ibid, pp. 339 & 340.
20. Ibid, pp. 340 & 341.
21. Ibid, pp. 341 to 343.
22. Ibid, p. 343.
23. Ibid, pp. 343 & 344.
24. Ibid, p. 344.

25. *Rup* Part I, p. 130 & Part II, pp. 281 & 10.
26. Vide Appendix, pp. 176 & 177.
27. *Rup* Part I, pp. 61, 65, 66, 67, 132, 133 & 134.
28. Vide Appendix, pp. 177 to 178.
29. Ibid, pp. 348 to 355.
30. Ibid, p. 177.
31. Ibid, pp. 348 to 350.
32. Ibid, p. 350.
33. Ibid, pp. 350 & 351.
34. Ibid, pp. 351 & 352.
35. Ibid, pp. 351 & 352.
36. Ibid, pp. 352 to 355.
37. Ibid, pp. 355 to 368.
38. 'tatra dhātupratyayeṣu yenubandhāḥ upadiśyante sarve kāryārthāḥ' (*Rup* Part II, p. 1).
39. 'irśabdaḥ irito vā (3-1-57) iti viśéṣaṇārthaḥ (*Rup* Part II, p. 2).
40. Vide Appendix, p. 192.
41. Ibid, pp. 369 to 376.
42. Ibid, Rules Nos. 1408 to 1574, 1575 to 1603, 1604 to 1642, 1643 to 1652 & 1653 to 1670.
43. Ibid, pp. 376 to 382.
44. Ibid, pp. 382 to 386.
45. Ibid, pp. 386.
46. Ibid, pp. 386 & 387.
47. Ibid, pp. 387 to 397.
48. 'tadyānyetāni catvāri padajātāni nāmākhyāte copasarganipātāśca . . .' (*Nirukta* P. 2.)
"catvāri vākparimitā padāni catvāri padajātāni-nāmāhyātopasarganipātāśca" (*Mbh* Paspaśāhnika, V.I, p. 32).
49. Vide Supra, p. 21.
50. Vide Supra, p. 48.
51. "varṇānāmupadeśastāvad / upadéśottarakāletsamjñā / itsamjñottarakāla 'ādirantyena sahetā' iti pratyāhāraḥ / prtyāhārottarakālā savarṇasamjñā / savarṇasamjñottarakālam 'aṇuditsavarṇasya cāpratyayaḥ' iti savarṇagrahaṇam /" (*Mbh* under var 'vākyāparisamāptervā' in the rule 1-1-10, Vol. I, p. 161).
52. *Rup* Part I, p. 3.

53. *Rup* Part I, pp. 6 & 7.
54. *Rup* Part I, p. 20.
55. "atha acāmeva sandhikārye prāpte prakṛitibhāva ucyate" (*Rup* Part I, p. 13).
56. *Rup* Part I, pp. 6 & 15.
57. "ayogavāhānāmaṭsu ṇatvam . . .' *śarṣu jaśbhāvaṣatve'* (*Mbh* Vol. I, Āhnika II, p. 89).
58. Vide Supra, p. 54.
59. "dakārāntāvapi yuṣmadasmad-śabdau aliṅgatvānnātra nirūpitau" (*Rup* Part I, p. 101) "atha halanteṣvalingau yuṣmadasmacchabdau ucyete / tayoścāliṅgatvāt triṣvapi liṅgeṣu samānam rūpam / katham ? tvam pumān, tvam strī, tvam napumsakam; aham pumān, aham strī, aham napumsakam; iti / " (*Rup* Part I, p. 123).
60. "atha aliṅgānyasaṅkhyānyavibhaktibhedānyavyayāni subantānīti atra samkṣepeṇopadiśyante / " (*Rup* Part I, p. 128).
61. "atha strīpratyayāntā nirdiśyante" (*Rup* Part I, p. 133).
62. "atha vibhaktyarthāḥ pradarśyante" (*Rup* Part I, p. 145) supra pp. 22 & 23 & infra p. 152.
63. "atha subantānāmeva padānām parasparasambandhinām samāsaḥ pradarśyate / sopi subantatvāt subantāśritatvācca subantānantaram samkṣepeṇopadiśyate / "(*Rup* Part I, p. 165).
64. "sa ca pūrvapadārthapradhānovyayībhāvaḥ, uttarapadārthapradhānastatpuruṣaḥ, anyapadārthapradhāno bahuvrīhiḥ; ubhayapadārthapradhāno dvandvaḥ; iti caturvidhaḥ" (*Rup* Part I, p. 165).
65. "kvacitsamāse vibhaktayaśśrūyante, purvotyarapadayoḥ rūpaviśeṣāśca/tatra samāso vā asamāsoveti sandeha upajāyate / atastannivṛtyarthamalugādhikāraḥ prathamam pradarśyate" (*Rup* Part I, p. 201).
66. "atha subantādapatyādyarthaviśeṣe taddhitotpattiḥ/ taddhitāntāḥ api subantānantaram samkṣepeṇopadisyante" (*Rup* Part I, p. 219).
67. Vide Supra, p. 54.
68. *Rup* Part II, pp. 1 to 3.
69. *Rup* Part II, pp. 3 & 4.
70. *Rup* Part II, p. 4.

71. "tatra śabvikaraṇeṣu bhvādiṣuprathamabhūtāt parasmaipadikāt akarmakāt bhū ityetasmāddhātoḥ parasya lakārasya sthāne tiṅvibhaktayo yojyante" (*Rup* Part II, p. 4).
72. "evamevātra neyānyanyānyapi ajantadhāturūpāṇi" (*Rup* Part II, p. 11).
73. "atha halantadhāturūpāṇi akārādyupadhākrameṇa pradarśyante" (*Rup* Part II, p. 11).
74. "idānīm bhāvakarmaṇoḥ laḍādayaḥ pradarśyante" (*Rup* Part II, p. 100).
75. "athaitebhya eva dhātubhyaḥ punaḥ kartari liṅādayaḥ pradarśyante" (*Rup* Part II, p. 108).

and

"athedānīm ciṇvadbhāvaprakaraṇe bhāvakarmaṇorliṅadayaḥ pradarśyante" (*Rup* Part II, p. 176).
76. "atha sanādyantaḥ pradarśyante" (*Rup* Part II, p. 186), "atha etebhya eva dhātubhyo yaṅvidhīyate" (*Rup* Part II, p. 200), "atha kvacidyaṅo lugvidhīyate" (*Rup* Part II, p. 206), "athaetebhya eva dhātubhyo ṇijvakṣyate" (*Rup* Part II. p. 212) & "atha subdhātava ucyante" (*Rup* Part II, p. 229).
77. *Rup* Part II, pp. 227 & 228.
78. "atha tiṅvibhaktyarthāḥ pradarśyante / atra lakārāṇām arthaviśeṣāh ucyante" (*Rup* Part II, p. 235).
79. "atha kṛdantāḥ pradarśyante" (*Rup* Part II p. 241).
80. Rarely he has included certain rules like ṅyāpossamjñā . . . (6-3-63) nonayati . . . (3-1-51) & *'chandasi sahaḥ'* (3-2-63), etc. which deal with Vedic Sanskrit (P-I - 209, P-II 165 & 221) and rules like *'uccairudāttaḥ'* (1-2-29), *'nicairanudāttaḥ* (1-2-30) and *'samāhāraḥ svaritaḥ'* (1-2-31) defining the three accents *udātta, anudātta* and *svarita*. (P-I p. 4).
81. *Rup* Part I, p. 51.
82. Vide *Mbh* under rules *'na bahuvrīhau,' 'na veti vibhāṣā*, Vol. I, pp. 215 to 217 & 243.
83. *Rup* Part I, pp. 39 & 41.
84. *Rup* Part I, p. 151.

85. "pakāraḥ anudāttau suppitau iti viśeṣaṇārthaḥ" (*Rup* Part II, p. 2).
86. Vide Appendix pp. 210 & 211.
87. Vide the latter part 'rūpāvatāramalpam sukalāpamṛjum kariṣyāmi' of the second introductory verse in *Rup* (Part I, p. 1).
88. *Rup* Part I, p. 145.
89. Ibid, p. 3.
90. Ibid, p. 6.
91. Ibid, p. 121.
92. *Rup* Part II, p. 242.
93. *Rup* Part I, p. 6.
94. "*chandobrāhmaṇāni* . . . (4-2-66) . . . ananyabhāvoviṣayārthaḥ" (*Rup* Part I, p. 238).
"paraḥ sannikarṣaḥ . . . (1-4-109) . . . parasabdotrātiśaye vartate ; sannikarṣaḥ pratyāsattiḥ." (*Rup* Part I, p. 6).
"ṣaṣṭhī śeṣe" (2-3-50) kaśca śeṣaḥ? uparyuktādanyo yaḥ saḥ śeṣah; karmādibhyonyaḥ prātipadikārthavyatiriktaḥ svasvāmibhāvādisambandhaḥ śeṣaḥ," (*Rup* Part I, p. 35) and also
"seṣe (4-2-92) kaśca śeṣa iti cet, apatyādibhyaścaturarthaparyantebhyo yonyorthaḥ sa śeṣaḥ" (*Rup* Part I, p. 240).
"arthavadadhāturapratyayaḥ . . . (1-2-45) abhidheyavacanorthaśabdaḥ" (*Rup* Part I, p. 23) &
"sambodhane ca (2-3-47) ābhimukhyakaraṇam sambodhanam" (*Rup* Part I, p. 145).
95. "āpādaparisamāpteḥ bhāvakarmādhikāraḥ" (Rup Part I, p. 273) &
"dhātoḥ (3-1-91) dhātorityadhikāroyam veditavyaḥ; yadita ūrdhvamanukramiṣyāmaḥ ātṛtīyādhyāyaparisamāpteḥ dhātorityeva tadveditavyam" (*Rup* Part II, p. 241).
96. "kālādhikāro nivṛttaḥ" (*Rup* Part I, p. 271).
97. *Rup* Part I, p. 79.
98. Ibid, pp. 95, 96 & 109.
99. *Rup* Part II, p. 245.
100. *Rup* Part I, pp. 204 & 280.
101. Ibid, p. 35.
102. Vide Infra, p. 129.
103. *Rup* Part I, pp. 47 & 48.

104. Ibid, p. 45.
105. Vide Infra, p. 124.
106. *Rup* Part I, p. 104.
107. Ibid, pp. 50, 66, 50 & 67. All the sutras repeatedly interpreted are noted as Rep in Appendix pp. 169 to 209.
108. *Rup* Part II, p. 120.
109. *Rup* Part I, p. 7.
110. Ibid, p. 7.
111. Vide Infra, pp. 87 to 94 & 106 to 136.
112. *Rup* Part I, p. 1.
113. Vide Infra, p. 130.
114. *Rup* Part I, pp. 30, 190 & 191.
115. Ibid, p. 30.
116. Ibid, pp. 190 & 191.
117. Ibid, p. 34.
118. Ibid, p. 42.
119. Ibid, p. 145.
120. Ibid, p. 177.
121. Ibid, p. 187.
122. Ibid, p. 240.
123. *Rup* Part II, pp. 74 & 75.
124. Ibid, p. 74.
125. Vide infra, pp. 125 & 126.
126. Ibid, pp. 81 & 82.

Chapter V

Dharmakīrti's Treatment of the Science of Grammar (Contd.)

While dealing with the science of grammar expounded in *Ast*, DK draws our attention to the most practical side of the same viz. *rūpa* and we find that it has been given the most significant role in his work. In this chapter we are, therefore, to discuss his mode of presentation of '*Rupa*' indicated by the title *Rūpāvatāra* and narration of the process of formation i.e. *prakriyā* of *rūpa*.[1] Lastly we are to turn our attention to certain other miscellaneous factors which have played an important role in his treatment of the science of grammar dealt with in *Ast*.

Mode of presentation of rūpas

Unlike the earlier grammatical works on *Ast*, the novelty with which *Rup* is endowed, is the mode of presentation of rupas i.e. the final level of utterance. In this work the student is in fact, given information about rupas and it is for pointing out the formation of the same that sutras of *Ast* are dealt with here, whereas, in the earlier works the aim of the authors was to explain and interpret sutras and it is for the illustration of these rules of *Ast*, that rupas are mentioned accidentally. The work of DK is therefore correctly titled as *Rupāvatāra*.

In the first section *Samjñāvatāra*, DK does not deal with any rupa, since it is meant to give certain preliminary information and it is in the *Samhitāvatāra* that he actually introduces sandhirupas.

Sandhirupas

In the first sub-section *tuksandhi* of *Samhitāvatāra* seven sandhirupas viz. *devacchatram, hrīcchaḥ, mlecchah, vadhūcchāyā, kumarīcchāyā, ācchādayati, mācchidat* are introduced as being derived from the seven instances viz. *deva + chatram, hrī + chāḥ, mle + chaḥ, vadhū + chāyā, āṅ + chādayati* and *māṅ + chidat* respectively.[2]

Of these the first *rūpa* is cited to illustrate the rule 'che ca' (6-1-73), the next two are introduced to illustrate the rule *'dīrghāt'* (6-1-75), the next two illustrate the rule *'padāntādva'* (6-1-76) and the last two are given as examples of the rule *'āṅmāṅośca'* (6-1-74).

In *svarasandhi,* DK cites many a *rupa* as examples of *acsandhi.* He points out that from the six instances *dadhi + atra, sámī + atra, madhu + atra, vadhū + ākṛtiḥ, pitṛ + arthah, ḷ + ākṛtiḥ* wherein the rule *'ikoyaṇaci'* (6-1-77) operates, eleven sandhirupas can be formed since the rule *'anaci ca'* (8-4-47) also has its optional function in them.[3] It is noteworthy that the number of rupas cited as illustrations for a single rule is significant. For example, the said rule *'ikoyaṇaci'* has its function in vowels like *'i', 'u', 'ṛ'* and *'ḷ'* irrespective of their varieties like *hrasva, dīrgha,* and *pluta* and in order to point out the same he chooses the above six instances wherein we get the *hrasva* varieties of all these (*'i', 'u', 'ṛ' & 'ḷ'* in *dadhi, madhu, pitṛ* and *ḷ* respectively) and the *dīrgha* varieties i.e. *'ī'* and *'ū'* (in *śamī* and *vadhū*) which thereby become the place of function for the said rule. So also while citing the function of a *sandhirūpa* as illustrating a particular *sandhi* rule, he also takes care to note the rest *sandhi* operations it undergoes. Thus in the instance *ardha + ṛcaḥ* and *tava + ḷkāraḥ* wherein the rule *'ādguṇaḥ'* (6-1-87) operates he notes the function of the rule *'uraṇraparaḥ'* (1-1-51) and the optional function of the rule *'aco rahābhyam dve'* (8-4-46) whereby four rupas viz. *ardharccaḥ, ardharcaḥ tavalkkāraḥ* and *tavalkāraḥ* are obtained.[4] So also in the instance *ye + āgatāh* and *pato + iha* he says that the rule *ecoyavāyāvaḥ* (6-1-78) operates and owing to the optional function of the rule *'lopaḥ śākalyasya'* (8-3-19) two sets of rupas *ya āgatāḥ* and *yayāgatāḥ, paṭa iha* and *paṭaviha* are got.[5] In this way the sandhirupas wherein all the vowels get either the euphonic combination or the *prakṛtibhāva* are explained at length.

In *vyañjanasandhi* DK cites a number of rupas to illustrate the same. He begins the same with instances *payas + śītam, nis + carati san + śambhuḥ, tat + cit* and says that these are the places of operation of the rule *'stoḥ ścunā ścuḥ'* (8-4-40) whereby the rupas *payaśśītam, niścarati, sañśambhuḥ, taccit* are got.[6] He adds that instances like *tad + jhaṣaḥ* and *tad + ñakāraḥ* are like-wise to be understood as *tajjhaṣaḥ, taññakāraḥ.*[7] He then gives the other rupas which regularly illustrate PAN's rules regarding the combination of consonants. In *visargasandhi* and *svādisandhi* also a number of rupas are cited likewise.

2. Vibhaktirupas

It is in the *vibhaktyavatāra* that DK has exposed all the declensional forms. His mode of presentation of rupas can be pointed out as such; i.e. he first of all gives the rupas of a stem ending in a particular letter and says that rupas of other stems ending in that particular letter are also to be declined likewise. The rupas of the stems which end in that particular letter, but have got certain variations in declension are next noted down with reference to the particular case and number wherein the disparity is evident.

While dealing with the rupas of the masculine stems ending in vowels, we find that DK first gives the rupas of akārānta stems like *vṛkṣa, nirjara, sarva, pāda, dvyahna* etc. which have dissimilar rupas. The rupas of the stem *somapā* and *hāhā* are explained while dealing with *ākārānta* stems. DK gives the rupas of the base *kavi* for the stems ending in *'i'* and the rupas of stems like *sakhi, dvi, tri, auḍulomi* are also dealt with one by one. The rupas of bases like *gramanī, vātapramī bahuśreyasī, sudhī* and *pradhī* are dealt with while dealing with *'ī'* stems. Then the *'u'* stems, *kāru* and *kroṣṭu* and *'ū'* stems like *khalapū, pratibhū, varṣābhū* and *punarbhū* are dealt with reference to their declensional rupas. After dealing with the rupas of *ṛkārānta* stems like *pitṛ, nṛ,* and *kartṛ,* he makes the remark 'ṝkāralkārāntāḥ śabdāḥ aprasiddhāḥ.'[8] He then deals with the rupas of stems like *se, go* and *glau* for dealing with stems ending in *'e,' 'o'* and *'au'* respectively.

While dealing with rupas of feminine stems ending in vowels, he begins to narrate the rupas of stems ending in *'ā'* because feminine stems ending in the short vowel *'a'* positively get a feminine suffix, *ṭāp* or the like. Then the rupas of stems ending in other vowels are also dealt with in order. He also points out that feminine stems ending in *'ṝ', 'ḷ'* and *'e'* are not in vogue.[9]

After dealing with the rupas of neuter stems in the *ajantanapumsakaliṅga* section of *vibhaktyavatāra,* DK passes on to the *halantapulliṅga* section. The rupas of the masculine stems ending in consonants are dealt with in the order in which the final consonants of these stems, occur in the fourteen Sivasutraṣ. DK also points out that masculine stems ending in *'y,' 'l,' 'ñ,' 'ṅ,' 'jh,' 'bh,' 'gh,' 'dh,' 'b,' 'g,' 'd,' 'kh,' 'ph,' 'ch,' 'th,' 't,'* & *'k'* are not in vogue.[10]

While citing the rupas of the feminine stems also, which end in consonants, DK follows the order of the consonants in the fourteen Sivasutras. He also points out that feminine stems ending in the consonants *y, l, ñ, ṅ, ṇ, jh, gh, ḍh, b, g, ḍ, kh, ph, ch, ṭh, ṭ* and *k* are not in usage.[11] The narration of the rupas of neuter stems ending in consonants is also done in the order in which their final consonants occur in the Sivasutras. He also notes that neuter stems ending in the consonants *y, l, ñ, ṅ, ṇ, jh, bh, gh, ḍh, dh, b, g, ḍ, kh, ph, ch, ṭh, th, ṭ, k* and *s* are little known.[12]

The grouping of the stems *yuṣmad* and *asmad* under the section, *aliṅga* is a peculiarity of *Rup.*[13] These stems have their own common declensional forms in the three genders since they do not denote any particular sex. That is why they are grouped as alingas.[14] The various declensional forms of each of these two stems are dealt with in all details by DK, in this section specially framed for the same.[15]

3. Avyayarupas

The avyayas which are really subantas wherein the *sup* suffixes get elided permanently, are enumerated in the *Avyayāvatāra*. After citing the rule *'svarādinipātamavyayam'* (1-1-37), he enumerates the sabdas comprehended in the *svarādigaṇa* referred to in this rule.[16] He further points out that the avyayas are to be divided into two groups, one comprising the original ones and the other comprising those got by the operation of Paninian rules and that the latter variety is of three types viz. *avyayībhāva, kṛdanta* and *taddhitānta* which are illustrated next.[17] He then mentions the nipatas coming under the ganas like *cādi, prādi*, etc. which also get the *avyayasamjñā* by the rule *'svarādi . . .'*[18]

4. Stripratyayantarupas

Under the section titled *'Strīpratyayāvatāra'*, DK gives the rupas which are feminine in gender.[19] He points out that there are eight suffixes viz. *ṭāp, ḍāp, cāp, ṅīp, ṅīṣ, ṅīn, ūṅ* and *ti* which are added to bases in order to denote the feminine gender.[20] Citing the relevant rules, he passes on to give the rupas, formed by these feminine suffixes in their order mentioned above.

5. Usage of vibhaktirupas in a sentence

DK not only introduces the vibhaktirupas but also points out their usage in a sentence. We find that in the section *Kārakāvatāra*, he shows the usage of the vibhaktirupas in a sentence in order to point out the varieties of sense which these rupas convey as per the relevant rules of *Ast.*[21]

6. Samastarupas

It is under the section *Samāsāvatāra* that DK introduces the samastarupas. This is one of the most useful parts in the text to a student studying the Sanskrit language. Before giving the rupas, he initially makes the student aware of the four varieties of samasas viz. *avyayībhāva, tatpuruṣa, bahuvrīhi* and *dvandva.*[22] Then he enumerates regularly the samastarupas coming under the four groups of samasas with the authority of the relevant rules of PAN.[23] After enumerating the rupas of these four-fold classification of samasas, he makes us aware of certain other samastarupas also, which, even though coming under the four groups of samasas mentioned previously, have got peculiarities which are accounted for by means of the *samāsānta* suffixes, non-elision of the component *sup* suffixes etc. These rupas are hence enumerated by him in the two sub-sections named *samāsānta* and *alugādisamāsāśrayavidhi.*[24]

7. Taddhitantarupas

The Taddhitantarupas which form a great majority are dealt with by DK in the section, *Taddhitāvatāra.* First of all he gives the *taddhidānta* forms like *aupagava, dākṣi, dākṣāyaṇa* etc. occurring in the sense of *apatya, gotrāpatya,* and *yuvāpatya.*[25] He then gives the rupas like *sālveya, gāndhāra* etc. got by the addition of *taddhita* suffixes named *'tadrāja'* occurring in the sense of *'tasya rājā'* as well as *'tasya apatyam.'*[26] Then rupas like *kāṣāyaḥ* (*paṭaḥ*), *taiṣī* (*rātriḥ*), *vāsiṣṭham* (*sāma*), *vāstraḥ* (*rathaḥ*), *sarāvaḥ* (*odanaḥ*) etc. where the various *taddhita* suffixes convey the varieties of sense like *'tena raktam,' 'nakṣatreṇa yuktaḥ kālaḥ,' 'dṛṣṭam sāma,' 'parivṛto rathaḥ, 'tatra uddhṛtam'* etc. taught by the various rules of *Ast.*[27] So also the rest manifold varieties of taddhitantarupas are cited by him with particular reference to the *taddhita* suffixes, their sense and the subantas to which these suffixes are added.[28] These taddhitantarupas also are dealt with by him citing the relevant rules of *Ast.*

8. Tinantarupas derived from the ten ganas of roots

It is in the second part of the work that DK presents the tinantarupas which are derived by the addition of *tiṅ* suffixes to the roots. He first of all gives the rupas of the root *bhū* in the *lakāra laṭ* and then passes on to narrate the rupas, in the same *lakāra*, of certain other roots coming under the ten ganas *i.e.* from *bhavādigaṇa* to *curādigaṇa*.[29]

DK then passes on to deal with the rupas in the *lakāra laṅ* of some roots coming under the ten ganas, beginning with' *bhū*.'[30] In this way the rupas in the lakaras *loṭ* and *vidhiliṅ* of certain roots coming under the ten ganas starting with *'bhu'* are also narrated by him.[31] After dealing with the above for lakaras occurring in the sense of *kartṛ*, he turns his attention to present the rupas of certain roots in the *lakāra laṭ* occurring in the sense of *karman, bhāva* and *karmakartṛ*.[32] Thus after citing the rupas in the four sarvadhatukalakaras in all details, he passes on to deal with the rupas of certain roots (coming under the ten ganas beginning with *'bhū'*) in the ardhadhatukalakaras, *āśirliṅ, liṭ, luṅ, luṭ, lṛṅ* and *lṛṭ* occurring in the sense of *kartṛ*.[33] He also gives the rupas of certain roots in the said ardhadhatukalakaras which occur in the sense of *bhāva* and *karman*.[34]

It is noteworthy that while citing the tinantarupas in different lakaras of the various roots, DK makes clear the conditions under which one and the same root is to take *parasmaipada* termination or *ātmanepada* termination or both of them. For example, after giving the parasmaipadarupas of the root *'ji'* in the *lakara laṭ*, he also cites the atmanepadarupas *vijayate* and *parājayate* quoting the relevant rule *'viparābhyām jeḥ'* (1-3-19) which ordains the *ātmanepada* termination to this root.[35]

So also the *ātmanepada* roots like *'ram'* which get the *parasmaipada* termination and the roots like *kṛñ* which get both *parasmaipada* and *ātmanepada* terminations are indicated by him giving the relevant rules of PAN.[36]

9. Tinantarupas derived from sanādyanta roots

DK next draws our attention to another category of tinantarupas which are characterised by the roots from which they are derived. Sounds which have at their end suffixes like *san, yaṅ, ṇic, kyaṅ, kāmyac, kvip, yak* and *kyaṣ* are designated as *dhātu* by the rule *'sanādyantā dhātavaḥ'* (3-1-32) and from these roots also one can get various tinantarupas, by the addition of *tiṅ* suffixes.[37] Thus an enormous number of tinantarupas like *jugupsate, mīmāṁsate, bubhuṣati, bubhūṣyate,* etc. derived from *sannata* roots, *bobhūyate, sosūcyate, aṭāṭyate* etc. derived from *yaṅanta* roots, *bobhavīti, bobhoti, pāpacīti, papakti* etc. derived from *yaṅlu ganta* roots, *bhāvayati, ed-*

hayati, pācayati, nandayati, etc. derived from *ṇijanta* roots, *bubhūsayati, bubhūṣyate, pipakṣayati, pāpacayati* derived by the addition of suffixes *san, ṇic,* etc. to one and same root one over the other, *putrīyati, rājīyati, carmīyati, aśvasyati* etc. derived from *subanta* roots are all dealt by him in detail without omitting any of their varieties.[38]

10. Usages of tinantarupas in a sentence

Dpp not only presents the tinantarupas, but also points out their usage in different varieties of meaning. The section named *'Tinvibhaktyartha'* is hence very useful to the student to understand the usage of tinantarupas in a sentence. With the authority of the rules of *Ast,* DK shows in this section how the tinantarupas can be used in a manifold variety of sense.[39]

11. Krdantarupas

Krdantarupas which are furnished by the addition of *kṛt* suffixes to the roots and which get *prātipadikasamjñā* by the rule *'kṛttaddhitasamāsāśca'* (1-2-46) and thereby become subantas by the addition of *sup* suffixes are dealt finally by DK, in the three sections as *śatrādiprakaraṇa, kṛtyaprakaraṇa* and *kṛtprakaraṇa* of *Kṛdantapariccheda.* In *śatrādiprakaraṇa,* DK deals with those krdantarupas wherein the *kṛt* suffixes substitute the lakaras. Hence rupas like *pacantam, pacamānam, pacan, vidyamānaḥ* etc. wherein the *kṛt* suffixes *śatṛ* and *śānac* replace the *lakāra laṭ,* rupas like *bhaviṣyan, bhaviṣyantī* wherein the *kṛt* suffix *śatṛ* replaces the *lakāra lṛt,* rupas like *babhūvan, edhāñcakṛvān,* etc. wherein the *kṛt* suffix *kvasu* replaces the *lakāra liṭ,* are enumerated by him.[40] He also includes here the rupas *pavamānaḥ maṇdayamānaḥ,* etc. which are pointed out as derived by the *kṛt* suffixes *śānan* and *cānaś,* though these suffixes do not replace any *lakāra.* DK next presents certain kṛdantarupas wherein the component *kṛt* suffix has got an additional technical name *'kṛtya.'*

In the section *kṛtyaprakaraṇa* concerned with them, he deals with rupas like *kartavyam, vāstavyam, snānīyam, pacelimāḥ, ceyam, hāryam, brahmodyam* etc. got by the addition of the various *kṛtya* suffixes, tavya, tavyat, *anīyar, kelimar, yat, ṇyat* and *kyap.*[41] In the next sub-section *kṛtprakaraṇa* which is comparatively very large, DK points out the remaining krdantarupas which are numerous in number and are got by the addition of various *kṛt* suffixes like *ṇvul, tṛc,* etc.[42]

Finally it deserves mention here that the originality of the work lies in the presentation of rupas for which the rules of *Ast* are rearranged by DK. The order, in which DK has presented the vibhaktirupas, samastarupas, etc. is followed by the authors of later recasts even though the order of tinantarupas is not adopted by them.[43] It can thus be found that the presentation of rupas is the most illustrious feature of *Rup* which won recognition and popularity in course of time.

Narration of prakriyā or the process of formation

The science of grammar is termed '*śabdānuśāsana*' in the sense that it expounds the sabdas discriminating the same from asādhuśabdās.[44] The accuracy and inaccuracy of sabdas are therefore, the main concern of grammar and this is attained by pointing out the *prakriyā* i.e. the process of formation of the parinisthitarupas. Hence to a student of grammar particularly to a beginner, the narration of *prakriya* or the process of formation is of immense value in the study of grammar. It is quite welcoming that *Rup* throws a flood of light in this regard. No one can deny the fact that DK deserves high appreciation in this respect also. We are now to turn our attention to the narration of the process of formation of rupas by DK.

1. Prakriyā of the sandhirupa

DK is very keen and vigilant while narrating the *prakriyā* or the process of formation. He deals with each and every stage while narrating the same. For example he begins the *samhitāvatāra* stating that 'deva + chatram iti sthite' and after dealing with the stages through which the said instance passes on to reach the final level of utterance devacchatram, says 'śliṣtoccāraṇam kartavyam, devacchatram iti siddham bhavati.'[45] The first step of *deva + chatram* in this direction is *devat + chatram* and the next and final step is *devacchatram*. These stages are clearly pointed out by giving the rules '*che ca*' (6-1-73) and '*stoḥ* . . .' (8-4-40) which ordain '*t*' and '*c*' here and in order to indicate the operation of these two rules, the necessary *paribhāṣā* rules and *samjñā* rules are also dealt with on the spot itself.[46] Hence a student does never feel giddy while grasping the process of formation of this *sandhirūpa*.

With regard to *svarasandhi, vyañjanasandhi, visargasandhi*, and *svādisandhi* also, he gives the *prakriyā* of sandhirupas very clearly and accurately. In the case of the instance *dadhi atra*, he not only deals with the four stages through which it passes on i.e., 1. *dadhyatra*, 2. *dadhdhyatra*, 3. *daddhyatra* and 4. *dadhyatra*, but also points out the contingency of the operation of the rule *saṃyogāntasya lopaḥ* (8-2-23) and averts the same pointing out the *paribhāṣā* 'asidham bahiraṅgam antaraṅge.'[47] It can be thus correctly stated that while narrating the different stages during the process of formation of a *rūpa*, he also pays attention to the probable contingency of the operation of any rule, involved therein and points out how such contingencies are to be averted scientifically. We meet with such numerous instances all through the work.

So also in the *vyañjanasandhi* while dealing with the *sandhiprakriyā* of the instances *vāk + hasati, ac + halau, ṣat + halāni, tat + hitam, triṣṭup + hutam,* he points out that the final consonant in all the previous forms in these instances gets *jaśtva* by the rule *'jhalām . . .'* (8-2-39) and then states that the rule *jhayo ho . . .* (8-4-62) is to function on the initial consonant *'h'* of the latter forms in these instances. And to point out the particular consonant which as per the above rule optionally replace the consonant *'h,'* DK narrates the *bāhyaprayatna* of each and every consonant and then makes the statement (mahāprāṇasya soṣmaṇo ghoṣavato nādavato hakārasya samvṛtakaṇṭhasya sthāne, pūrvasavarṇo mahāprāṇavān soṣmavān nādavan ghoṣavaṃśca vargacaturtho bhavati.[48] Thus he arrives at the final level of utterance *vāgghasati vāghasati* etc. Here it is to be noted that unless one is aware of the *bāhyaprayatna* of consonants, the process of combination of these instances can never be understood and DK helps the student by equipping him with this readymade knowledge at his finger-tips.

2. Prakriyā of vibhaktirūpa

The *prakriyā* of the *vibhaktirūpa* is dealt in all minute details by DK. He narrates the same very clearly and orderly. Perhaps one may only feel that he could have made it more concise in certain instances.[49] Hence nowhere he cannot be accused of obscurity.

With regard to the narration of the *prakriyā* of vibhaktirupas it can be seen that he gives all the details of the process of formation of the vibhaktirupas formed from the masculine stem *vṛkṣa* which is taken first for elaboration. In order to give the *prakriyā* of the nominative singular form, *vṛkṣaḥ,* he starts from the *prātipadikasaṃjñā* of the stem *vṛkṣa* stating "vṛkṣa iti sthite (arthavattvāt) prātipadikasamjñāyām svādyutpattiḥ" and after dealing with each and every step in the process of formation, concludes the same with the remark "tasmāt vṛkṣaḥ yathā vṛkṣastiṣṭhati."[50] In this way he delcines all the rupas of the stem *vṛkṣa* with clear reference to the process of formation of the same. After dealing with the vibhaktirupas of the *vṛkṣaśabda*, he passes on to deal with other masculine stems ending in '*a*' having peculiar rupas unlike *vṛkṣaśabda* and the *prakriyā* of these peculiar rupas are clearly narrated then and there. In this way the process of formation of the vibhaktirupas of the masculine, feminine and neuter stems ending in vowels and consonants are delineated accurately. We cannot but appreciate the clarity and ease with which he gives the *prakriyā* of the vibhaktirupas.

3. Prakriyā of strīpratyayāntarūpa, samastarūpa and taddhitāntarūpa

The process of formation of *strīpratyayāntarūpa samastarūpa*, and *taddhitāntarūpa* is narrated clearly by DK. With regard to the *prakriyā* of *strīpratyayāntarūpa* and *taddhitāntarūpa* got by the addition of feminine as well as *taddhita* suffixes to nominal and sup-inflected bases respectively, there is not so much intricacy as in the *prakriyā* of vibhaktirupas. Yet, DK does not confine himself to the mere narration of these rupas, but pays attention to give the *prakriyā* of them individually.[51] So also, he gives the *prakriyā* of each and every *samastarūpa* pointing out the peculiarity, if any, it presents, from the *prakriyā* of the *samastarūpa* mentioned previously. For example, while dealing with the *prakriyā* of the *samastarūpa*, *kaṣṭaśritaḥ* he says, "pūrvavat supo luk; kaṣṭaśabdasya dvitīyeti sūtre prathamānirdiṣṭatvādupasarjanatayā pūrvanipātaḥ; svādyutpattiḥ; kaṣṭaśrito devadattaḥ."[52]

4. Prakriyā of tiṅantarūpa and kṛdantarūpa

With regard to the narration of the *prakriyā* of tinantarupas we find that DK has devoted much care on the same as on the *prakriyā* of vibhaktirupas. The *prakriyā* of the tinantarupas of the *parasmaipada* root *bhū* and the *ātmanepada* root '*edh*' in each and every *lakāra*, is narrated in all details. The *prakriyā* of the tinantarupas of certain other roots coming under the ten ganas is also described when the deviation of the same from the *tiṅantarūpa* mentioned just previous to it is met with. He makes clear the *prakriyā* of the *sanādyanta* roots also. Here also the root *bhū* is taken first for narrating the *prakriyā*. The *kṛdantarūpa* does not present much difficulty in their process of formation. Yet, the *prakriyā* of the same is also given due attention.[53]

Other Miscellaneous factors

It has been already stated that, in his treatment of the science of grammar expounded in *Ast*, DK has made use of certain other miscellaneous but relevant factors also.[54] They are the *vars*, the istis of PAT, the unadisutras, the paribhasas, verses of his own as well as of other grammarians, ganapāṭha, and ganasutras. Among these the vars and verses mentioned in *Rup*, are taken up for detailed study in the following chapters.[55] Therefore, we are now, to deal with the istis of PAT, paribhasas, unadisutras, ganapathas and ganasutras.

Istis of Patanjali

The istis of PAT are the foremost one among the several factors that contribute to the greatness of his work, *Mbh*.[56] These istis are accepted to be the authority par excellence in the science of grammar. In his work, DK has made use of 2 istis from the *Mbh*.[57] It deserves mention that DK does not quote the exact wording of these istis as given in *Mbh*, but only comprehends the idea in similar statements.

Gatikāraketarapūrvapadasya yaṇ ṇeśyate

('gatikārakapūrvasyaiveṣyate' - iṣṭi under rule 6-4-82)

This statement 'gatikāraketarapūrvapadasya yaṇ neṣyate' is made by DK while dealing with the declensional rupas of *ikārānta* stems like *pradhī*, *śuddhadhī* and *paramanī*.[58] It means that the substitute *yaṇ* taught by the rule '*eranekāco* . . . (6-4-82) and replacing the vowel '*i*' at the end of a root, does not function when the root is preceded by forms other than those designated as '*gati*' or '*kāraka*.' DK points out that with regard to the base *pradhī*, the substitution by '*y*' (*yaṇ*) of the vowel '*i*' as per the above rule, can take place since the *pūrvapada* '*pra*' in *pradhī* has the designation *gati* and hence has the rupas *pradhyau* etc. in nominative dual onwards whereas in regard to the bases *śuddhadhī* and *paramanī*, the same does not take place since the purvapadas *su* and *parama* in the said instances are neither *gati* nor *kāraka* and has the declensional rupas *paramaniyau* and *śuddhadhiyau* etc. in the dual number of nominative case onwards, wherein it is the *iyaṅ* which comes as the substitute of the final vowel '*i*.'

It is noteworthy here that this statement of DK is drawn from the *iṣṭi* of PAT given as 'gatikārakapūrvasyiyate meaning **"with regard to the** *yaṇādeśa* taught by the rule *'eranekāco'* (6-4-82) it is desirable that the same, while substituting the vowel *'i,'* of a root having a *pūrvapada*, does so only if that *pūrvapada* be *gati* or *kāraka*.[59] The idea of this *iṣṭi* is hence given by DK as 'gatikāraketarapūrvapadasya yaṇ neṣyate.'

Sūtrāntādakalpāderiṣyate

(Vidyālakṣaṇakalpasūtrāntādakalpāderikak smṛtaḥ — isti under rule 4-2-60)

DK makes the statement 'sūtrāntādakalpāderiṣyate' while dealing with the *rūpa 'kālpasūtraḥ'* meaning 'kalpasūtram adhīte vetti vā' i.e. 'one who learns or knows the *kalpasūtra*.'[60] Though the rule *'kratūkthādisūtrāntāṭṭhak'* (4-2-60) ordains to bases ending with *'sūtra,'* the *taddhita* suffix *ṭhak* to denote the sense *'tadadhīte'* or *'tadveda'* the base *kalpasūtra* does not procure it since the base beginning with *'kalpa'* and ending with *'Sūtra'* is excluded from the scope of the suffix *ṭhak* as per this statement. Hence by the addition of the original *taddhita* suffix *aṇ*, one gets the form *kālpasūtraḥ* to denote the idea of one knowing or learning *kalpasūtra*.

This statement 'sūtrāntādakalpāderiṣyate' found in *Rup* is the outcome of the *iṣṭi* we get in *Mbh* under the rule 4-2-60.[61] PAT gives his *iṣṭi* as 'vidyālakṣaṇakalpasūtrāntādakalpāderikak smṛtaḥ' and after explaining the same, he cites the *rūpa kālpasūtraḥ* saying "akalpāderiti kimartham? kālpasūtraḥ." PAT means that bases which have, at their end, sounds like *vidyā*, *lakṣaṇa*, *kalpa* and *sūtra* get the suffix *ṭhak* and the base having *'sūtra'* at the end and *'kalpa'* in the beginning does not procure *ṭhak* and hence gets the original suffix *aṇ* alone, whereby the form *kālpasūtraḥ* is obtained.

Paribhasas

In addition to the *paribhāṣā* rules found in *Ast*, DK has comprehended certain other paribhasas or postulates in his work. These paribhasas facilitate the easier understanding of the process of formation of rupas as well as the meaning of the rules of *Ast* and are accepted in the science of grammar on the authority of the *vars* of KAT and *Mbh* of PAT.[62] It is praiseworthy that DK has adhered to the needs of *'bāla,'* the beginner by introducing these paribhasas in relevant places for giving the interpretation or rules or narrating the *prakriyā* of rupas. The paribhasas which he has selected for his work number 32 and a few of them are now briefly dealt with so as to show how these paribhasas are interwoven by DK in his work to interpret a rule or narrate the *prakriyā* of a *rūpa*.

Ekadeśavikṛtamananyavad bhavati

This *paribhāṣā* is cited by DK to point out that the nipatas *āṅ* and *māṅ*, even when stripped of the *anubandha 'ṅ'* can be treated as *āṅ* and *māṅ* and hence in the instances *ā (ṅ)+ chādayati* and *mā (ṅ)+ chidat* the rule *'āṅmāṅośca'* (6-1-74) can very well operate treating the *'ā'* and *'mā'* here to be *āṅ* and *māṅ*.[63] As per this paribhāṣā, a sound incurring a change in its minor part, does never become any other one. In spite of this minor change, it can therefore be treated as the same as it was before. DK adds that a dog, even when one of its limbs like tail, ears, etc. is cut off, does not become a horse or a donkey but, is the dog itself.

Asiddham bahiraṅgam antaraṅge

While dealing with the euphonic combination of *dadhi* and *atra* into *dadhyatra*, DK cites this *paribhāṣā* which makes *bahiraṅga* rules invalid from the point of view of *antaraṅga* rules.[64] The elision, of the letter *'y'* in *dadhyatra,* contingent by the rule *'saṃyogāntasya lopaḥ'* (8-2-23) is averted by this *paribhāṣā* according to which the substitute *'y'* (of the letter *i*) taught by the *bahiraṅga* rule *'iko yaṇaci'* (6-1-77) becomes invalid with respect to the *antaraṅga* rule *'saṃyogāntasya lopaḥ'* and hence the substitute *'y'* does not get elided by the rule *'saṃyogāntasya.'*

Pratyayagrahaṇe yasmātsa vihitaḥ tadādestadantasya grahaṇam

and

Samjñāvidhau pratyayagrahaṇe tadantagrahaṇam na bhavati

Both these paribhasas are cited by DK while interpreting the rule *'suptiṅantaṃ padaṃ'* (1-4-14).[65] There he points out that in the existence of the *paribhāṣā* 'pratyayagrahaṇe yasmāt sa vihitaḥ tadādestadantasya grahaṇam' which means 'whenever an affix is employed it denotes the part which begins with that, to which the affix had been added and ends with the affix itself,' the part *'anta'* in the rule is an excess and hence it indicates the *paribhāṣā* 'samjñāvidhau pratyayagrahaṇe, tadantagrahaṇam na bhavati' meaning 'an affix, when employed in a rule which teaches the meaning of a technical term, does not denote a wordform ending with the affix.' As a result, the *ghasamjñā* taught by the rule *'taraptamapau ghaḥ'* (1-1-22) relates only to the suffixes *tarap* and *tamap* and not to *tarabanta* and *tamabanta.* Therefore in the sentence 'gaurī brāhmaṇitarā' the *hrasva* taught by the rule *'gharūpa . . .'* (6-3-43) occurs only to the *pūrvapada brāhmaṇī* which is followed by *tarap* having *ghasamjñā* and not to *gaurī* which is followed by *brahmaṇitarā* i.e. *tarabanta* which does not have the *ghasamjñā.*

Padāṅgādhikāre tasya ca tadantasya ca

and

Nirdiśyamānasyādeśā bhavanti

While narrating the *prakriyā* of the nominative dual form *nirjarasau* of the masculine base *nirjara,* DK refers to both of these paribhasas.[66] According to the *paribhāṣā,* 'padaṅgādhikāre tasya ca tadantasya ca,' a substitute coming to a word or base, governed by a rule studied under the *adhikāra, padasya* or *aṅgasya* comes to that part also which ends with that word or base. Hence the *'jaras'* taught as a substitute of *jarā* by the rule *'jarāyā jarasanyatarasyām* (7-2-101) can have its function in the base *nirjara* by the favour of this *paribhāṣa* which allows the rule to function on *jarā* as well as on a base ending with *jarā* since this rule comes under the scope of the *adhikāra* rule *'aṅgasya'* (6-4-1). However the substitute *jaras* replaces the part *jarā* alone of *nirjara* and not the whole base *nirjara,* in accordance with the *paribhāṣā,* 'nirdiśyamānasyādeśā bhavanti' by which a substitute can take the place of that alone which is actually enunciated in a rule. This *paribhāṣā* is referred to by DK while giving the *prakriyā* of the accusative plural *dvipadaḥ* of the *'d'* stem *dvipād* also.[67] While interpreting the rule *'iṣṭa-keṣīkāmālānām . . .'* (6-3-65) DK once again refers to the *paribhāṣā* 'padāṅgā . . .'[68]

It is clear from the paribhasas dealt with just now, that the introduction of paribhasas in this work by DK, helps to interpret the rules or narrate the *prakriyā* of rupas or to point out the rules which act as the jnapakas of these paribhasas. Moreover by incorporating the paribhasas, DK has achieved the purpose of making the reader acquainted with these technical postulates which would help for an advanced study in the science of grammar.

Uṇādi rules

We find that DK has made use of 15 *uṇādi* rules for interpreting the rules of *Ast* and narrating the *prakriyā* of rupas. He has given the meaning of most of these rules and we are now concerned with the relevance of these rules in this work.

1. Pāterdatiḥ (uṇādi : IV - 58)

Before dealing with the declensional rupas of the *'i'* stem *pati*, DK cites this rule.[69] He points out that the stem *pati* is got by the addition of the suffix *ḍati* taught by this *uṅādi* rule, to the root *'pā'* wherein the *'ā'* gets elided on the basis of the *anubandha 'ḍ'* in *ḍati* as per the rule *'ṭeḥ'* (6-4-143).

2. Si - tani - gami - masi - saci - avi - dhāñ - kruśibhyastun (u ṇ ādi: I - 69)

Before dealing with the declensional rupas of the *'u'* stem *kroṣṭu*, DK cites this rule, gives its meaning and says that the stem *kroṣṭu* derived from the root *kruś* by the addition of the suffix *tun* taught by this *uṇādi* rule, is a *kṛdanta* stem endowed with the *prātipadikasamjñā*.[70]

3. Glainudibhyāmḍauḥ (uṇādi : II - 65)

Before dealing with the declensional rupas of the stem *'glau'* DK cites this rule and gives its meaning to point out that the masculine stem *glau* is derived by the addition of the suffix *ḍau* to the root *'glai.'*[71]

4. Bhāterḍavatuḥ (uṇādi : I - 63)

It is for pointing out the derivation of the *'ī'* stem, *bhavatī*, that DK mentions this rule and gives it meaning.[72] Thus he makes the reader aware of the fact that the root *'bhā'* added with the suffix *ḍavatu* procures the *kṛdanta* stem *bhavat* and by the addition of the feminine suffix *ṅīp*, the stem *bhavatī* is got.

5. Lakṣermuṭ ca (uṇādi : III - 160)

The derivation of the *'ī'* stem *lakṣmī* is got by this rule which is cited by DK before dealing with the declensional rupas of this stem.[73] The meaning of the rule is that the root *'lakṣ'* gets the suffix *'ī'* as well as the augment *muṭ* and thus we get the stem *lakṣmī*.

6. Styāyaterḍrarṭ : (uṇādi : IV - 167)

As per this *uṇādi* rule, the root *'styai'* gets the suffix *ḍraṭ*. This rule is cited by DK to point out the derivation of the 'ī' stem *strī*.[74] He states that the *anubandha 'ḍ'* in the suffix *ḍraṭ* causes the elision of the letter *'ai'* and the form *stra* got thereby, gets the feminine suffix *nīp* by the force of the rule *'ṭiṭḍhāṇañ . . .'* (4-1-15) and thus the stem *strī* is arrived at.

7. Patastha ca (uṇādi : IV - 12)

DK points out that the *nakārānta* stem *pathin* is derived as per this rule which gives the suffix *'in'* and the final substitute *'th'* to the root *'pat'* to get the stem pathin.[75]

8. Parau vrajeḥ ṣaśca padānte (uṇādi : II - 60)

This *uṇādi* rule means that the root *'vraj'* gets the suffix *kvip* and the lengthening of its vowel *'a'* when it has the *upapada 'pari'* and that the base *parivrāj* got thereby, is subject to the substitution by *'ṣ'* of its final consonant *'j'* when *'j'* becomes the final one of a *pada*. It is to point out the nominative singular forms *parivrāṭ* and *parivrāḍ* of the *'j'* stem *parivrāj* that DK cites this *uṇādi* rule in his work.[76]

9. Vartamāne pr̥ṣat - br̥hat - mahat - śatr̥vat (uṇādi: II - 85)

DK cites this rule to point out that the base *mahat*, derived by the addition of the *uṇādi* suffix *ati* to the root *'mah,'* gets the operations enjoined to the suffix *śatr̥*.[77] DK points out that the base *mahat*, as per the *śatr̥vadbhāva* enjoined by this *uṇādi* rule gets the suffix *num* taught by the rule *'ugitacām . . .'* (7-1-70), when followed by the suffix *su*; hence its nominative singular form is obtained as *mahān*.

10. Vaśeḥ kanasiḥ (uṇādi : IV - 240)

The base *uśanas* is derived from the root *'vaś'* added with the suffix *kanasi* ordained by this rule which is cited by DK before dealing with the declensional rupas of *uśanas*.[78]

11. Ñamantāḍḍaḥ (uṇādi : I - 119)

This rule teaches the suffix *'ḍa'* to roots ending in consonants, viz. *ñ, m, ṅ, ṇ* and *n* which come under the *pratyāhāra 'ñam'*. DK cites this rule only to point out the fact that the consonant *'m'* is comprehended by the *pratyāhāra ñam* referred to in the part *ñamanteṣu* of the verse beginning with 'yamirñamanteṣvaniḍeka . . .' which is an *aniṭkārikā*.[79] He states that in this verse the reference to the root *'yam'* as *ñamanta* is quite appropriate since its final consonant *'m'* is one among the letters comprehended by *ñam* which is understood as a *pratyāhāra* from this *uṇādi* rule itself.

12. Jṛśṛstṛjāgṛbhyaḥ svin (unādi : IV - 55)

While interpreting the rule *'jāgrovicinnalṅitsu* (7-3-85), DK states that the rule teaches *guṇa* to the root *jāgṛ* when it is not followed by the suffixes *vi, ciṇ, ṇal* and *ṅit*. It is in order to illustrate the same, that he presents this *uṇādi* rule which teaches the suffix *svin* to the root *jāgṛ.*[80] He continues that the suffix *svin* when stripped of the anubandhas becomes *vi* and hence the root *jāgṛ* added with this suffix *vi* does not get *guṇa* by the part *avicinnalṅitsu* of the rule *'jāgro . . . '* and we get the resultant form *jāgṛviḥ.*

13. kṛvāpājimisvadisādhyaśūbhya'uṇ (uṇādi : I - 1),

14. Gamerḍoḥ (uṇādi : II - 67)

and

15. Sarvadhātubhyosun (uṇādi : IV - 188)

These three *uṇādi* rules are dealt by DK while interpreting the rule *'uṇādayo bahulam'* of *Ast* (3-3-1).[81] The suffixes beginning with *uṇ* are referred to in the rule *'uṇādayo . . . '* and hence DK cites as examples these three rules among the many which ordain the *uṇādi* suffixes. Of these three *uṇādi* rules the first, *'kṛvā . . . '* ordains the suffix *uṇ* to the roots *kṛ, vā, pā, ji, mi svad, sādh* and *aś* etc. whereby forms like *kāruḥ, vāyuḥ, pāyuḥ, jāyuḥ, māyuḥ, svāduḥ, sādhuḥ* and *āśuḥ* are got. The *uṇādi* rule *'gamerḍoḥ*, cited next by DK, teaches the suffix *ḍo* to the root gam, to procure the stem *'go*. The rule *'sarva . . . '* enjoins to all the roots the suffix *asun* and DK cites the forms like *saraḥ, tejaḥ, manaḥ, tamaḥ* etc. as examples.

Ganapathas and ganasutras

DK's avowed aim in creating a recast of *Ast* was to bring the rupas within the easy reach of the students of grammar. Hence his work gives, as stated earlier, more importance to rupas. Therefore, when a rule of *Ast*, selected for his work, refers to ganas or list of nominal stems which behave alike grammatically, he gives the *gaṇapāṭha* for ready reference. Thus we find that DK has enumerated ganas like *svarādi, prādi, ajādi*, etc. referred to in rules like *'svarādinipātamavyayam'* (1-1-37) *'prādayaḥ'* (1-4-58) *'ajādyataṣṭāp'* (4-1-4) etc. respectively.[82] In addition to these he has enumerated certain ganas though he has omitted in his work, the rules which refer to these ganas. They are the ganas like *uryādi*, the *gaṇa* headed by the word *sākṣāt* etc. He had not mentioned in his work, the rules *'uryādicviḍācaśca'* (1-4-61) and *'sākṣātprabhṛtīni ca'* (1-4-74) which endow the two groups of sabdas headed by *ūrī* and *sākṣāt*, with the *nipātasamjñā*.[83] These nipatas are enumerated by him to point out that they get the *avyayasamjñā* taught by the rule *'svarādinipātamavyayam'* which is interpreted by him.

However it deserves mention that in certain instances DK does not enumerate all the stems or roots coming under the ganas which are referred to in the Paninian rules selected by him, but gives only a few among them. For instance, in the ganas like *nadyādi, utkarādi*, etc. referred to in rules like *'utkarādibhyaśchaḥ'* (4-2-90) *'nadyādibhyo ḍhak'* (4-2-97) etc. respectively, we find that forms *utkarīyam, śapharīyam* and *pippalīyam* derived from certain stems *utkara, śaphara* and *pippala* coming under the *utkarādigaṇa* and the forms *nādeyam, māheyam* and *vārāṇaseyam* derived from a few stems *nadī, māhī* and *vārāṇasī* coming under the *nadyādigaṇa*, are only mentioned by him.[84] So also with regard to the ten ganas of roots, *bhvādi, adādi* etc., he does not enumerate all the roots coming under these ganas but cites only a few of them under the respective ganas, in course of narrating their verbal forms in the various sections concerned with them.[85]

Again DK has made mention of certain ganasutras for giving the rupas of certain stems which have some speciality from the other stems occurring in the same gana.[86] For example, he mentions the *gaṇasūtra nṛnarayorvṛddhiśca* to point out the fact that in addition to the feminine suffix *ṅīn* enjoined by the rule *śārṅgaravādyaño ṅīn* (4-1-73) to the stems *'śārṅgaravā, kāpatava, nṛ,* and *nara* etc. coming under the *'śārṅgaravādigaṇa'* the stems *nṛ* and *nara* alone, get an initial *vṛddhi* also whereby the form *nārī* is arrived at.[87] So also other ganasutras like *'sarvatoktin-narthādityeke,' 'arhato num ca,' 'māraṇatoṣaṇaniśāmaneṣu jñā'* etc. are cited to point out the rupas like *rājiḥ, rājī, ārhantyam jñapayati* etc.[88]

Notes and References

1. Vide Supra, pp. 20 & 21.
2. *Rup* Part I, pp. 6 & 7.
3. The eleven sandhirupas are *daddhyatra, śammyatra, maddhvatra, vaddhvākṛtiḥ, pittrarthaḥ, lākṛtiḥ, dadhyatra,*

śamyatra, madhvatra, vadhvākṛtiḥ & pitrarthaḥ. (*Rup* Part I, p. 8).

4. *Rup* Part I, p. 9.
5. Ibid, p. 12.
6. Ibid, pp. 15 & 16.
7. Ibid, p. 16.
8. Ibid, p. 58.
9. ṝkāra ḷkāra ekārāntā aprasiddhāḥ (Part I, p. 71).
10. *Rup* Part I, pp. 87 to 106.
11. Ibid, pp. 113 to 117.
12. Ibid, pp. 118 to 127.
13. "atha halanteṣvaliṅgaprakaraṇam" (*Rup* Part I, p. 123).
14. Vide Supra, pp. 56 & 57.
15. *Rup* Part I, pp. 123 to 127.
16. Ibid, p. 128.
17. "atra kānicidavyayāni svarūpato nipātitāni kānicil-lakṣaṇalabdhāni/lakṣaṇalabdhāvyayāni tredhā bhavanti avyayībhāva - kṛdanta - taddhitānta-bhedena" (*Rup* Part I, pp. 128 & 129).
18. *Rup* Part I, pp. 130 & 131.
19. Ibid, pp. 132 to 144.
20. "ke punaḥ strīpratyayāḥ ? ṭāp, ḍāp, cāp, ṅīp, ṅis, ṅīn, uṅ, ti ityete strīpratyayāḥ" (*Rup* Part I, p. 132).
21. *Rup* Part I, pp. 145 to 164.
22. Vide Supra, pp. 57 & 58.
23. *Rup* Part I, pp. 165 to 191.
24. Ibid, pp. 192 to 218.
25. Ibid, pp. 219 to 227.
26. Ibid, pp. 227 to 229.
27. Ibid, pp. 229 & 230.
28. Ibid, pp. 231 to 308.
29. *Rup* Part II, pp. 4 to 50.
30. Ibid, pp. 51 to 73.
31. Ibid, pp. 74 to 99.
32. Ibid, pp. 100 to 107.
33. Ibid, pp. 108 to 176.
34. Ibid, pp. 176 to 186.
35. Ibid, p. 9.
36. Ibid, pp. 77 & 153.

37. Vide Supra, p. 60.
38. *Rup* Part II, pp. 186 to 235.
39. Ibid, pp. 235 to 241.
40. Ibid, pp. 241 to 247.
41. Ibid, pp. 247 to 253.
42. Ibid, pp. 254 to 306.
43. Vide Infra, pp. 153 & 154.
44. śabdāḥ anuśiṣyante asādhuśabdebhyo vivicya bodhyante iti śabdānuśāsanam.
45. *Rup* Part I, p. 7.
46. Here the *saṃjñā* rule '*paraḥ* . . . ' (1-4-109) is interpreted to explain the word *saṃhitāyām* which is got by *anuvṛtti* in the rule '*che ca*.' So also the *paribhāṣā* rules '*ṣaṣṭhī* . . . ' (1-1-49) and '*ādyantau* . . . (1-1-46) are interpreted here since they help to understand the meaning of the rule '*che ca*.' The rule '*stoḥ* . . . ' teaches *cavarga* as the substitute of *tavarga* and hence the *paribhāṣā* rule '*yathā* . . . ' (1-3-10) is also interpreted, since it determines the particular letter i.e. '*c*' which among the *cavarga* is to replace '*t*' here. (*Rup* Part I, p. 7).
47. *Rup* Part I, p. 8 & Vide Supra, p. 49.
48. *Rup* Part I, p. 17.
49. Vide Supra, p. 42.
50. *Rup* Part I, p. 29.
51. For example we may go through the *prakriyā* of *bahurājñī* (strīpratyayāntarūpa) and *aupagavaḥ* (*taddhitāntarūpa*) as narrated by DK :

    "bahurājan ityatra, an upadhālopinonyatarasyām (4-1-28) upadhālopinaḥ annantāt bahuvrīheḥ ṅīppratyayo bhavatyanyatarasyām / yaci bham (1-4-18) iti bhasamjñāyām, alloponaḥ (6-4-134) ityakāralopaḥ; stoḥ ścunā ścuḥ (8-4-40) iti cutvam ; bahurājñī nagarī" (*Rup* Part I, p. 133).

    "upagu + ṅas+aṇ ityatra ittvāṇṇalopė 'taddhitāḥ' iti taddhitasamjñāyām supo luk bhavati /upagu + a iti jāte, 'aṅgasya' (6-4-1), 'mṛjervṛddhiḥ' (7-2-114), 'aco ñṇiti' (7-2-115), iti vartamāne, taddhiteṣvajāmādeḥ (7-2-117) ñiti, ṇiti ca taddhite paratoṅgasyā-cāmāderaco vṛddhirbhavati / aṅgasya (6-4-1), bhasya (6-4-129), nastaddhite (6-4-114) iti vartamāne, orguṇaḥ (6-4-116), uvarṇāntasyāṅgasya bhasya guṇo bhavati taddhite parataḥ/ iti aupagavaḥ" (*Rup*. Part I, p. 219).

52. *Rup* Part I, p. 171.
53. For example, we may go through the narration of the *prakriyā* of the *kṛdantarūpa 'bhavan'* :
"idānīm śatrādau kṛte, kartari śap iti śapi, sārvadhātukārdhadhātukayoḥ iti guṇaḥ; avādeśaḥ; atoguṇe iti pararūpatvam/bhavat iti jāte, kṛdantatvena prātipadikasamjñāyām svādayo bhavanti . . . /halṅyādisamyogāntalopau; bhavan" (*Rup* Part II, p. 242).
54. Vide Supra, p. 66.
55. Vide Infra, pp. 106 to 113.
56. Vide Nāgeśabhaṭṭa, "mahābhāṣyeti - vyākhyātṛtvepyasyeṣṭyādikathanenānvākhyātṛtvādit -arabhāṣyavailakṣaṇyena mahatvam" (*Udyota* of *Mbh*. Vol. I, *Prathamakhanda,* p. 2).
57. In his index (vārtikaparibhāṣādisūci) to the edition of *Rup*, Prof. Rang has wrongly noted some more statements as the istis of PAT. But when we refer to *Mbh* under the relevant rules, it can be clearly understood that these statements of *Rup* are based on the vars of *Mbh* or the views of other grammarians cited in *Mbh* and they are not based on any istis of PAT. For example, Rang gives the statement (in *Rup*) 'prathamaliṅgagrahaṇam ca'as the *iṣṭi* of PAT, but when we refer to *Mbh* under the rule *'yū stryākhyau nadī* (1-4-3) it can be clearly understood as var. (*Rup* Part I, p. 50 & *Mbh*, Vol. I, Dvitīyakhaṇda, p. 221).
58. *Rup*. Part I, p. 52.
59. *Mbh* (Vol. II), under rule 6-4-82, Vol. II, p. 942.
60. *Rup* Part I, p. 237.
61. *Mbh*, Vol. II, p. 421.
62. Vide Nageśabhatta, "prācīnavaiyākaraṇatantre vācanikānyatra pāṇinīyatantre jñāpakanyāyasiddhāni bhāṣyavārtikayornibaddhāni yāni paribhāṣarūpāni . . ./" (*Paribhāṣenduśekhara*, p. 1).
63. *Rup* Part I, p. 8.
64. Ibid, p. 9.
65. Ibid, p. 24.
66. Ibid, p. 36.

67. Ibid, pp. 100 & 101.
68. Ibid, p. 209.
69. Ibid, p. 46.
70. Ibid, p. 53.
71. Ibid, p. 60.
72. Ibid, p. 67.
73. Ibid, p. 68.
74. Ibid, p. 697.
75. Ibid, p. 97.
76. Ibid, p. 100.
77. Ibid, p. 105.
78. Ibid, p. 109.
79. *Rup* Part II, p. 111.
80. Ibid, p. 165.
81. Ibid, pp. 289 & 290.
82. Rup Part I, pp. 128, 130 & 132.
83. Ibid, pp. 130 & 131.
84. Ibid, pp. 240 & 241.
85. *Rup* Part II, pp. 4 to 241.
86. Scholars are of opinion that the so called ganasutras do not have the status of a *sūtra* which is defined as "alpākṣaramamasandigdham . . . ". They are to be more appropriately called ganavakyas which are interpolations made in the *gaṇapāṭha* by later authors. For further details, Vide Kapiladeva Sastry *'Samskrta vyakaran mem ganapath ki parampara aur acary Panini,'* pp. 84 to 91.
87. *Rup* Part I, p. 143.
88. *Rup* Part I, pp. 140 & 273, Part II, pp. 46 & 218.

Chapter VI

Readings of the Sūtras and Vārtikas in Rūpāvatāra

We now turn our attention to the sutras and vartikas found in the *Rup* which present slight variations from the same found in earlier grammatical works. The sutras in *Rup* are discussed in this chapter with regard to the variations in their readings from earlier works where as vartikas are discussed with reference to the extent to which they follow or differ from the earlier works.

Readings of the Sutras

The text of *Ast* has always been a source of inspiration for study not only for its contents but also for its verbal form which to a certain extent get variations in *Mbh, K* and the recasts of *Ast* like *Rup, PK, PS, SK* etc. We now examine the altered versions of the text of *Ast* found in *Rup*.

The readings of the sutras in *Rup* differ in many cases with that of the text of *Ast*. These variant readings can be grouped on the basis of the mode of variation. In one group the difference in reading relates to the addition, omission or variation of words. In another group the variation in reading relates to the component letters of the roots mentioned in the sutras. In yet another group the variation in reading of the sutras is mainly brought about either by the operation or non-operation of *sandhi* rules.

Difference in reading involving addition, omission or variation of words

Sutra 1-1-5 : *Mbh* reads the rule as *'kiṅiti ca'* wherein the letter *'k'* occurs once only. But under the rule *'glāgisthaśca ksnuḥ* (3-2-139) PAT speaks of the two kakaras that occur in this rule, *"kakāre gakāraścartvabhūto nirdiśyate - kkiṅiti ceti.*[1] *Rup* gives the same reading as *Mbh* by mentioning *'k'* once and while explaining the forms *glāsnuḥ, jiṣṇuḥ, sthāsnuḥ, bhūṣṇuḥ*, says *'giccāyam pratyayo na kit; tena* *stha ikārādeśo na bhavati"/kṅitica ityatrāpi gakāraścartvabhūto nirdiśyate, tena guṇo na bhavati'*[2] K reads the rule as *'kkiṅiti ca'* wherein two kakaras are given.

Sutra 2-3-5 : In *Mbh* and *K* this rule is read as *'kālādhvanoratyantasamyoge'* where as *Rup* reads the rule as *'kālādhvanoratyantasamyoge dvitīyā.'*[3] The addition of the word *dvitīyā* in this rule when the same can be got by *anuvṛtti* from the previous rule *karmaṇi dvitīyā* (2-3-2) may be to avoid the *anuvṛtti* of the word *tṛtīyā* from the previous rule *'tṛtīyā ca . . .'* (2-3-3) and it can be pointed out that the same is not necessary to achieve the said purpose. This is because the absence of the *anuvṛtti* of the word *tṛtīyā* from the rule 2-3-3 to the rule 2-3-4 and 5 can be inferred on the basis of the fact that the next rule *apavarge tṛtīyā* (2-3-6) has got the word *tṛtīyā* in it and if the word *tṛitīyā* were to be got by anuvṛtti from the rule 2-3-3 to 2-3-4 & 5, the same can be got by *anuvṛtti* in the rule 2-3-6 also and there is no necessity of the mention of the word *tṛtīyā* in *apavarge tṛtīyā* (2-3-6). Hence the addition of the word *dvitīyā* in 2-3-5 found in *Rup* is not essential to prevent the anuvṛtti of the word *tṛtīyā* from the previous rule and the word *dvitīya* can be got by *anuvṛtti* in *'kālādhvanor*. . . (2-3-5) from *'karmaṇi dvitīyā'* (2-3-2). Thus by the addition of the word *dvitīyā, Rup* makes the reading more explanatory as opposed to the concise nature of a *sūtra* well-known from the verse beginning with "alpākṣaramasandigdham. . . ."

Sūtra 2-3-33 : *K* reads this rule as *'karaṇe ca stokālpakṛcchrakatipayasyāsatvavacanasya.' Mbh* does not comment on this *sūtra. Rup* omits the part *'karaṇe ca'* and gives the reading of the rule as *'stokālpakṛcchrakatipayasyāsatvavacanasya.'*[4] However the word *Karaṇa* is included by DK while giving the *vṛtti* of this rule. The word *karaṇe* cannot be said to have got by the ordinary mode of *anuvṛtti* since the same is not seen in the just previous rules. Hence as per the reading of *Rup* one has to explain the connection of the word *karaṇe* in this rule only by virtue of a special kind of *anuvṛtti* technically known as *maṇḍūkapluti* from the distant previous rule *'kartṛkaraṇayostṛitīyā'* (2-3-18). Since the reading of the rule in *Rup* demands the strenuous effort of *maṇḍūkapluti* for getting the connection of the word *karaṇe* in the rule, the reading presented by *K* seems more acceptable.

Sūtra 3-1-111 : *K* and *Rup* read this rule as *'ī ca khanaḥ'* according to which the root *khan* gets the suffix *kyap* and the substitution by the vowel 'ī' in the place of its final consonant '*n*.'[5] PAT suggests the reading '*i ca khanaḥ*.' He contends that the form *kheyam* which is to be derived by this rule, can well be obtained even if the substitute enjoined by the rule be the short vowel '*i*' instead of '*ī*.'[6]

Sūtra 3-2-54 : *K* reads this rule as '*śaktau hastikapāṭayoḥ*' whereas *Rup* given the rule as '*śaktau hastikavāṭayoh*' wherein we find the word *kavāṭa* in the place of '*kapāṭa*' in *K*.[7] *Mbh* does not give this rule. However the word *kavāṭa* or *kapāṭa* denote the same sense and hence the variant reading in *Rup* does not affect the meaning of the rule. *PS* follows the reading of this rule found in *Rup*.[8]

Sūtra 4-2-42 : As per *Mbh* and *K*, this rule has the reading '*brāhmaṇamāṇavabāḍavādyan*' whereas *Rup* read this rule '*brāhmaṇamāṇavabāḍavādyat*' wherein we get *yat* in the place of '*yan*.'[9] *PS* has the reading of *Rup*.[10] The form of the suffix be *yan* or *yat*, it does not make any difference in the accomplishment of the words *brāhmaṇyam, māṇavyam* and *bāḍavyam* which are to be derived by this rule. If it is *yan*, then by the rule *ñnityādirnityam* (6-1-197), the words formed will have *udātta* in the beginning, while if it is *yat* then by '*titsvritam*' (6-1-85) they will have *pratyayasvara*, viz. *svarita*.

Sūtra 4-3-34 : *Mbh* and *K* read this rule as '*śraviṣṭhāphalgunyanurādhāsvātitiṣyapunarvasu hastaviśākhāṣaṭhābahulālluk*' whereas *Rup* reads *anūrādhā* for *anurādhā* in the rule.[11] In *PS* also we get the same reading.[12]

Anurādhā or *Anūrādhā* is the name of a star and hence the variation in reading in *Rup* does not affect the sense of the rule.

Sūtra 4-3-103 : *K* reads this rule as '*kāśyapakauśikābhyām ṛṣibhyām ṇiniḥ*'. *Mbh* does not explain this rule. Though DK omits the word *ṛṣibhyām* in the reading of the rule, he takes the words *Kāśyapa* and *Kauśika* as denoting *ṛṣi* while giving the meaning of the rule.[13] Hence the variant reading in *Rup* does not effect any change in meaning.

Sūtra 4-3-143 : *Mbh* reads this rule as '*mayaḍvaitayorbhāṣāyāmabhakṣācchādanayoḥ*' wherein the word *abhakṣa* occurs.[14] But *K* and *Rup* read the rule with the word *abhakṣya* in the place of *abhakṣa*.[15] Anyhow *abhakṣya* is used to denote the sense conveyed by the expression *abhakṣa* and hence the variant reading in *K* and *Rup* does not bring about any change in the idea conveyed by the rule.

Sūtra 4-4-20 : *K* reads the rule as *'ktrermamnityam'* which means that the bases ending with the suffix *'ktri'* enjoined by the rule *'ḍvitaḥ ktriḥ'* (3-3-88) gets the suffix *map. Mbh* reads the rule as *'trermamnityam'* which is followed in *Rup* also.[16] Though the suffix *'ktri'* is referred to in *Mbh* & *Rup* as *'tri'* devoid of the *anubandha 'k,'* there is no difference in the meaning of these two readings.

Sūtra 5-1-66 : In *K* this rule is read as *'daṇḍādibhyaḥ'* which ordains the suffix *'yat'* taken by *anuvṛtti* from the previous rule *'śīrṣachedādyacca'* (5-1-65). This rule is not seen in *Mbh*. But in *Mbh* under the rule *aco yat* (3-1-97) there is an indication that it is *yat* which is applied to *daṇḍādi.*[17] *Rup* reads the rule as' *daṇḍādibhyo yaḥ.'*[18] Since the word *yat* can be got by *anuvṛtti* from the previous rule, the insertion of the word *yaḥ* in this rule is treated as an interpolation by some commentators.[19]

Sūtra 5-3-5 : *Mbh* reads this rule as 'etadon' which enjoins the substitute *'an'* in the place of *'etad.'* But *K* and *Rup* read the rule as *'etadoś'* by which it is the substitute *'as'* which replaces the base *'etad.'*[20] It is here noteworthy that both the substitutes *'an'* and *'as'* serve the same purpose inasmuch as both become *sarvādeśa* by the force of the rule *'anekalśitsarvasya'* (1-1-55) the former on the basis of *anekāltva* and the latter on the basis of *śitva.*[21]

Sūtra 6-1-124 : This rule is read as *'indre ca nityam'* in *K* and *Rup.*[22] *Mbh* gives a variant reading as *'indre ca'* omitting the word *nityam.* In *Prauḍhamanorama* BD accepts the reading found in *Mbh* and speaks of the reading *'indre ca nityam'* as defective.[23]

Sutra 6-3-13 : *Mbh* and *K* read this rule as *'bandhe ca vibhāṣā'* whereas *Rup* alone gives a variant reading as *'bandhe vibhāṣā'* omitting the word ca.[24] This rule enjoins the optional non-elision of the locative case suffixes *'ni,' os* & *sup'* of the *pūrvapada* when followed by the *uttarapada 'bandha.'*

Sūtra 7-1-94 : *K* reads this rule as *'ṛduśanaspurudamsonehasām ca'* where we get the consonant *'s'* in the base *purudams.* But in the reading of the rule in *Rup,* we find *'ś'* instead of *'s,'* by mentioning the base as *purudamś.*[25] *Mbh* does not explain this rule.

Variation in roots

In *Mbh, K, Rup* etc. roots mentioned in certain sutras present slight variations. They are now being discussed.

Sūtra 1-2-6 : In *Mbh* we get the reading of this rule as *'indhibhavatibhyam ca'* which is given in *Rup* also.[26] In *K* the root *'indhi'* is read as *'īndhi'* as per the reading *'īndhibhavatibhyām ca.'*

Sūtra 1-2-24 : In this *sūtra*, *Rup* mentions the root *'luñc'* without the vowel *'i'* prescribed by the var *'ikstipau dhātunirdeśe'* and reads the rule as *'vañciluñcṛtaśca.'*[27]

Mbh and *K* read the *sūtra* as *'vañciluñcyṛtaśca'* where the root *'luñc'* is mentioned with the vowel *'i'* which gets the substitute 'y' (*yaṇ*) by the rule *'iko yaṇaci'* (6-1-77). This *sūtra* is not mentioned in *Mbh*. It is at the end of the *Bhāṣya* passage under the rule *'pūṅah ktvā ca'* (1-2-22) that we get this reading of the rule 1-2-24.[28] However the mention of the root without the vowel *'i'* in *Rup* does not bring about any change in the form to be derived from it.

Sūtra 3-1-90 : *Mbh* and *K* mention this root as *'raj'* by giving the reading *'kuṣirajoḥ prācām śyan parasmaipadam ca.' Rup* reads this root as *'rañj'* giving the rule as *'kuṣirañjoḥ . . . .'*[29]

Sūtra 3-2-155 : *Rup* reads this rule as *'jalpabikṣakuṭṭaluṇṭhavṛṅaḥ ṣākan'* wherein we get the root *'luṇṭha.'* But *K* reads the root as *luṇṭa* by giving the rule as *'jalpabhikṣakuṭṭaluṇṭavṛṅaḥ ṣākan.'*[30] *Mbh* does not comment on this rule.

Sūtra 3-2-46 : *K* mentions the root *tṝ* in this *sūtra* read as *'samjñāyām bhṛtṝvṛjidhārisahitapidamaḥ.'* But *Rup* mentions the root as *'tṛ'* instead of *'tṝ.'*[31] *Mbh* does not have this rule.

Sūtra 3-2-163 : *K* mentions the root *naś* in this rule with the reading 'iṇnaśji. . . .' *Rup* mentions the root as *naśi* and reads the rule as *'iṇnaśiji. . . .'*[32] *Mbh* does not comment on this rule.

Sūtra 7-2-60 : *K* mentions the root *'kḷp'* in this *sūtra* which is read as *'tāsi ca kḷpaḥ.' Mbh* under the *sūtra 'na vṛdbhyaḥ. . . .'* (7-2-59) notes a *var 'catustāsikḷpigrahaṇānarthakyam ca'* which refers to this rule and in this *var* PAT refers to this root as *'kḷp.'* Quite different from this, *Rup* mentions this root as *'kṛp'* giving the reading *'tāsi ca kṛpaḥ.'*[33]

Sūtra 7-4-95 : *K* mentions the root *'dṛ'* in this *sūtra*, *atsmṛdṛtvaraprathamradastṝspāsam.'* But *Rup* gives the root with the lengthened vowel, as *dṝ*. This rule is not seen in *Mbh.*[34]

Sūtra 8-4-34 : *Mbh* and *K* mention the root *pyāyī* in this rule read as *'na bhābhūpūkamigamipyāyīvepām.' Rup* gives the root as *pyāyi* without the lengthening of the vowel *'i.'*[35]

Variation caused by optional sandhisutras

It is to be noted that *sandhi* rules like *'padāntādvā'* (6-1-76) which are optional, bring about variation in the reading of a number of Paniniyan sutras found in *K* and *Rup*. We find that such variations are caused by the operation and non-operation of optional sandhisutras, on the sutras of *Ast* found in these works. A few examples of the same are pointed out below.

Sūtra 1-2-27 : The *sandhisūtra, 'jhayohonyatarasyām'* (8-4-62) optionally enjoins *pūrvasavarṇa* as a substitute of the consonant *'h'* when preceded by the consonants coming under the *pratyāhāra 'jhay.' Mbh* and *Rup* read the rule 1-2-27 as *ukālojjhrasvadīrghaplutaḥ'* wherein the initial consonant *'h'* of *hrasva* is substituted by the *pūrvasavarṇa 'jh'* by the function of the said optional rule.[36] But *K* gives the reading *'ūkāloj hrasvadīrghaplutaḥ'* wherein the consonant *'h'* of *hrasva* is not substituted by the *pūrvasavarṇa* optionally enjoined by the rule *'jhayo. . . .'*

Sūtra 3-1-115 : The rule *'anaci ca'* (8-4-47) teaches an optional reduplication of the consonants grouped under the *pratyāhāra 'yar'* and preceded by vowels. By the optional function of this rule, we get two different readings of the rule 3-1-115. In *K* this rule is read as *'bhidyoddhyau nade'* wherein the consonant *'dh'* occurring after *'o'* gets doubled as *dh dh* by the rule 8-4-47 and the former one among them is replaced by *'d'* as per the rule *'jhalām jaś jhaśi'* (8-4-53). *Rup* reads the rule as *'bhidyodhyau nade'* where *'dh'* is not doubled, owing to the non-operation of the optional rule 8-4-47.[37]

Sūtra 4-1-55 : The *var 'otvoṣṭhayossamāse vā pararūpam vaktavyam'* read under the rule *'eṅi pararūpam'* (6-1-94) in *Mbh*, optionally enjoins *pararūpa* i.e. *'o'* as *ekādeśa* in the place of the vowel *'a'* and the following diphthong *o* which is the initial letter of the base *otu* or *oṣṭha*. In the reading of the rule *'nāsikodaroṣṭhajanghādantakarṇaśṁgācca'* (4-1-55) found in *Rup* we notice that this *pararūpa 'o'* has come as *ekādeśa* in the place of the vowel *'a'* of *udara* and *'o'* of *oṣṭha.*[38] But in *Mbh* and *K* this rule is read as *'nāsikodarauṣṭha. . . .'* wherein we find that the substitution by the *pararūpa 'o'* has not functioned owing to the optional nature of the *var* and hence the *'a'* of *udara* and *'o'* of *oṣṭha* are replaced by the *vṛddhi* vowel *'au'* as per the rule *'vṛddhireci'* (6-1-88).

Sūtra 5-4-117 : The rule *'vā padāntasya'* (8-4-59) optionally enjoins *parasavarṇa* as substitute of *anusvāra* occurring at the end of a *pada* and followed by the consonants grouped under the *pratyāhāra 'yay.'* As per this optional rule, we get two variant readings of the rule 5-4-117. In *Rup* this rule is read as *'antarbahibhyāñcalomnaḥ'* wherein the *anusvāra* occurring as the final of the compound word *antarbahibhyāṁ* is replaced by the *parasavarṇa, ñ.*[39] But *K* reads the rule as *'antarbahibhyāṁ ca lomnaḥ* wherein *parasavarṇa* does not function on the *anusvāra* of *antarbahibhyāṁ.*

Sūtra 7-3-36 : The *sūtra 'yaronunāsikenunāsiko vā'* (8-4-45) optionally enjoins nasals as substitutes of consonants coming under the *pratyāhāra 'yar'* and followed by nasal sounds. The function of this optional rule is clear in the reading of the rule 7-3-36 found in K. *K reads this rule as 'artihrīblīrīknūyīkṣmāyyātām puṅṇau* wherein the consonant *g* of *pug* is replaced by the nasal sound *ṅ*. But *Rup* reads this rule as *'artihrīblīrīknūyīkṣmāyyātām pugṇau'* wherein the *g* of *pug,* though followed by the nasal sound *ṇ* is not substituted by the nasal sound owing to the optional nature of the *sandhisūtra 'yaronunāsikenunāsiko vā.*[40]

Sūtra 7-4-41 : The *sandhi* rule *'padāntādvā'* (6-1-76) enjoins optionally the augment *'t'* to the final long vowel *ā* of a *pada* when followed by the consonant *ch. Mbh* reads the rule 7-4-41 as *'śācchoranyatarasyām'* wherein the vowel *ā* of *śā* gets the augment *'t'* by the operation of the optional *sandhi* rule quoted first (6-1-76) and the augment *'t'* has changed into *'c'* by the rule *'stoścunā ścuḥ* (8-4-40). *K* and *Rup* reads the rule as *'śāchoranyatarasyām'* wherein the vowel *ā* does not get the augment *'t'* owing to the non-operation of the optional *sandhisūtra 'padāntādvā. . . .'*[41]

It is between *Mbh* and *K* that we get the maximum number of variations in the readings of the rules of *Ast*. Most of these have been classified and discussed by *Kielhorn* in his *'Notes on the Mahābhāṣya.'*[42] They come under four categories namely 1. *Yogavibhāga* where a *sūtra* of PAN is split up into two, 2. one or more words added to the original text of a *sūtra,* 3. the wording of sutras altered otherwise than by the addition of one or more words, and 4. whole sutras added to the original text of *Ast*. It is possible to know that in every one of these cases the change is brought by incorporating wholly or partly into the sutras certain vars or PAT's observations or changing the form taking his suggestions. In his *'Notes on the Mahābhāṣya'* Kielhorn notices 58 such instances of variation in the reading of the rules found in *Mbh* and *K. Rup* closely following *K* in almost all respects, presents exactly the same readings given in *K* for the text of *Ast* with regard to these 58 instances noted by Kielhorn.

Vartikas of Rūpāvatāra

A study of the vartikas shows that the work closely follows *K* in that respect also. There are more or less 450 vars in *Rup*. Of these, about 150 vars are adopted from *Mbh* without any change and are just the same found in *K* while about 105 vars are adopted from *K* differing from *Mbh*. The rest of the vars in *Rup* present minute variations from those of *K*. However it can be seen that these variations are merely verbal in nature and hence do not affect the sense. We also find certain rare instances where *Rup* follows *Mbh* differing from *K*. Based on the vars of *K* and *Mbh*, the vars found in *Rup* are discussed in a three-fold manner.

1. Vartikas adopted from Kāśikā

It has been already stated that about 105 vars of *Rup* are adopted from *K* differing from *Mbh*. They are being discussed now.

Mbh under the rule 3-1-112 gives the *var 'samaśca bahulam'* which means that the root *bhṛñ* when preceded by the *upasarga 'sam'* gets the suffix *'kyap'* optionally. The idea of this var is given in a different wording in *K* and *Rup* as 'sampūrvādvibhāṣā.'[43]

A similar instance is cited here :

Mbh (under rule 6-3-21) :

'ṣaṣṭhīprakaraṇe vāgdikpaśyadbhyo

yuktidaṇḍahareṣu upasaṅhyānam'

K and Rup[44]

'ṣaṣṭhīprakaraṇe vāgdikpaśyadbhyo yuktidaṇḍa-

hareṣu yathāsaṅkhyam alugvaktavyaḥ'

Sometimes we find that the vars refuted by PAT are found adopted in *K* and *Rup*. For instance : In *Mbh* under the rule kaṛtṛkaraṇayostṛtīyā (2-3-18) we get the *var* 'tṛtīyāvidhāne prakṛtyādibhya upasaṅkhyānam.' PAT refutes this *var* since the instances of this *var* are got by the rule 2-3-18 itself. *K* adopts this *var* and reads it under the same rule, as 'tṛtīyāvidhāne prakṛtyādīnāmupasaṅkhyānam." *Rup* also adopts this *var* with the reading 'tṛtīyāvidhāne prakṛtyādibhya upasaṅkhyānam.'[45]

In some cases, *Rup* follows the vars of *K* but these vars are not at all seen in *Mbh*. It is evident here that Rup has adopted them as vars since they are treated to be so in *K*. For instance, in *K* under 2-4-17 we get two vars 'akārāntottarapado dviguḥ striyām bhāṣyate' and 'pātrādibhyaḥ pratiṣedho vaktavyaḥ.' In *Mbh* rule 2-4-17 is not explained and we do not get these two vars there. But *Rup* has adopted them from *K*.[46] A few vars which are found in *K* and *Rup* but not seen in *Mbh* are listed below :

1. 'śvaśurasyokārākāralopśca vaktavyaḥ'[47]
2. 'śatasahasrau pareṇeti vaktavyam'[48]
3. 'yamācceti vaktavyam'[49]
4. 'guṇādibhyo grāmajvaktavyaḥ'[50]
5. 'ādeśceti vaktavyam' and 'avodhasorlopaśca'[51]
6. 'samsiduhiguhibhyo veti vaktavyam'[52]
7. 'pāṇau srjerṇyadvaktavyaḥ' and 'samavapūrvācca'[53]
8. 'sahitapidameḥ samjñāyām'[54]
9. 'bhavateśceti vaktavyam'[55]
10. 'bhage ca dāreritivaktavyam'[56]
11. 'vyadheḥ samprasāraṇam kuracca vaktavyaḥ'[57]
12. 'śradantarorupasargavadvṛttiḥ'[58]
'śradantarorupasargavadvṛttirvaktyaḥ'[59]

While explaining certain rules *Mbh* suggests certain amendments. These modifications of PAT are given as vars in *K* and *Rup*. For instance under the rule 8-4-42 PAT says : 'atyalpamidamucyate anāmiti anāmnavatinagarīṇām ceti vaktavyam' ṣaṇṇām, ṣaṇṇavatiḥ ṣaṇṇagaryaḥ.' Here PAT points out that as per the rule 8-4-42 the prohibition of *ṣṭutva* excludes *nām* alone and opines that this exclusion is to be more comprehensive, i.e. the prohibition should exclude not only *nām* but also *navati* and *nagarī*. This statement of PAT is given as *var in K* and *Rup*. *K* reads the *var* as 'anāmnavatinagarīṇāmiti vaktavyam' under the same rule and *Rup* reads it as 'anāmnavatinagarīṇāmiti vācyam.'[60]

Similarly in *K* and *Rup* we get the following vars; but when we go through *Mbh* it can be seen that they are originally the statements of PAT amending the idea of the rules.

1. 'vergro vaktavyaḥ'[61]
2. 'vyāsavaruḍaniṣādacaṇḍālabimbānāmiti vaktavyam'[62]
3. 'pathyadhyāyanyāyavihāramanuṣyahastiṣviti vaktavyam'[63]
4. 'vismitapratighatayośeti vaktavyam'[64]

While discussing certain sutras, PAT cites the views of other grammarians and we find that such views cited in *Mbh* are treated as vars in *K* and *Rup*. For example in the passage 'apara āha - akākārayoḥ prayoge pratiṣedho neti vaktavyam' under the rule 2-3-66, PAT cites a view of other grammarians and the same is read as a *var* in *K* and *Rup* in the form 'akākārayoḥ strīpratyayayoḥ prayoge neti vaktavyam.'[65] Two more vars in *K* and *Rup* which are likewise based on the views cited in the *Mbh*, are mentioned below :

1. upāddevapūjāsaṇgatikaraṇamitrīkaraṇapathiṣviti vācyam'[66]
   'upāddevapūjasaṅgatikaraṇamitrakaraṇapathiṣviti vaktavyam'[67]

Mbh on rule 1-3-25 :

'aparaāha - upāddevapūjāsaṅgatakaraṇamitrakaraṇa-pathiṣu'

2. 'sarvaprātipadikebhya ityeke'[68]

Mbh on rule 3-1-11 :

'apara āha - sarvaprātipadikebhya ācāre kibvā vaktavyaḥ.'

In certain instances *Mbh* explains the meaning of the rules in such a way that they help to refute the modifications of the rules suggested by KAT. Such explanations of PAT in regard to the meaning of the rules are given the form of a *var* in *K*. Such vars are adopted by DK in his work. *Mbh* refutes the modification 'āṅodovyasanakriyasya' suggested by KAT by explaining the idea of the part '*anāsyaviharaṇe*' of the rule '*āṅodonāsyaviharaṇe*' (1-3-20), as 'iha āṅo donāsya' itīyatā siddham / soyamevam siddhe sati yadviharaṇagrahaṇam karoti tasyaitatprayojanam - āsyaviharaṇasamānakriyādapi yathā syāt" and this explanation is given as a *var K* under the same rule as 'āsyaviharaṇasamānakrīyādapi pratiṣedho vaktavyaḥ.' Replacing the word *vaktavyaḥ* with bhavati, *Rup* adopts this var.[69]

In certain other instances *K* supplements the *vars* of *Mbh*. It is this modified *var* that is followed by *Rup*. For example under the rule 5-2-107, *Mbh* gives the *var* 'nagācca.' *K* supplements the *var* as 'nagapāmsupāṇḍubhyaśceti vaktavyam.' Here *Rup* has followed K.[70]

Sometimes *K* omits certain words in the vars in *Mbh* and such vars are adopted by *Rup*. For example, in *Mbh* under the rule 6-3-3 we get the *var* 'pumsānujo januṣāndho vikṛtākṣa iti ca.' The word *vikṛtakṣa* in the *var* is omitted by *K* which gives the *var* as 'pumṣānujo januṣāndha iti vaktavyam.' *Rup* adopts this reading of *K*.[71]

There are some more vars in *K* and *Rup* wherein we find that certain words originally found in the vars of *Mbh* are omitted. They are :

1. *Mbh* on rule 4-3-23 'agrādipaścāḍḍimac smṛtaḥ' *K* and *Rup* 'agrapaścāḍḍimac' (*ādi* - omitted).[72]
2. *Mbh* on rule 4-2-43 'gajasahāyābhyām ca' *K* and *Rup* 'gajācceti vaktavyam.' It may also be noted here that though the word '*sahāya*' is omitted, it is included in the rule 4-2-43 itself which is read in *K* and *Rup* as 'grāmajanabandhusahāyebhyastal.'[73]
3. *Mbh* on rule 3-2-8: 'bahulam taṇi'

K & *Rup* 'bahulam chandasīti vaktavyam.' Though the word '*taṇi*' denoting *saṃjñā* and *chandas* is omitted, it is replaced by the word *chandasi* and hence only a part of the idea conveyed by the word '*taṇi*' is omitted here.[74]

We meet with certain instances wherein the vars given in *K* and *Rup* are actually *Bhāṣya* passages explaining the vars. For instance, the *Var* 'akṣādūhinyām' in *Mbh* under rule 6-1-89 is followed by the *Bhāṣya* passage 'akṣādūhinyām vṛddhiravaktavyā.' We find that this passage is read as a *var* in *K* and *Rup*.[75] Similar instances are given below :

1. Passage in *Mbh* - 'otvoṣṭhayoḥ samāse vā pararūpam vaktavyam' on the *var* 'otvoṣṭhayoḥ samāse vā' (6-1-94). *K* and *Rup* 'otvoṣṭhayoḥ samāse vā pararūpam vaktavyam.'[76]
2. Passage in *Mbh* -'*tatsthaiśca guṇaiḥ ṣaṣṭhī* samasyata iti vaktavyam' on the *var* 'tatsthaiśca guṇaiḥ' (2-2-8) *K* on rule 2-2-9 & *Rup* ' tatsthaiśca guṇaiḥ ṣaṣṭhī samasyata iti vaktavyam.'[77]
3. Passage on *Mbh* -'ivena saha samāso vibhaktyalopaḥ pūrvapadaprakṛtisvaratvam ca vaktavyam' on the var 'ivena vibhaktyalopaḥ purvapadaprakṛtisvaratvam ca' (2-2-18) *K* & *Rup* 'ivena saha samāso vibhaktyalopaḥ purvapadaprakṛtisvaratvam ca vaktavyam.'[78]
4. Passage on *Mbh* -'jyotirudgamane iti vaktavyam' on the *var* 'jyotiṣāmudgamane' (1-3-40)

K & *Rup* 'jyodirudgamana iti vaktavyam.'[79]

5. Passage on *Mbh* -'prādibhyo dhātujasya bahuvrīhirvaktavyaḥ / uttarapadasya ca vā lopo vaktavyaḥ' on the *var* 'prādibhyo dhātujasya vā' (2-2-24) *K* and *Rup* 'prādibhyo dhātujasyottarapadasya lopaśca vā bahuvrihīrvaktavyaḥ.'[80]

Certain vars in *K* and *Rup* are based on the idea of the *Bhāṣya* passage following the vars. In the passage "evam tarhi yogavibhāgaḥ kariṣyate - kṛtyānām prayoge ṣaṣṭhī na bhavatīti," PAT speaks of the *yogavibhāga* of the rule *'kṛtyānām kartari vā'* (2-3-71). The rule as a single *yoga* means 'ubhayaprāptau kṛtye kartari ṣaṣṭhī vā bhavati.' As the result of the *yogavibhāga* the idea additionally got is 'ubhayaprāptau kṛtye ṣaṣṭhyāḥ pratiṣedho bhavati.' *K* does not speak of this *yogavibhāga,* but taking the idea additionally got by the *yogavibhāga* reads a *var* in the form 'ubhayaprāptau kṛtye ṣaṣṭhyāḥ pratiṣedho vaktavyaḥ.' *Rup* adopts this *var of K.*[81]

In certain cases we find that a single *var* in *Mbh* is given as two or three vars in *K* and *Rup.* For instance in *Mbh* under rule 4-3-60, we get the *var* 'samānasya tadādeśca adhyātmādiṣu ceṣyate.' *K* gives this as three different vars 'samānaśabdāṭṭhañ vaktavyaḥ,' 'tadādeśca' and 'adhyātmādibhyaśca.' Following *K, Rup* also gives the three vars with slight difference in the form as 'addhyātmādibhya upasaṅkhyānam', 'samānācca ṭhañ vaktavyaḥ,' and 'tadādeśca.'[82]

Vartikas adopted from Mahābhāṣya :

Certain vars in *Rup,* closely follow *Mbh* varying from what is found in *K.* Thus it is clear that DK has adopted vars from *Mbh* also. For instance, under the rule 5-2-122, PAT cites the var *'śītoṣṇatṛprebhyastanna sahate'* which enjoins a *taddhita* suffix *ālu* in the sense of *'tanna sahate.'* He then gives two more vars 'himācceluḥ,' *'vātātsamūhe ca.'* By virtue of the *nipāta 'ca'* found in these vars, PAT comprehends the sense *'tanna sahate'* in these two vars from the *var* 'śītoṣṇa. . .'. Following *Mbh* DK gives these two vars with the same reading. He then makes the remark 'cādasahanepi' and thus admits the view of PAT that the *nipāta 'ca'* comprehends the sense *'tanna sahate'* from the var 'śītoṣṇa. . .'[83] *K* gives the var 'śītoṣṇa. . .' but reads the latter in a different manner as 'tanna sahata iti himācceluḥ,' 'vātātsamūhe ca' and 'vātam na sahata iti ca.' Similar instances are given below :

	Mbh and Rup	*K*
1.	'kārakārhāṇām ca kārakatve' (2-3-36)[84]	'kārakārhāṇām ca kārakatve saptamī vaktvyā'
2.	'akārakārhāṇām cākārakatve' (2-3-36)[85]	'akārakārhāṇām ca akārakatve saptamī vaktavyā'
3.	'tadviparyāse ca' (2-3-36)[86]	'tadviparyāse ca saptamī vaktavyā'

Vartikas which differ from Mahābhāṣya and Kāśikā

Here we deal with certain vars which differ from *Mbh* and *K* as well. Under rule 6-1-89 *Mbh* gives the vars, 'pravatsatarakambalavasanānām carṇe' and 'ṛṇadaśābhyām ca.' *K* also gives these two vars as 'pravatsatarakambalavasanānāmṛṇe vṛddhirvaktavyā and 'ṛṇadaśābhyām vṛddhirvaktavyā.'

Quite differently DK combines these two vars into a single one as 'pravatsatarakambalavasanadasārṇānāmṛṇe.'[87]

In *Mbh* under rule 8-4-45 there is the *var* 'yaronunāsike pratyaye bhāṣāyām nityavacanam.' *K* gives the *var* as 'yaronunāsike pratyaye bhāṣāyām nityavacanam kartavyam.' DK specifies the suffix mentioned in it to be *taddhita* suffix and reads the *var* as 'yaronunāsike taddhitapratyaye parataḥ bhāṣāyām nityamiti vaktavyam.'[88] Here the deviation from *Mbh* and *K* can be seen as a specification only and it does not contradict the idea of the *var* given in *Mbh* and *K* since the examples given in *Mbh* and *K* justify this specification.

Under rule 6-4-84, PAT cites the *var* 'varṣābhūpunarbhvaśca' and explains that in the rule '*varṣābhvaśca*' (6-4-84) which deals with the *prātipadika varṣābhū*, mention of the *prātipadika punarbhū* is also to be made. On the basis of this statement *K* draws a *var* in the form 'punarbhvaśceti vaktavyam.' *Rup* presents this *var* in a different form 'punaḥ pur̄vasya bhuvo yaṇ vaktavyaḥ.'[89]

In *Mbh* under the rule 5-2-122 we get a *var* 'sarvatrāmayasya' which means that the suffix *vini* comes after the word *āmaya* both in *chandas* and *bhāṣā*. *K* adopts this *var* from *Mbh* with the reading 'sarvatrāmayasyopasaṅkhyānam.' *Rup* reads the *var* differently as 'amayasyopaṅkhyānam' omitting the word *sarvatra.*[90] The reason for this may be that DK, as a rule, omits the rules relating to Vedas and deals with words of the Classical Sanskrit only.

Under the rules *ṝta iddhātoḥ*' (7-1-100), '*upadhāyāśca*' (7-1-101) and *udoṣṭhyapūrvasya* (7-1-102) which are taken combinendly for explanation in *Mbh*, we get a statement 'itvotvābhyām guṇavṛdhī bhavato vipratiṣedhena.'

But *K* gives it as a *var* with the same reading under the rule 7-1-102. Though *Rup* has followed *K* by accepting the same as *var*, it makes a slight deviation in the form of a specification of *vipratiṣedha* to be *pūrvavipratiṣedha. Rup* thus reads the *var* as 'itvotvabhyaṁ guṇavṛdhī pūrvavipratiṣedhena.'[91]

In *Mbh* under the rule 3-2-1, we get a *var* 'śīlikāmibhakṣyācaribhyo ṇaḥ pūrvapadaprakṛtisvaratvam ca.' *K* gives the same reading except for the addition of the word 'vaktavyam' at the end. Different from these two, *Rup* notes the *var* as 'śīlikāmibhakṣyācaribhyo ṇaḥ' omitting the part 'pūrvapadaprakṛtisvaratva, ca.'[92] The reason may be that the omitted part deals with the accent of the Vedic words and he has omitted almost all the rules relating to Vedas.

Under the rule 3-3-108 we get the *var* 'iṇajādibhyaḥ in *Mbh* and *K*. This *var* enjoins the suffix *iṇ* to the roots *aja* and the like. But *Rup* reads the *var* as 'iñajādibhyaḥ' by which it is the suffix '*iñ*' that is enjoined to the root '*aja*.'[93] Though there is thus a difference in the suffix enjoined by *Rup* from that of *Mbh* and *K*, it is noteworthy here that the resultant form *ājiḥ* etc. can be derived by the addition of the suffix *iṇ* or *iñ*. The *anubandha* '*ṇ*' or '*ñ*' too does not make no difference in the form *ājiḥ* etc. since both these bring *upadhāvṛddhi* to the root by the force of the rule '*ata upadhāyāḥ*' (7-2-116).

Finally, certain vars refuted by PAT and omitted by *K* are found adopted by DK in his work. For instance, in *Mbh* under the rule 1-3-7, we get the var 'ira upasaṅkhyānam' meaning that the part '*ir*' in roots is to be deemed as '*it*.' The next *var* 'avayavagrahaṇātsiddham' refutes the above *var* since '*i*' and '*r*' can individually get *itsamjñā*. Following *Mbh, K* too does not mention this *var*. But *Rup* has accepted the *var* with the reading 'ira itsamjñā vācyā' by mentioning the same with reference to the root '*dṛsir*' in 'luṅprakaraṇa.'[94]

In *Mbh* under the rule *vano ra ca* (4-1-7), there is a *var* 'ravidhāne bahuvrīherupasaṅkhyānam,' 'pratiṣiddhatvāt' which means that the feminine suffix *ṅīp* and the substitute *'r'* ordained optionally by the said rule must be optionally enjoined to the *bahuvrīhi* compound, ending in *'van.'* PAT refutes this *var* since by virtue of the word *'anyatarasyām'* in the rule 'ḍābūbhābhyāmanyatarasyām' (4-1-13), *bahuvrīhi* compounds ending in *'van'* can get optionally the feminine suffix *ṅīp* and the substitute *'r.'*[95] K too accepts this view of PAT.[96] Without mentioning the purpose served by the word *anyatarasyām* while interpreting the rule *'ḍābubhābhyām. . . .'. . . .'* DK quite differently reads under the rule 4-1-7 a *var* in the form 'bahuvrīhau *vā'* in order to secure the same purpose.[97]

Notes and References

1. *Mbh*, Vol II, p. 196.
2. *Rup* Part II, pp. 16 & 284.
3. It is to be noted here that in the Mss. of *Rup* (No. 368) found in the Oriental Mss. Library, Government Sanskrit College, Tripunithura, Kerala the rule is read as *'kālādhvanoratyantasamyoge.'* The above variation is pointed out as per the reading in the printed text (*Rup* Part I, p. 146).
4. 'stoka alpa krcchra katipaya ityetebhyosatvavacanebhyaḥ karaṇe kārake pañcamī vibhaktirbhavati' (Part I, pp. 201 & 202). The reading of the rule given in the printed text differs from that of the Mss. of *Rup* (No. 368) in the Oriental Manuscripts Library, Government. Sanskrit College, Tripunithura, Kerala where it is given as *'karaṇe ca stokālpakṛcchrakatipayasyāsatvavacanasya.'*
5. *Rup* Part II, p. 251.
6. *"'dīrghoccāraṇam kimartham? na 'i ca khanaḥ' ityevocyeta / kā rūpasiddhiḥ? kheyam/ ādguṇena siddham. . . tasmād 'i ca khanaḥ' ityeva vaktavyam /"* (*Mbh*, Vol. II, pp. 133 & 134.
7. *Rup* Part II, p. 268.
8. *PS* Part I, p. 124.
9. *Rup* Part I, p. 234.
10. *PS* Part III, p. 51.
11. *Rup* Part I, p. 245.
12. *PS* Part III, p. 77.

13. 'kāśyapakauśikaśabdābhyam ṛṣibhyām proktārthe ṇinipratyayo bhavati' (*Rup* Part I, p. 251.
14. In *Mbh* this rule is numbered as 4-3-142.
15. *Rup* Part I, p. 254.
16. Ibid, p. 257.
17. 'taddhito vā punareṣa bhaviṣyati vadhamarhatīti vadhyaḥ' (Vol. II, p. 130).
    The *Pradīpa* and *Udyota* on this *Bhāṣya* passage is also noteworthy here :
    'vadhamarhatīti / daṇḍādibhya iti yatpratyayaḥ' (*Pradīpa*)

'yatpratyaya iti / etena daṇḍādibhyo ya iti vṛttipātha etadbhāṣyaviruddha' iti bhāvaḥ'

18. *Rup* Part I, p. 269.
19. " 'daṇḍādibhyaḥ' daṇḍādibhyo ya iti pāṭhe ya iti prakṣiptam" (*Ast* edited by Kṣemarājasrīkṛṣnadās, p. 59. Footnote 4).
20. *Rup* Part I, p. 289.
21. Kaiyaṭa speaks of these two readings under the said rule : 'iha kecit aśam paṭhanti kecit anam / tatrottarapāṭhāpekṣo vicāraḥ' (*Pradīpa* on *Mbh* Vol II, p. 600).
22. *Rup* Part I, p. 13.
23. "ārambhasāmarthyānnityamidam 'indre ca nityam' iti pāṭhastu bhāsyāsammatatvādupekṣitaḥ" (p. 123).
24. *Rup* Part I, p. 204.
25. *Rup* Part I, p. 53.
26. *Rup* Part II, pp. 119 & 127.
27. Ibid, p. 300.
28. *Mbh* Vol. I, Dvitīyakhaṇḍa p. 18.
29. *Rup* Part II, p. 107.
30. Ibid, p. 287.
31. Ibid, p. 267.
32. Ibid, p. 287.
33. Ibid, p. 176.
34. Ibid, p. 217.
35. *Rup* Part I, p. 32.
36. Ibid, p. 3.
37. *Rup* Part II, p. 252.
38. *Rup* Part I, p. 142.
39. Ibid, p. 200.

40. *Rup* Part II, p. 46.
41. Ibid, p. 281.
42. Vide '*Indian Antiquary*,' Vol. XVI (1887), pp. 178-84.
43. *Rup* Part II, p. 251.
44. *Rup* Part I, p. 205.
45. Ibid, pp. 150 & 151.
46. Ibid, p. 177.
47. *K* under rule 4-1-68 & *Rup* Part I, p. 144.
48. *K* under rule 2-1-39 & *Rup* Part I, p. 174.
49. *K* under rule 4-1-85 & *Rup* Part I, p. 222.
50. *K* under rule 4-2-37 & *Rup* Part I, pp. 233 & 234.
51. *K* under rule 4-3-8 & *Rup* Part I, pp. 243 & 244.
52. *K* under rule 3-1-109 & *Rup* Part II, p. 251.
53. *K* under rule 3-1-110 & *Rup* Part II, p. 251.
54. *K* under rule 3-1-134 & *Rup* Part II, p. 256.
55. *K* under rule 3-1-143 & *Rup* Part II, p. 258.
56. *k* under rule 3-2-41 & *Rup* Part II, p. 266.
57. *K* under rule 3-2-162 & *Rup* Part II, p. 287.
58. *K* under rule 3-3-106.
59. *Rup* Part II, p. 295.
60. *Rup* Part I, p. 16.
61. *Mbh* & *K* under rule 5-4-119 and *Rup* Part I, p. 194.
62. *Mbh* & *K* under rule 4-1-97 and *Rup* Part I, pp. 223 & 224.
63. *Mbh* & *K* under rule 4-2-129 and *Rup* Part I, p. 242.
64. *Mbh* & *K* under rule 7-2-29 and *Rup* Part II, p. 280.
65. *Rup* Part I, p. 160.
66. *K* on rule 1-3-25.
67. *Rup* Part II, p. 79.
68. *K* on rule 3-1-11 and *Rup* Part II, p. 232.
69. *Rup* Part II, p. 29.
70. *Rup* Part I, p. 285.
71. Ibid, p. 202.
72. Ibid, p. 245.
73. Ibid, p. 234.
74. *Rup* Part II, p. 261.
75. *Rup* Part I, p. 10.
76. Ibid, p. 13.
77. Ibid, p. 174.
78. Ibid, p. 181.
79. *Rup* Part II, p. 13.

80. *Rup* Part I, p. 183.
81. Ibid, p. 160.
82. Ibid, p. 247.
83. Ibid, p. 287.
84. Ibid, p. 163.
85. Ibid, p. 163.
86. Ibid, p. 163.
87. Ibid, p. 10.
88. Ibid, p. 17.
89. Ibid, p. 56.
90. Ibid, p. 287.
91. *Rup* Part II, p. 30.
92. Ibid, p. 259.
93. Ibid, p. 296.
94. Ibid, p. 148.
95. "vakṣyati ḍābubhābhyāmanyatarasyāmityatrānyatarasyām grahaṇasya prayojanam ḍāppratiṣedhābhyām mukte ṅībrāvapi yathā syātāmiti" (*Mbh* on rule 4-1-7)
96. "anyatarasyām grahaṇam kimartham? bahuvrīhau 'vano ra ca' ityasyāpi vikalpoyathā syāt" (*K* on rule 4-1-13).
97. *Rup* Part I, pp. 133 & 134.

Chapter VII

Verses in Rūpāvatāra

In addition to the rules of PAN, their explanation and illustration, *Rup* comprises in it numerous verses. We get a complementary reference to these verses in *Rup* in the commentary of Guṇasāgara to Amitasagara's *'yāpparuṅgala-k-kārikai,* a Tamil work. Guṇasāgara in his commentary says that the work *Yāpparuṅgala-k-kārikai* is composed as a beautiful pendant to the work on prosody, called *Yāpparuṅgala,* in the Tamil language.[1] He points out many reasons for having given the title *yāpparuṅgala-k-kārikai* to the work by Amitasāgara. One of the reasons is that it contains verses similar to the leading stanzas (*nītakusloka*) which decorate *Rup,* 'urūpāvatārattiṟku nītakacculōkamē pōlavam . . . alaṅgāramuḍaittāgac-ceyya-ppaṭṭamaiyāl Yāpparuṅgalakkārikai eṉṉum peyarttu.' A perusal of the slokas that occur frequently in the course of the *Rup* and of the mnemonic verses in the Yāpparuṅgala-k-kārikai will show clearly the aptness of Gunasagara's comparison.

Verses cited from previous works

The verses in *Rup* can be distinguished as those taken from previous works and those of the author himself. Among them verses quoted from previous works like *Pāṇinīya Śikṣā, Mbh, Vak, K, Nyāsa, Pradīpa* and *Padamañjarī* are dealt with first.

Verses quoted from Pāṇinīya Śikṣā

> hakāram pañcamairyuktamantasthābhiśca samyutam /
> urasyam tam vijanīyāt kanṭhyamāhurasamyutam //
> aṣṭau sthānāni varṇānāmuraḥ kaṇṭhaḥ śirastathā /
> jīhvāmūlam ca dantāśca nāsikoṣṭhau ca tālu ca[2] //

These two verses are taken from *Paṇinīya Śikśā* wherein the verse 'aṣṭau . . . ' is given first followed by the other one.[3] The verse 'aṣṭau . . . ' enumerates the different places of articulation of phonemes. The verse hakāram . . . points out the place of articulation of the letter *'h'* when combined with vargapancamas, antasthas and also when uttered alone.

Verses taken from Mbh

Among the verses quoted from *Mbh*, we find that some are 'slokavartikas and they are dealt with first.

> nāmi dīrgha āmi cet syāt kṛte dīrghe na nuḍ bhavet /
> vacanādyatra tannāsti nopadhāyāśca carmaṇām[4] //

This is a *ślokavārtika* found in *Mbh* under the rule *nāmi* (6-4-3). *Rup* quotes this verse after interpreting the rule *'nāmi'* along with the explanation of the formation of the word *vṛkṣāṇām*. This *var* points out the purpose served by the rule *'nāmi'* instead of reading the rule as *'āmi.'*

> ubhasarvatasoḥ kāryā dhiguparyādiṣu triṣu
> dvitīyāmreditānteṣu tatonyatrāpi dṛśyate[5] //

This is a *ślokavārtika* found in *Mbh* under the rule *'karmaṇi dvitīyā* (2-3-2). *Rup* too adopts the said *var* in the same context. This deals with the instances where the *dvitīyāvibhakti* is to be used.

> apatye kutsite mūḍhe manorautsargikaḥ smṛtaḥ /
> nakārasya ca mūrdhanyaḥ tena sidhyati māṇavaḥ[6] //

This is a *slokavārtika* found in *Mbh* under the rule 'manorjātāvañyatau . . . ' (4-1-161). It derives the form *māṇava* by enjoining the suffix *'aṇ'* to the base *manu* and the substitution of *'n'* by *ṇ* in *manu*. This verse finds its place under the same rule in *Rup*.

> amehakvatasitrebhyastyabvidhiryovyayāt smṛtaḥ /
> ninirbhyām dhruvagatyośca praveśo niyame tathā[7] //

Mbh under the rule *'avyayāttyap'* (4-2-104) reads the *var* 'amehakvatasitrebhyastyabvidhiryovyayātsmṛtaḥ.' After illustrating this *var*, PAT says, 'tyabnerdhruve / tyabnerdhruve vaktavyaḥ / nityaḥ //niso gatau / tyabvaktavya iti / niṣṭyaḥ' // meaning that the suffix *tyap* mentioned in this *var* is to be enjoined from *ni* and *nis* in the sense of *dhruva* and *gati*. In K and *Rup*, we get the above verse, wherein the said *var* forms the first half and the idea mentioned in the *Bhāṣya* passage is given in the latter half.

> tasyedamityapatyepi bādhanārtham kṛtam bhavet /
> utsargaśśeṣa evāsau vṛddhānyasya prayojanam[8] //

This *ślokavārtika* is found in *Mbh* under the rule *'tasyāpatyam'* (4-1-92). It deals with the purpose of composing a separate rule *'tasyāpatyam'* (4-1-92) instead of comprehending the same by the rule *'tasyedam'* (4-3-120) or combining it with the rule *'ata iñ'* (4-1-95). *Rup* quotes this under the same rule.

bhūvādīnām vakāroyam maṅgalārthaḥ prayujyate /
bhuvo vārthem vadantīti bhvarthā vā vādayasmṛtāḥ[9] //

Mbh gives a *var* 'bhūvādinām vakāroyam mangalārthaḥ prayujyate' under the rule *'bhūvādayo dhātavaḥ'* (1-3-1). In *K* and *Rup* we find that this *var* is given as the first half of the verse quoted above. This verse deals with the part *bhūvādaya* of the rule *'bhūvādayo . . . .'*

ciṇvadvṛdhiryuk ca hanteśca ghatvam
dīrghaścokto yo mitām vā ciṇīti
iṭ cāsiddhastena me lupyate nir-
ṇityaścāyam valnimitto vighāti[10] //

Towards the end of the *ciṇvadbhāvuprakaraṇa,* DK gives this *var* with the introductory remark *'tatra saṅgrahaślokaḥ.'* Accordingly it summarises the operations that occur in roots ending in vowels and also in roots like *han, gṛh* and *dṛś,* as a result of the *ciṇvadbhāva* attributed to them by the rule *'syasic . . .'* (6-4-62). This *ślokavārtika* is taken from *Mbh* (under rule 6-4-62) which reads the first line as 'vṛddhiściṇvadyukca hanteśca ghatvam.' The variant reading of the first line of the verse seen in *Rup* is adopted from *K.*

samjnāyām pumsi dṛṣtatvānnate bhāryā prasidhyati /
striyām bhāvādhikarosti tena bhāryā prasidhyati[11] //

This *ślokavārtika* is mentioned in *Mbh* under the rule *'bhṛño' samjñāyām* (3-1-112). It deals with the question as to how the word *bhāryā* can be derived. *Rup* quotes this under the same rule.

ksnorgitvānna stha īkāraḥ kṅitorītvaśāsanāt
guṇābhāvastriṣu smāryaḥ śrukoniṭtvam gakoritoḥ[12] //

This *ślokavārtika* mentioned by PAT under the rule *'glājisthaśca ksnuḥ'* (3-2-139) describes the purpose of treating the suffix *snu,* enjoined by the said rule to be *git. Rup* has adopted this *var* under the same rule.

Now we turn our attention to the verses quoted from *Mbh* which are in the form of sangrahaslokas. By the word *saṅgrahaśloka,* we mean those which summarise the discussions regarding the application of Paninian rules.

īsadarthe kriyāyoge maryādābhividhau ca yaḥ /
etamātam ṅitam vidyādvākyasmaraṇayoraṅit[13] //

Under the rule *'nipāta ekājanāṅ'* (1-1-14) PAT mentions this verse which points out the different kinds of meaning while denoting which the *nipāta ā* is to be treated as *ṅit* to *aṅit*. Rup quotes this verse under the same rule.

etvam bhisi paratvāccedata ais kva bhaviṣyati /
kṛtepyetve bhautapaurvyādaistu nityastathā sati[14] //

This *saṅgrahaśloka* is found in *Mbh* under the rule *'ato bhisa ais'* (7-1-9). It summarises the discussion under the said rule. *Rup* gives it after interpreting the same rule along with the explanation of the formation of the word *vṛkṣaiḥ*.

sadṛsam triṣu liṅgeṣu sarvāsu ca vibhaktiṣu /
vacaneṣu ca sarveṣu yanna vyeti tadavyayam[15] //

This verse is given in *Mbh* under the rule *'svarādinipātamavyayam* (1-1-37). It gives the idea conveyed by the technical term *avyaya*. In *Mbh* PAT treats this *samjñā* to be *anvarthasamjñā*. Hence after explaining the idea of this *samjñā*, PAT quotes this verse summarising the explanation of the term *avyaya*. DK at the outset of *avyayāvatāra* says 'atha aliṅgānyasaṅkhyānyavibhaktibhendānyavyayāni subantānīti atra saṅkṣepeṇopadiśyante tathā coktam' and gives this verse.

adravam mūrtimat svāṅgam prāṇisthamavikārajam /
atatstham tatra dṛṣṭam cet tena cet tat tathā yutam[16] //

This verse is given in *Mbh* under the rule *'svāṅgaccopasarjanāt* (4-1-54). It explains the part *svaṅga* in the rule. DK quotes it in the same context to serve the same purpose.

ākṛtigrahaṇā jātirliṅgānām ca na sarvabhāk /
sakṛdākhyātanirgrāhyā gotrañca caraṇaissaha[17] //

This verse defines the word *jāti* referred to in the rule *'jāterastrī . . .'* (4-1-63). *Rup* quotes the same verse under the same rule.

ūrdhvamānam kilonmānam parimāṇam tu sarvataḥ /
āyāmastu pramāṇam syāt saṅkhyā bāhyā tu sarvataḥ[18] //

This verse is mentioned by PAT under the rule *'ārhādagopucchasaṅkhyāparimāṇāṭṭhak'* (5-1-19). It describes as to what *parimāṇa* (mentioned in the rule) is, clearly discriminating the same from *unmāna, pramāṇa* and *saṅkhyā*. *Rup* quotes this verse under the same rule.

bhumanindāpraśamsāsu nityayogetiśāyane /
samsargestivivakṣāyām bhavanti matubādayaḥ[19] //

This verse is mentioned by PAT under the rule *'tadasyāstyasminniti matup'* (5-2-94) and it deals with the different kinds of meaning in which the suffix *matup* occurs. *Rup* quotes this verse under the same rule.

vācya ūrṇorṇuvadbhāva yaṅprasidhiḥ prayojanam /
āmaśca pratiṣedhārthamekācaśeḍupagrahāt[20] //

This verse is mentioned twice by PAT, first under the rule *'dhātorekāco . . .'* (3-1-21) and again under the rule *'ijādeśca . . .'* (3-1-36). It deals with the *nuvadbhāva* of the root *ūrṇu* and *Rup* has adopted it.

śaiṣikānmatubarthīyācchaiṣiko matubarthikaḥ /
sarūpapratyayo neṣṭaḥ sannantānna saniṣyate[21] //

This verse is mentioned PAT under the rule *'tadasyāstyasminniti matup'* (5-2-94) to point out that the suffix *san* need not be added to a *sannanta* root (i.e. a root having the suffix *san* at its end) and a suffix in the sense of *matup* need not be added to a base which already has a suffix in the sense of *matup*. This verse is quoted by DK.

dhātuprakaraṇāddhātuḥ kasya cāsajjanādapi /
āha cāyamimam dīrgham manye dhāturvibhāṣitaḥ[22] //

This verse mentioned by PAT under the rule *'kaṇḍvādibhyo yak'* (3-1-27), points out that the *kaṇḍvādi* sounds referred to in the said rule, are to be treated as both roots and pratipadikas. *Rup* quotes this verse under the same rule.

tānte doṣo dīrghatvam syāt dānte doṣo niṣṭhānatvam /
dhānte doṣo dhatvaprāptisthāntedoṣastasmātthāntam[23] //
avadattam vidattam ca pradattam cādikarmaṇi /
sudattamanudattam ca nidattamiti ceṣyate[24] //

These two verses are mentioned by PAT under the rule *'do dad ghoḥ'* (7-4-46). The former one gives the reason for treating the substitute enjoined by the said rule as *dath* instead of *dat, dad* or *dadh*. The latter one states that in the five instances, *avadattam, vidattam, pradattam, sudattam, anudattam* and *nidattam* the rule *'aca upasargāttaḥ.'* (7-4-47) does not function. These reason is that the sounds *ava, pra, vi, su, anu* and *ni,* found in these instance, are not real upasargas but avyayas which resemble the upasargas *ava, pra, vi, su, anu* and *ni* (i.e. *upasargapratirūpaka*). *Rup* quotes the verse, 'tānte......' under the rule 7-4-46. The verse *'avadatta......'* is found quoted in *Rup* under the rule *'prāgrī.....'* (1-4-56) and *do dadghoḥ* (7-4-46).

> jagdhau siddhentaraṅgatvāttikitītilyabucyate
> jñāpayatyantaraṅgāṇām lyapā bhavati bādhanam[25]

PAT under the rule *'ado jagdhir......'* (2-4-36) quotes a *kārikā* or Vyāghrabhūti and says that the verse 'jagdhau Siddhe.....' conveys the same sense.[26] It is this verse 'jagdhau siddhe......' that is quoted in *Rup* under the said rule. The verse points out that *lyap,* which is the substitute of the suffix *ktvā,* has got priority over *antaraṅga* rules as opposed to the *paribhāṣā* 'asiddham *bahiraṅgamantaraṅge*'

Now we are to deal with the verses of *Rup* which are quoted from *Mbh* and are illustrative in character.

> duhi, yāci, rudhi, pracchi, bhikṣi, ciñāmupayoganimittamapūrvavidhau
> bruvi, śāsi, guṇene ca yat sacate tadakīrtitamācaritam kavinā
> nī, vahyorharateścaiva gatyarthānām kṛṣestathā
> dvikarmakeṣu grahaṇam siddham vāpyanyakarmaṇaḥ[27]

These two verses found in *Rup,* are taken from *Mbh* where they are given under the rule *'akathitam ca'* (1-4-51). The former one is given as a reply to the question *'kimudāharanam'* (of the said rule). Again under the same rule to the question 'ke punardhātūnām dvikarmakāḥ' PAT gives as reply the verse;

> nīvahyorharteścāpi gatyarthānām tathaiva ca
> dvikarmakeṣu grahaṇam draṣṭavyamiti niścayaḥ

In *Mbh* this verse is followed by a *var* 'siddham *vāpyanyakarmaṇaḥ'* which points out another view with regard to these, *dvikarmaka* roots. The *var* 'siddham vāpyanyakarmaṇaḥ' is given as the fourth *pāda* in the verse given in *Rup.* We also find that PAT does not mention the root *'kṛṣ'* in this verse whereas *Rup* mentions it.

> vātāya kapilā vidyudātapāyātilohinī
> pītā varṣāya vijñeyā durbhikṣāya sitā bhavet[28]

PAT gives this verse as example to the *var* 'utpātena jñāpyamāne' given under the rule *'caturthī sampradāne'* (2-3-13). There the latter part of the verse is read as 'kṛṣṇā sarvavināśāya durbhikṣāya sitā bhavet.' The reading in *Rup* is in accordance with the reading found in *K* under the same rule.

carmaṇi dvīpinam hanti dantayorhanti kuñjaram /
vāleṣu camarīm hanti sīmni puṣkalako hataḥ[29] //

This verse given in *Mbh* under the rule *'saptyamyadhikaraṇe'* (2-3-36), points out the instances where the locative case enjoined by the var 'nimittātkarmayoge' operates. *Rup* gives this in the same context with a variant reading as *vāleṣu* instead of *keśeṣu* found in the reading of *Mbh*.

Verses quoted from Vākyapadīya

vastūpalakṣaṇam yatra sarvanāma prayujyate /
dravyamityucyate sortho bhedyatvena vivakṣitaḥ //
svarūpeṇāthavā jātyā guṇenāpyatha saṅkhyaya /
sambadhyate yadā vastu taddravyam parikīrtitam[30] //

These two verses denote the nature of *dravya* and are quoted by the author under the rule *'cādayosatve'* (1-4-57). The first is quoted from *Vak.*[31] But the latter one is not found in the present editions of *Vak*.

nirvartyañca vikāryañca prāpyañca trividham matam /
karturyat kriyayā vyāptam kaṭakāṇḍagṛhādivat[32] //

This verse is quoted from *Vak* where the latter half is read as, 'tatrepsitatamam karma caturdhānyattu kalpitam.'[33] The verse found in *Rup*, explains the three-fold division of *karma* and illustrates the same. Under the rule 1-4-49, *Padamañjarī* quotes this verse. The reading of the verse in *Rup*, is similar to that of *Padamañjarī*.

Verses quoted from K

ekasmān ṅañaṇavaṭā dvābhyām ṣastriphya eva kaṇamāḥ syuḥ /

jñeyau cayau caturbhyo raḥ pañcabhyaḥ śalau ṣaḍbhyaḥ[34] //

While dealing with the pratyaharas to be formed by the anubandhas in the fourteen Sivasutras, DK says that such pratyaharas number 41 and gives this verse as an authority for the same. This is taken from K where it occurs under the *Māheśvarasutra 'hal.'*

samyogāntasya lope hi nalopādirna sidhyati /
rāttu tenaiva lopaḥ syāt // halastasmādvidhīyate[35]

This verse establishes the necessity of the part *hal* in the compound 'halṅyābhyaḥ' of the rule *'halṅyābhyo . . .'* (6-1-68). This verse is adopted in *Rup* from K.

apṛktaścedamo doṣo nivṛtte ḍatarādiṣu /
adḍītvāḍḍatarādīnām na lopo na ca dīrghatā[36] //

This is a verse explaining the purpose served by the *anubandha 'ḍ'* and the vowel *'a'* in the substitute *'adḍ.'* In K this verse is given under the rule *'adḍḍatarādibhyaḥ . . .'* (7-1-25) and is quoted in *Rup* under the same rule.

sambodhane tūśanasastrirūpam
sāntam tathā nāntamathāpyadantam /
mādhyamdinirvaṣṭi guṇam tvigante
napumsake vyāghrapadām variṣṭhaḥ[37] //

While dealing with the declensional forms of the base *'uśanas,'* DK cites this verse which give the vocative singular forms of the said base. This verse is quoted from K where it is mentioned under the rule *'ṛduśanas . . .'* (7-1-94)

pañcamyāśca caturthyāśca ṣaṣṭhīprathamayorapi /
yānyadvivacanānyatra śeṣe lopo vidhīyate[38] //

This verse is given in K under the rule *'śeṣe lopaḥ'* (7-2-90). It explains the idea conveyed by the word *śeṣe* in the rule. *Rup* too mentions this verse in the same context.

satve niviśatepaiti pṛthagjātiṣu dṛśyate /
ādheyaścākriyājaśca sosatavaprakṛtirguṇaḥ[39] //

This verse explains the meaning of the word *'guṇa'* referred to in the rule *'voto guṇavacanāt'* (4-1-44). K gives this verse under the said rule and is quoted by DK in the same context.

susūkṣmajaṭakeśena sulabhājinavāsasā /
putrī parvatarājasya kuto hetorvivāhitā[40] //

This verse seen in *Rup*, is taken from *K* in order to point out the purpose of the word *aneka* in the rule *'anekamanyapadārthe'* (2-2-24).[41]

kṛṣṇodakpāṇḍupūrvāyāḥ bhūmeracpratyayaḥ smṛtaḥ /
godāvaryāśca nadyāśca saṅkhyāyā uttare yadi[42] //

This verse points out instances where the *samāsānta* suffix *ac* occurs in addition to the instances pointed out by the rule *'acpratyanvavapūrvāt* (5-4-75). *Rup* adopts this verse from *K*.

dugāgamoviśeṣeṇa vaktavyaḥ kārakacchayoḥ /
saṣṭhītṛtiyayorneṣṭaḥ āśīrādiṣu saptasu[43] //

This verse, given in *K*, summarises the idea of the *Bhāṣya* passage under the rule *'aṣaṣṭhyatṛtīyāsthasya . . .'* (6-3-99) and is quoted by DK.[44]

varṇāgamo varṇaviparyayaśca dvau cāparau varṇavikāranāśau /
dhātostadarthātiśayena yogastaducyate pañchavidham niruktam[45] //

This verse points out the five-fold irregularities from the point of view of grammar that can be noticed in the group of words headed by *pṛṣodara* referred to in the rule *'pṛṣodarādīni . . .'* (6-3-109). The said rule treats these sounds with the above irregularities to be correct. This verse is adopted in *Rup* from *K*.

pṛthum mṛdum bhṛśam caiva kṛśam ca dṛḍhameva ca /
paripūrvam vṛḍham caiva ṣaḍetān ravidhau smaret[46] //

Under the rule *'ra ṛto halāderlaghoḥ'* (6-4-161), PAT says, 'evam tarhi parigaṇanam kriyate 'pṛthumṛdu-bhṛśakṛśadṛḍhaparivṛdhānāmiti vaktavyam' which specifies the six bases wherein the rule *'ra ṛto halādeḥ'* functions. Taking the idea of this statement in *Mbh*, *K* gives the above verse under the same rule and *Rup* has adopted it in the same context.

tātaṅi ṅitvam saṁkramakṛt syādantyavidhiścettacca tahā na /
heradhikāre heradhikāro lopavidhau tu jñāpakamāha
tātāno ṅitvasāmarthyānnāyamantyavidhismṛtaḥ /
na tadavadanaṅādīnām tena tentyavikārajāḥ[47] //

K gives this verse under the rule *'tuhyostātaṅ . . .'* (7-1-35). It deals with the purpose served by the *anubandha ṅ* in *tātaṅ* as opposed to the purpose served by the same in other substitutes like *anaṅ* etc. While in the former, the *anubandha ṅ* brings about the prohibition of *guṇa* and *vṛddhi*, it serves the purpose of '*antyadeśatva*' in the latter. The reason for the same is also given in this verse. This is quoted by DK in *Rup* in the same context.

karmasthaḥ pacaterbhāvaḥ karmasthā ca bhideḥ kriyā /
māsāsibhāvaḥ kartṛsthaḥ kaṛtṛsthā ca gameḥ kriyā[48] //

This verse dealing with the two varieties of *kriyā* into *karmasthā* and *kartṛsthā*, is mentioned under the rule '*karmavatkarmaṇā* . . .' (3-1-87) in *Rup* as in *K*.

The eleven verses starting from the verse 'aniṭ svarānto bhavatiti, dṛśyatam . . .' known as anitkarikas are wholly adopted from *K* by DK in his work.[49] These verses enumerate the roots which do not get the augment '*iṭ*' for their *ārdhadhātuka* suffixes and which are hence known as '*aniṭ*'

āmomitvamadantatvātdaguṇatvam videstathā /
āskāsorāmvidhānācca pararūpam katantavat[50] //

This verse taken from *K* deals with the suffix *āma* enjoined by the four rules beginning from '*kāspratyayāt* . . .' (3-1-35), with particular reference to the final vowel *a* which helps to prohibit *itsamjñā* for the penultimate *m*.

lumpedavaśyamaḥ kṛtye tum kāmamanasorapi /
samo vā hitatatayormāmsasya paci yuḍghañoḥ[51] //

Under the rule '*aparasparāḥ kriyāsātatye*' (6-1-144) PAT notes three vars, 'hitatatayorvālopaḥ; samtumunaḥ kāme' and 'avaśyamaḥ kṛtye.' Under the second *var* he adds a statement 'manasi ceti vaktavyam.' The idea of these vars and the *Bhāṣya* passage is given in the first three lines of this verse whereas the fourth line states that the word *māmsa* gets the elision of the final vowel when preceded by words like *pacana* and *pāka*. This verse found in *K* is quoted in *Rup*.

Now verses that are illustrative in character and quoted from *K* are dealt with.

dhūmāyanta ivāśliṣṭāḥ prajvalantīva saṅgatāḥ /
ulmukānīva memī svā jñātayo bharatarṣabha[52] /

This verse given under the rule '*svamajñātidhanākhyāyām*' (1-1-35) in *K*, illustrates the prohibition of *sarvanāmasamjñā* enjoined by the part 'ajñātidhanākhyāyām.' *Rup* also gives the same verse of *K* in the same context.

rudre viśveśvaro devo yuvayoḥ kuladaivatam /

sa eva nātho bhagavān āvayoḥ śatrukarśanaḥ[53] //

This verse illustrates the purpose of the word *apadādau* which is got by *anuvṛtti* in the rule *'yuṣmadasmadoḥ . . .'* (8-1-20). K gives this verse with *yuṣmākam* and *asmākam* in the place of *yuvayoḥ* and *āvayoḥ* and cites this verse under *'anudāttam sarvamapādādau* (8-1-18). The difference in the reading between *Rup* and *K* in this respect is significant. It makes clear the author's effort to make the necessary modifications suitable to his work even when he adopts *K*. *K* explaining the rules in the order of *Ast* does not pay any heed to the order of deriving the case ending of one and the same base. Hence while explaining this *adhikārasūtra*, *K* points out the purpose served by the part *apādādau* by citing as the illustrations the forms of *yuṣmad* and *asmad* in the plural number of the genitive case. But *Rup* as its name suggests, seeks to the order and number of the case endings while dealing with *yuṣmad* and *asmad* and in order to point out the first variant forms of *yusmad* and *asmad* in the dual number of the genitive case cites the rule *'yuṣmadasmadoḥ'* (8-1-20) and refers to rule *'anudāttam sarvamapādadau'* (8-1-18) as an *adhikārasūtra* which supplements the same. He then explains the purpose served by the part *apādādau* got by *anuvrtti* in the rule 8-1-20 saying 'apādādāviti kim ? rudro . . . .' Since the rule 8-1-20 deals with the dual number of the genitive case, he gives in this illustrative verse the forms of *yuṣmad* and *asmad* in the dual number of the genitive case.

aśmānam dṛṣadam manye kāṣṭhamulūkhalam /

andhāyāstam sutam manye yasya matā na paśyati[54] //

This verse is given in *K* to point out instances where the rule *'manyakarmaṇyanādare'* (2-3-17) does not operate on account of the word *'anādare'* in it. *Rup* also gives the same in the same context.

vinā vātam vinā varṣam vidyutprapatanam vinā /

vinā hastikṛtān doṣān kenemau pātitau drumau[55] //

This verse is given in *Rup* to point out the fact that the indeclinables like *vinā* and *nānā* govern *dvitīyāvibhakti.* DK is of opinion that the rule *'pṛthagvinā . . .'* (2-3-32) which enjoins *pañcamī* and *tṛtīyāvibhakti* optionally, also prescribes *dvitīyāvibhakti* to be governed by the above said indeclinables. The *dvītīyāvibhakti* is to be achieved by the *yogavibhāga* of the rule 2-3-32. This is in accordance with *K* where we get this verse as well as the idea of *yogavibhāga.*[56]

kṣudrajanturanasthiḥ syādathavā kṣudra eva yaḥ /
śatam vā prasṛtau yeṣām kecidānakulādapi[57] //

This verse describes as to what the ksudrajantus, mentioned in the rule *'kṣudrajantavaḥ'* (2-4-8) are. This verse is taken from *K*. Though this is not seen in *Mbh* the verse closely follows the idea of the *Mbh* passages under the said rule.[58]

śrotriyasyeva te rājan mandakasyālpamedhasaḥ /
anuvākahatā buddhirnaiṣā tatvārthadarśinī[59] //

This verse is taken in *Rup* from *K* to point out the purpose of the word *nityam* in the rule *'nityamasic . . .'* (5-4-122). In the compound word *alpamedhasaḥ* mentioned in this verse, the *samāsānta* suffix *ac* has operated by virtue of the word *nitya* in the said rule.

haridrureṣām prathamastataśchagalitumburū /
ulapena caturthena kālāpakamihocyate /
ālambiścarakaḥ prācām palaṅgakamalāvubhau /
ṛcābhāruṇitāṇḍyāśca madhyamīyāstrayopare /
śyāmāyana udīcyeṣu uktaḥ kaṭhakalāpinoḥ[60] /

These verses mention the disciples of Kalāpi and vaiśampāyana mentioned in the rule *'kalāpi. . .'* (4-3-104). DK takes this verse from *K*.

Verses quoted from Nyāsa

praparāsamanvavanirdurvyāṅnyadhayopyatisūdabh-ayaśca
pratinā saha lakṣayitavyāḥ paryupayorapi lakṣaṇamatra[61] //

This verse in *Rup* is quoted from *Nyāsa* where it is given under the rule *'nipāta ekājanāṅ'* (1-1-14). The nipatas coming under *prādi* are enumerated in this verse.

kvacitpravṛttiḥ kvacidapravṛttiḥ kvacidvibhāṣā kvacidanyadeva /
vidhervidhānam bahudhā samīkṣya caturvidham bāhulakam vadanti[62] //

This verse is found quoted in *Nyāsa* under *'uṇādayo bahulam'* (3-3-1). It explains the idea conveyed by the word *bahulam* used in the sutras.

Verses quoted from Pradīpa

guṇo vṛdhirguṇo vṛddhiḥ pratiṣedho vikalpanam /
punarvṛddhirniṣedhoto yaṇpūrvāḥ prāptayo nava[63] //

Kaiyaṭa gives this verse in his *Pradīpa* on *Mbh* under rule 7-2-5.[64] Under the rule *'jagrovicinṇalṅitsu . . .'* (7-3-85) DK quotes this verse. It points out that in instances like *ajāgarīt* (the aorist first person singular of the root *jāgṛ*) where the *guṇa* enjoined by the rule operates, there is the contingency of the function of nine rules ordaining *yaṇādeśa, guṇa, vṛddhi,* the prohibition and option of *vṛddhi. Paḍamañjarī* also quotes this verse with the introductory remark *'āha ca.'*[65]

Verses quoted from Paḍamañjarī

radhirnaśistṛpidṛpī druhiṣṇuhimuhiṣṇihāḥ /
radhādayomī paṭhitā divādiṣvaṣṭa kṛṣṭibhiḥ[66] //

This verse quoted from *Paḍamañjarī* enumerates the eight roots coming under *radhādi* mentioned in the rule *'radhādibhyaśca'* (7-2-45). In *Paḍamañjarī* this verse is given under the rule 7-2-45 with the introductory remark *'āha ca.'*

Some other verses

Besides the verses quoted from the texts mentioned above we get certain other verses in *Rup* with the introductory remark *'tathā coktam'* which lead us to the assumption that they are quotations. Such verses are now dealt with.

ekamātrojbhavedghrasvo dvimātro dīrgha ucyate /
trimātrastu pluto jñeyo vyañjanam tvardhamātrakam[67] //

While explaining the rule *'ukālojjhrasva . . .'* (1-2-27) DK cites this verse. It describes the nature of short, long and prolate vowels.

bhedyabhedakayoścāpi sambandhonyonyamiṣyate /
dviṣṭho yadyapi sambandhaḥ ṣaṣṭhyutpattistu bhedakāt[68] //

While explaining the rule *'ṣaṣthī śeṣe,* (2-3-50), DK says that *śeṣa* means *sambandha* just as *svasvāmibhāva* and the like. He then continues that since *sambandha* involves two things, *ṣaṣṭhīvibhakti* comes after that *sambandhin* which among these two qualifies the other. To give weight to his statement he quotes the above verse.

ekājūrṇuñadantānām dīdhīvevyośca jīryateḥ /
jāgarteśca daridrāternānunāsaḥ prayujyate[69] //

In this verse, roots which do not possess the *anunāsika* vowel are pointed out. As a result, these roots do not get, for their vowels, the *itsamjñā* enjoined by the rule *'upadeśejanunāsika it'* (1-3-2). This verse is cited by DK with the introductory remark *'tathā ca vakṣyati.'*

Verses of the author

Apart from the verses from *Mbh, K, Vak*, etc. *Rup* contains a number of verses. In the case of these verses one is inclined to believe them to be the original verses of DK himself since there is no negative proof for the same. Moreover these verses are not given with the introductory remark *'tathā coktam'* which favour the above conclusion. However this cannot be a positive proof since certain verses which are quoted from the works mentioned above are also given without this introductory remark. From the narrative style of the text it seems safer to assume them as those of the author himself. These verses are very simple and discrete and they help very much to serve the purpose of the context.

dhātusūtragaṇoṇādi vākyaliṅgānuśāsanam /
āgamapratyayādeśā upadeśāḥ prakīrtitāḥ[70] //

DK gives this verse while interpreting the rule *'halantyam'* (1-3-3). After giving the meaning, that the final consonant of an *upadeśa* gets the designation *it*, he passes on to explain what is conveyed by the term *upadeśa*. He narrates that *dhātu, sūtra, gaṇa, uṇādi*, etc. are what are known as *upadeśa*. He then gives this verse which clearly enumerates those that are known as *upadeśa*.

pade tu samhitā nityā nityā dhātūpasargayoḥ /
samāse ca tathā vākye sā vivakṣāmapekṣate[71] //

At the outset of *samhitāvatāra*, DK explains *samhitā* by interpreting the rule *'paraḥ sannikarṣaḥ samhitā'* (1-4-109) and in addition, gives this verse to point out where *samhitā*, the source of *sandhi* is to be treated as invariable (*nitya*) or optional (*vivakṣādhīna*).

tuk svaraḥ prakṛtiścaiva vyañjanaśca tataḥ param /
tato visarjanīyaśca svādiḥ ṣaṭsandhirucyate[72] //

This is the concluding verse of *samhitāvatāra* which enumerates the six types of sandhis viz. *tuksandhi, svarasandhi, prakṛtisandhi, vyañjanasandhi, visarjanīyasandhi* and *svādisandhi* dealt by him already.

tasyābhāve nimittasya nityabhāvo na vidyate /
liṅgamasya prayogasya kaṣṭāyeti prakīrtitam[73] //

In this verse DK deals with the *anityatva* of the maxim 'sannipātalakṣaṇo vidhiranimittam tadvighātasya' and points out that this *anityatva* is indicated by the usage *kaṣṭāya* in the rule '*kaṣṭāya kramaṇe*' (3-1-14)

vṛkṣastiṣṭhatikānane kusumitā vṛkṣam latā samśritā /
vṛkṣeṇābhibhato gajo nipatito vṛkṣāya deyam jalam //
vṛkṣādānaya mañjarīmabhinavām vṛkṣasya śākhonnatā/
vṛkṣe nīḍamidam kṛtam śakuninā he vṛkṣa kim kampase[74] //

In the section *ajantapulliṅga* of *vibhaktyavatāra* after explaining all the declensional forms of the word *vṛkṣa*, DK gives this verse in which all the declensional forms of the masculine base *vṛkṣa* including the vocative case are employed in simple sentences.[75]

sarvādiḥ sarvanāmākhyo na cedgauṇothavābhidhā /
pūrvādiśca vyavasthāyām samotulyentaropuri /
paridhāne bahiryoge svorthajñatyanyavācyapi[76] //

Here DK gives an information regarding the *sarvādi* stems which are designated as *sarvanāman*. This verse follows the discussion regarding the statement '*samjñopasarjanībhūtāstu na sarvādayaḥ*' in *Mbh* under the rule *sarvādīni sarvanāmāni*' (1-1-27). So also the idea of the ganasutras under the *sarvādigaṇa* viz. *pūrvaparāvaradakṣiṇottarāparādharāṇi vyavasthāyāmasamjñāyām,*' '*svamajñātidhanākhyāyām* and *antaram bahiryogopasaṅkhyānayoḥ*' are comprehended here. In addition, it is stated that *sama* which comes under *sarvādi* gets the designation when it does not denote the sense of the stem *tulya*.

dhātvartham bādhate kaścit kaścittamanuvartate /
tameva viśinaṣṭyanya upasargagatistridhā[77] //

After giving the meaning of the *sūtra* '*upasargāḥ . . .*' (1-4-59), DK gives this verse in which it is stated that, among the upasargas which are added to roots, some help to convey a sense just opposite to the original sense of the root while some others help to convey the same sense conveyed by the root whereas yet another group modify the sense of the root.

> svasā tisraścatasraśca nanāndā duhitā tathā /
> yātā māteti saptaite svasrādaya udāhṛtāḥ[78] //

While interpreting the rule *'na ṣaṭsvasrādibhyaḥ'* (4-1-10) he gives this verse which enumerates the sounds included under the *svasrādigaṇa.* This verse of DK is quoted by BD in SK.[79]

> eko vai datarantaśca datamāntastathāparaḥ /
> anyetaru tarāntonyaḥ sūtre pañcavidham smṛtam[80] //

The *sūtra 'adḍḍatarādibhyaḥ . . .'* (7-1-25) prescribes the substitute *adḍ* to the suffixes *su* and *am* which are added to the five bases beginning from *datara.* In the above verse DK specifies those five bases.

> ubhayoridamanyatarat kataradyatarattatarat punarekataram /
> itaratpunaranyadathānyatamam katamatprabhṛtiṣvidamekatamat[81] //

In this verse DK gives the illustrative forms of the rule *'adḍḍatarātibhyaḥ . . .'* (7-1-25). In these examples we find the substitute *adḍ* has replaced the suffixes *su* and *am* added to the five stems viz. *itara, anya, anyatara, datarānta* and *datamānta.* However, KAT has prohibited the function of the substitute in regard to the stem *ekatara* which comes under the *datarānta* stems.[82] This fact is pointed out in this verse by giving the form *ekataram* where the substitute has not replaced the suffix *su* or *am.* In addition he also gives the form *anyatamam* in this verse. This is to point out that the stem *anyatama* does not come under the *datamānta* stems and hence it does not get the substitute *adḍ* for the suffixes *su* or *am* added to it.

> vaṣṭi bhāgurirallopamavāpyorupasargayoḥ /
> āpañcaiva halantānām yathā vācā niśā diśā[83] //

DK concludes the *avyayāvatāra* with this verse. In this verse he points out that according to the grammarian Bhāguri, the vowel *'a'* of the upasargas *ava* and *api* gets elision. So also the feminine bases like *vācā, niśā,* etc. gets the elision of the vowel *'ā'* which is indicative of the feminine gender and thus becomes *halanta* stems like *vāc, niś,* and *diś.* This verse of DK is quoted by BD in *SK.*[84]

yaḥ kriyāvyāptitaḥ sthānam kurute mukhyabhāvataḥ /
aprayuktaḥ prayukto vā sa kartā nāma kārakam //
samuddiṣṭakriyāsiddhau yatprakṛṣṭopakārakam /
karaṇam bāhyamanyatra netrādi vividham matam[85] //

These two verses, mentioned by DK under the rules *'svatantraḥ kartā'* (1-4-54) and *'sādhakatamam karaṇam'* (1-4-42) explain the *kartṛkāraka* and *karaṇakāraka.*

hiraṇyam kuṇḍalāyedam dāru rūpāya yujyate /
yajñāya paśavo nītā jāta viprāḥ svakarmaṇe //
samyamāya śrutam dhatte dharmāya sa yamam pumān/
dharmam mokṣāya medhāvī dhanam dānāya bhuktaye[86] //

These two verses are given by DK to elucidate the function of *caturthīvibhakti* in the sense of *tādarthya.* These examples are very simple and very clearly illustrates the idea of the *vār 'tādarthye caturthī vaktavyā'* noted under the rule *'caturthī sampradāne'* (2-3-13).

kṛṣṇāya slāghate gopī hnute kṛṣṇāya tiṣṭhate /
śapate cāpi tasmai sā jñīpsyamānaya kāmataḥ[87] //

This verse is given by DK to illustrate the function of the dative case taught by the rule *'slāghahnuṅ . . .'* (1-4-34).

kamalena samam vaktram vaktrasya sadṛśaḥ śaśī /
sadṛkṣaḥ śaśinā rājā tasya bhāsvān prabhāvataḥ[88] //

This verse is given to illustrate the alternate function of *trtīyā* and *ṣaṣṭhīvibhakti* enjoined by the rule *'tulyārthair . . .'* (2-3-72).

āste kaṭe devadatto gagane vihagaścaret /
puṣpe gandhaḥ sute prītiḥ vāṭe gāvaḥ suśerate[89] //

In this verse, DK gives forms illustrating the function of the locative case enjoined by the rule *'saptamyadhikaraṇe ca'* (2-3-36). According to him locative case denotes the four types of adharas viz. *aupaśleṣika, vaiṣayika* and *abhivyāpaka* and *pratyāsatti bhedavat.* The locative case functioning in the four categories noted above are illustrated in the above verse.

kimapi bahūnām vadatām svayam guṇī yāti sādhumārgeṇa /
sādhu vadatsvapi satsu svayamaguṇī yātyasādhumārgeṇa[90] //

This verse is given by DK to illustrate the function of the *ṣaṣṭhīvibhakti* and *saptamīvibhakti* taught by the rule *'ṣaṣṭhī cānādare'* (2-3-38). The example given in this verse very clearly illustrate the idea of the rule.

saha sākalyasādṛśyayaugapadyasamāptiṣu
samṛdhau cāpi sampattau sahaśabdaḥ prakīrtitaḥ[91] //

In this verse DK denotes the different varieties of sense conveyed by the *nipāta 'saha.'* This verse is noted by him while interpreting the rule *'avyayībhāve cākāle'* (6-3-81) which deals with the *nipāta, 'saha.'*

upasargeṇa dhātvartho balādanyatra nīyate /
prahārāharasamhāravihāraparihāravat[92] //

While giving the forms of the root *hṛ* in the present tense, DK gives this verse. In this verse he states that the combination of *upasarga* seriously affects the sense of a root and illustrates the root *hṛ* as conveying different varieties of sense when prefixed with different upasargas. This is quoted by BD in his *SK.*[93]

roditisvapitiścaiva śvasitiḥ praṇitistathā //
jakṣitiśceti vijñeyo rudādiḥ pañcako gaṇaḥ[94] //

In the rule *'rudādibhyaḥ sārvadhātuke'* (7-2-76) PAN mentions *rudādi* only and does not specify them to be five. DK while giving its meaning specifies them to be five and then enumerates those five roots in the above verse.[95]

jakṣi jāgṛ daridrā śās dīdhī vevī cakās tathā /
abhyastasamjñāsaptaite sābhyāsā ye ca dhātavaḥ[96] //

In this verse DK enumerates those which are designated by the term *abhyasta.* This verse comprehends the idea of the rules *'ubhe abhyastam'* (6-1-5) and *jakṣityādayaḥ ṣaṭ'* (6-1-6)

muñcatirlumpatiścaiva vidirlimpatireva ca /
siciḥ kṛtiḥ kṣidiścaiva piśiścāṣṭau mucādayaḥ[97] //

In this verse DK enumerates the eight roots which come under the *mucādigaṇa* mentioned in the rule *'śe mucādīnām'* (7-1-59).

sankyackāmyackyankyaṣothācārakvip ṇijyanau tathā /
yagāya īyan ṇin caite bhavanti hi sanādayaḥ[98] //

The *sanādi* suffixes referred to in the rule '*sanādyantā dhātavaḥ*' (3-1-32) are enumerated in this verse by DK.

Yajo vapo vahiścaiva vyeñveñau śvayatistathā /
vadvasau hvayatiścaiva smṛtā nava yajādayaḥ[99] //

This verse given by DK under the rule '*vacisvapiyajādīnām kiti*' (6-1-15) enumerates the nine roots to be comprehended by the word *yajādi* in the said rule.

kriyamāṇantu yatkarma svayameva prasidhyati /
sukaraissvairguṇairyasmāt karmakarteti tadviduḥ[100] //

While concluding the *yakprakaraṇa* of *sārvadhātukapariccheda*, DK gives a vivid description of *karmakartṛ* referred to in the rule '*karmavatkarmaṇā* . . . (3-1-87).

halassetṣici vṛddirnātō halāderlaghostu vā /
syāllrāntasya vadavrajyoḥ na śvasa kṣaṇahmyeditām[101] //

Under the rule '*ato halāderlaghoḥ*' (7-2-7) DK gives this verse with the introductory remark '*tatra saṅgrahaślokaḥ*.' Accordingly it summarises the idea conveyed by the rules '*atolrāntasya*' (7-2-2) '*vadavrajahalantasyācaḥ*' (7-2-3) and *neṭi* (7-2-4) '*hmyantakṣaṇa* . . .' (7-2-5) and '*ato halāderlaghoḥ*' (7-2-7).

śamistamirdamiścaiva śramirbhramiḥkṣamistathā /
klamirmādyatirevaite smṛtāḥ śamyādayoṣṭadhā[102] //

The rule '*śāmāmaṣṭānām* . . .' (7-3-74) prescribes the lengthening of the penultimate vowel of the eight roots beginning from *śam* when followed by the suffix *śyan*. These eight roots are enumerated by DK in this verse.

gatvā snātvā ca dadhyannam bhuktvā pītvāmbu śītalam /
vaṭe sayitvā krīḍitvā yāto mandātape sukhī[103] //

The rule '*samānakartṛkayoḥ* . . .' (3-4-21) teaches the fact that the suffix *ktvā* can be added to a root, in case the action denoted by that root is previous to another action done by the same person. (*kartṛ*) DK points out in this rule that the suffix *ktvā* can be added to many a root when the many actions denoted by those roots are previous to another one among themselves done by a single person (*kartṛ*). Hence he says that the dual number in *samānakartṛkayoḥ* of the rule 3-4-21 is not intended by PAN. To illustrate this fact, he gives this verse wherein the suffix *ktvā* is added to many a root, the actions denoted by which are done in a previous time in relation to the action denoted by the root *'yā'* is the word *yātaḥ*.

> īkṣamīkṣam tadā bālā rodamrodam camūmanu /
> āyamāyam nivṛttāyā jīvedekākinī katham //
> nalinyā iva tanvaṅgyāstasyāḥ padmamivānanam /
> mayā madhuvrateneva pāyampāyamaramyata[104] //

In these two verses the usages *īkṣamīkṣam, rodam rodam, āyamāyam* and *pāyam pāyam* illustrate the *ṇamulanta* forms derived by the rule *'ābhīkṣṇye ṇamul ca'* (3-4-22) and the reduplication enjoined by the rule *'nityavīpsayoḥ'* (8-1-4).

> bhvādyadādi juhotyādi divādisvādayasthathā /
> tudādiśca rudhādiśca tanakryādi curādayaḥ[105] //

It is with this verse that DK concludes the second part of the work. In this verse he points out that the roots can be grouped into ten ganas viz. *bhvādi, adādi, juhotyādi, divādi, svādi, tudādi, rudhādi, tanādi, kryādi* and *curādi*.

Notes and References

1. Vide Nīlakaṇṭha Śāstry, 'A Note on Rūpāvatāra,' *Journal of Oriental Research Institute*, Madras, July-September 1934, pp. 277 to 280.
2. *Rup* Part I, pp. 4 & 5.
3. Vide Supra, p. 24.
4. *Rup* Part I, p. 36.
5. *Rup* Part I, p. 146.
6. Ibid, p. 227.
7. Ibid, p. 241.
8. Ibid, p. 253.
9. *Rup* Part II, p. 5.
10. Ibid, p. 185.
11. Ibid, p. 251.
12. Ibid, p. 285.
13. *Rup* Part I, p. 15.
14. Ibid, p. 33.
15. Ibid, p. 128.
16. Ibid, p. 141.

17. Ibid, p. 143.
18. Ibid, p. 267.
19. Ibid, p. 283.
20. *Rup* Part II, p. 110.
21. Ibid, p. 228.
22. Ibid, p. 235.
23. Ibid, p. 281.
24. *Rup* Part I, p. 130 & Part II, p. 281.
25. *Rup* Part II, p. 303.
26. 'jagdhividhirlyapi yattadakasmātsiddhamadasti kitīti vidhānāt /
    hiprabhṛtīmstu sadā bahiraṅgo lyabbharatīti kṛtam tadu viddhi //
    (*Mbh* Vol. I, Dvitīyakhaṇḍa, p. 553).
27. *Rup* Part I, pp. 147 & 148.
28. Ibid, p. 153.
29. Ibid, p. 163.
30. Ibid, p. 14.
31. Vide Supra, p. 24.
32. *Rup* Part I, p. 146.
33. Vide Supra, pp. 24 & 25.
34. *Rup* Part I, p. 2.
35. Ibid, p. 45.
36. Ibid, p. 74.
37. Ibid, p. 110.
38. Ibid, p. 123.
39. Ibid, p. 140.
40. Ibid, p. 184.
41. In *Mbh* under the rule 2-1-1 we get a somewhat similar verse :
    susūkṣmajaṭakeśena sunatājinavāsasā
    samantaśitirandhreṇa dvayorvṛttau na siddhyati //
    This verse points out that compounds like *susūkṣmajaṭa keśena sunantājinavāsasā, samantaśitirandhreṇa* cannot be achieved, if *samāsa* is treated to be relating to two words alone.
42. *Rup* Part I, p. 193.
43. Ibid, p. 212.

44. "evam tarhyaviśeṣeṇa 'anyasya duk chakārakayoḥ' ityuktvā tato vakṣyāmi - 'aṣaṣṭhyatṛtīyāsthasyāśīraśāsthāsthitotsukotirāgeṣu' iti" (*Mbh* under rule 6-3-99)
45. *Rup* Part I, p. 213.
46. Ibid, p. 298.
47. *Rup* Part II, p. 74.
48. Ibid, p. 106.
49. Ibid, pp. 109 to 114.
50. Ibid, p. 120.
51. Ibid, p. 249.
52. *Rup* Part I, p. 40.
53. Ibid, p. 126.
54. Ibid, p. 156.
55. Ibid, p. 159.
56. pṛthagvinānānābhiriti yogavibhāgo dvitīyārthaḥ' (*K* under rule 2-3-32).
57. *Rup* Part I, p. 189.
58. "kṣudrajantavaḥ ityucyate /
    ke kṣudrajantavaḥ ? kṣottavyā jantavaḥ kṣudrajantavaḥ / /
    yadyevam yūkālikṣam kīṭapipīlikam damśamaśakamiti na sidhyati /
    evam tarhyanasthikāḥ kṣudrajantavaḥ /
    athavā yeṣām svam śoṇitam nāsti te kṣudrajantavaḥ /
    athavā yeṣāmāsahasrādañjalirna pūryate te kṣudrajantavaḥ /
    atha vā yeṣām gocarmamātram rāśim hatvā na patati te kṣudrajantavaḥ /
    atha vā nakulaparyantāḥ kṣudrajantavaḥ" (*Mbh*, Vol. I, *Dvitīyakhaṇḍa* pp. 536 & 537).
59. *Rup* Part I, p. 200.
60. Ibid, pp. 251 & 252.
61. Ibid, p. 51.
62. Ibid, p. 95.
63. *Rup* Part II, p. 165.
64. Vide *Mbh*, Vol. III, p. 103.
65. Yudhiṣṭhira Mīmāmsaka takes this as the main proof for assigning Kaiyaṭa to a period previous to that of

Haradatta, the author of *Paḍamāñjarī* (Op. cit. Part I, p. 366)

66. *Rup* Part II, p. 145).
67. *Rup* Part I, p. 4.
68. Ibid, p. 35.
69. *Rup* Part II, p. 5.
70. *Rup* Part I, p. 1.
71. Ibid, p. 6.
72. Ibid, p. 28.
73. Ibid, p. 34.
74. Ibid, p. 36.
75. Infra, p. 323.
76. *Rup* Part I, p. 40.
77. Ibid, p. 51.
78. Ibid, p. 65.
79. *SK* Part I, p. 322.
80. *Rup* Part I, p. 74.
81. Ibid, p. 74.
82. Vide the *var* 'itarācchandasi pratiṣedha ekatarātsarvatra' (*Mbh*, Vol. III, p. 29).
83. *Rup* Part I, p. 131.
84. *SK* Part I, p. 492.
85. *Rup* Part I, p. 150.
86. Ibid, p. 153.
87. Ibid, p. 154.
88. Ibid, p. 161.
89. Ibid, p. 162.
90. Ibid, p. 163.
91. Ibid, p. 168.
92. *Rup* Part II, p. 10.
93. *SK* Part III, p. 54.
94. Ibid, p. 24.
95. 'rudādibhyaḥ pañcabhyo dhātubhyaḥ parasya valādessārvadhātukasya iḍāgamo bhavati' (*Rup* Part II, p. 24).
96. *Rup* Part II, p. 25.
97. Ibid, p. 38.
98. Ibid, p. 45.
99. Ibid, p. 104.
100. Ibid, p. 107.

101. Ibid, p. 146.
102. Ibid, p. 243.
103. Ibid, p. 300.
104. Ibid, pp. 303 & 304.
105. Ibid, p. 306.

Part III

Observations

Chapter VIII

Rūpāvatāra in Comparison with Kāśikā and Later Recasts

In this chapter a comparative study of *Rup*, is attempted with its earlier and later works. Since *Rup* is a quite different attempt with respect to the earlier works on *Ast*, the merits and demerits of the same to be discussed only in the background of those earlier works. The works of later authors who imbibed the idea of their creation from *Rup*, also deserve a comparative study with it, so that the influence of *Rup* on them can be brought out. Hence in this chapter let us turn our attention to a comparative study of *Rup* mainly with *K* and *SK* which are respectively the most prominent ones among the earlier and later works on Ast.

Rūpāvatāra in comparison with Kāśikā

Rup deserves special appreciation when studied in comparison with *K*. It is very clear that *Rup* closely follow *K* in many respects. It is always to be borne in mind that the purpose of *Rup* is not an exposition of PAN's rule but the composition of a preliminary text for the beginners of Sanskrit grammar so as to make the accomplished forms within their easy reach and hence all that suit this purpose are taken from *K*, the source of which is *Ast* itself.

Again *K* is the first one to explain all the Paninian rules in the order of *Ast* and *Rup* is the first one which explains the Paninian rules (though not all of them) in a different order. This fact too is responsible for a comparison of *Rup* with *K*. Therefore we now attempt a comparative study of *Rup* with *K* based on the form of sutras, their interpretation and illustration.

Form of sutras

We find that *Rup* closely follows *K* with regard to the form of sutras. Based on the *yogavibhāga* of certain rules suggested by PAT, *K* treats those single rules to be pairs of rules. In such cases it can be seen that DK considers those sutras to be separate ones just as they are given in *K*. For instance the pairs of rules *aut* and *acca gheḥ* (7-3-118 & 119) '*prādayah* and *upasargāḥ kriyāyoge* (1-4-58 & 59), *vibhṣā* and *apaparibahirañcavaḥ' pañcamyā* (2-1-11 & 12) and *hvassamprasāraṇam* and *abhyastasya ca* (6-1-32 & 33) are treated as separate rules by DK as in *K*.[1]

Interpretation of rules

With regard to the interpretation of rules in *Rup* and *K*, it deserves mention at the outset that all the rules of *Ast* are interpreted in *K* whereas only 2381 of them are interpreted in *Rup*.[2] Again when we view these rules of *Ast* interpreted in *Rup*, it can be understood that great majority of them present similarity in interpretation with *K* while some others given simplified or detailed versions of the interpretation given in *K* and only, a few others expose slight difference in interpretation. Instances of all such varieties are detailed below.

Similarity in interpretation

The rules of *Ast*, interpreted in *Rup* and exhibiting similarity in the interpretation of the same with *K*, can be classed into two groups. The former group includes those rules the interpretation of which is exactly the same as given in *K* while in the letter group though there is a difference in wording the similarity in idea, is kept in tact. For instance rules like *taparastatkālasya* (1-1-70) have exactly the same wording of *K* with regard to their interpretation given in *Rup*.[3] But rules like '*igyaṇaḥ samprasāraṇam*' (1-1-45), '*adar śanam lopah*(1-1-60) etc. found in *Rup* have similar interpretation with *K* in a different wording.[4] It is to be repeated here that a great majority of the rules in *Rup* are similar to *K* in interpretation.

Simplification or elaboration in interpretation

In the case of certain rules, we find that the interpretation given by DK is the simplification of what is detailed in *K* under the said rules. For instance the rule '*halonantarāḥ samyogaḥ*' (1-1-7) is interpreted in *Rup* as 'ajbhiravyavahitāḥ halaḥ samyogasamjñāḥ syuḥ.' It can be seen that this is the simplified extract of the interpretation given in *K*, 'bhinnajātīyairajbhiravyavahitāḥ śliṣṭoccāritā. halaḥ samyogasamjñā bhavanti, samudāyaḥ samjñī/jātau cedam bahuvacanam tena dvayorbahūnām ca samyogasamjñā siddhā bhavati.'[5] Other rules like '*ṣaṣṭhī sthāneyogā*' (1-1-49) can also be pointed out as examples for this.[6]

At the same time, we find that DK gives a more detailed explanation with regard to certain rules. For instance *K* simply gives the meaning of the rule *'ādhārodhikaraṇam'* (1-4-45) with a brief description of *'ādhāra.'* But in *Rup* DK not only gives the meaning of the rule but also makes mention of the four types of adharas. He explains these four types and illustrates them.[7]

Difference in interpretation

Though DK has closely followed *K* while interpreting the rules of *Ast,* rarely we meet with certain instances where there is difference in the interpretation given to the rules in *Rup* and *K.* A few instances of this kind are given below.

arhe kṛtyatṛcaśca (3-3-169)

Rup interprets this rule as teaching the sense *'arha'* to the *Kṛt* suffix *tṛc* and *kṛtya* suffixes.[8] But in *K* it is stated that this rule by virtue of the word *ca* found in it, teaches the sense *'arha'* not only to *tṛc* and *kṛtya* suffixes but also to the lakara *liṅ*. Thus *Rup* differs from *K* here in as much it does not mention the idea comprehended by the word *ca,* pointed out in *K.*

ḍhaki lopaḥ (4-1-133)

This rule enjoins the elision of the final letter of the base *'pitṛṣvasṛ'* when followed by the suffix *ḍhak*. Here it is to be noted that it is the suffix *chaṇ* that is ordained to this base *'pitṛṣvasṛ'* by the rule *'pitṛṣvasuśchaṇ'* (4-1-132) and we do not get any rule ordaining the suffix *ḍhak* to this base *pitṛṣvasṛ*. Hence it is pointed out in *K* that this rule (*ḍhaki lopaḥ*) itself is the authority for the addition of the suffix *ḍhak* to the base *pitṛṣvasṛ* since it speaks of the elision of the final letter of the base *pitṛṣvasṛ* when followed by the suffix *ḍhak.*

DK while interpreting this rule expresses the same opinion. But he adds that the authority for the addition of the suffix *ḍhak* is to be sought in another way also.[9] According to him the rule *'ḍhaki lopaḥ* is to be split into two parts (*yogavibhāga*) one consisting of the word *ḍhaki* and other consisting of the word *lopaḥ.* The former consisting of the single word *ḍhaki* along with the *anuvṛtti* of the word *pitṛṣvasuḥ* from the rule *'pitṛṣvasuśchaṇ'* must be interpreted as teaching the suffix *'ḍhak'* to the base *pitṛṣvasṛ.* The latter part consisting of the single word *lopaḥ,* along with the help of the word *'ḍhaki'* of former split rule and of the word *pitṛṣvasuḥ* got from the previous rule *'pitṛṣvasuśchaṇ,'* can be construed in such a way so as to teach the elision of the final letter of the base *pitṛṣvasṛ'* when followed by the suffix *ḍhak*. This is an innovation made by DK.

idamasthamuḥ (5-3-24)

The rule *idamasthamuḥ* enjoins to the base *idam,* the suffix *thamu* which is termed *vibhakti* by the rule *'prāgdiśo vibhaktiḥ* (5-3-1). Here *K* points out that the final vowel *'u'* in *thamu* helps the penultimate consonant *'m'* from being designated as *'it.'* If the suffix *thamu* were devoid of the final vowel *'u,' 'm'* would have been the final consonant of the suffix and hence it would have been designated as *'it'* by the rule *'halantyam'* (1-3-3). Hence it is said in *K 'ukāro makāraparitrāṇārthaḥ'*. DK draws an indication here. He states 'atra ukāro makāraparitrāṇārthaḥ /etadevokārakaraṇam jñāpakam na vibhaktau tusmāḥ (1-3-4) ityasya anityatvasya; tena kimot (5-3-12) ityatra takārasya itsamjñā bhavati.'[10] According to him even if the consonant *'m'* were the final letter of the suffix *'thamu'* termed *vibhakti,* it won't get the designation *'it'* by virtue of the rule *'na vibhaktau tusmāḥ'* (1-3-4) by which the consonants, coming under *tavarga, 's'* and *'m'* in a suffix termed *vibhakti,* are prohibited from being designated as *'it.'* Hence the unnecessary effort of providing the suffix with a final vowel *'u,'* is to be understood as indicative of the fact that the prohibition of *itsamjñā* to *tavarga, 's'* and *'m'* by the rule *'na vibhaktau tusmāḥ'* is *anitya* (i.e. not invariable) and hence does not function in certain instances. The *itsamjñā* by the rule *'na vibhaktau tusmāḥ'* being thus *anitya,* the consonant *'m'* in the suffix has got a chance of being designated as *'it'* if it were the final letter of the suffix. If so, it will get elided by the rule *'tasya lopaḥ'* (1-3-9) and one cannot attain the form *itham.* Hence the consonant *'m'* is provided with a final vowel *'u'* to protect the same from *itsamjñā* and consequent *lopa.*

DK cites an instance which is benefited by this indication (*jñāpanam*). It is the indeclinable *kva* which is derived by the addition of the *taddhita* suffix *'at'* to the base *kim* by the rule *'kimot'* (5-3-12). The suffix *at* is termed *vibhakti* by the rule *'prāgdiśo vibhaktiḥ'* and hence its final consonant *'t'* ought to undergo the prohibition of *itsamjñā* by the rule *'na vibhaktau tusmāḥ.'* But on the basis of the indication of *anityatva* of the rule *'na vibhaktau tusmaḥ,'* the final consonant *'t'* of the suffix *'at'* does not undergo *itsamjñāniṣedha.* It therefore can be designated as *'it'* and gets elided. Thereby the form *kva* can be arrived at.

ciṇo luk (6-4-104)

This rule is interpreted in *K* an ordaining the elision, i.e., *'luk'* of the suffix that occurs as latter to *'ciṇ,'* which comes as the substitute of the suffix *cli.*[11] But in *Rup* DK specifies that this rule teaches the elision of the suffix *'ta'* occurring as latter to *cin.*[12] This is because the rule *'ciṇbhāvakarmaṇoḥ,'* ordains the substitute *ciṇ* in the place of *cli* only when *cli* is followed by the suffix *'ta'* (*āt-manepada* — first person singular). Hence when followed by other *dvivacana* and *bahuvacana* suffixes *'cli'* gets replaced by other substitutes like *'sic'* and so on and thereby the *ekavacana* suffix *'ta'* alone can occur as latter to *ciṇ.* Hence DK interprets this rule as teaching the elision of the suffix *'ta.'* Here we find that DK differs from *'K'* in the interpretation of this rule by way of accurate specification.

tṝphalabhajatrapaśca & phaṇām ea saptāmām (6-4-122 & 125)

While interpreting these two rules which ordain the vowel *'e'* as the substitute of the component vowel in roots like *tṛ phal,* etc. along with the *abhyāsalopa* of these roots, *K* cites as *the nimitta* for the same, *liṭ* which is *kit* and *ṅit* and *thal* which is *seṭ.*[13] But while dealing with these two rules, DK cites as *nimitta liṭ* which is *kit* and *thal* which is *seṭ.* He does not mention the *nimitta* viz. *liṭ* which is *ṅit.*[14]

oto gārgyasya (8-3-20)

While interpreting this rule enjoining elision, *K* points out that the *lopa* enjoined as per this rule operates on the consonant *'y'* whereas DK interprets this rule as enjoining the elision of two consonants *'y'* and *'v.'*[15] It is from the words *vyoḥ* of the rule *'vyorlaghuprayatantaraḥ . . .'* (8-1-18) that *'y'* is got by *anuvṛtti* for the rule *'oto gārgyasya'* and since there is the mention of both the consonants *'y'* and *'v'* in the part *vyoḥ* that DK seems to interpret this rule as enjoining the elision of both the consonants *'y'* and *'v.'*

Illustration of sutras and presentation of rupas

In the second introductory verse to *K* we find that the work is referred to as *vyutpannarūpasiddhi* meaning that it helps to arrive at the rupas by giving their *vyupatti* or derivation.[16] When we go through *K* we find that each and every *sūtra* is illustrated as part of interpretation. Many a rule is provided with rupas which form their examples and counter examples. But in *Rup* we find that DK gives more importance to the citation of rupas and it is for this purpose that the sutras of *Ast* are selected and interpreted in *Rup*. Hence when we make a comparison between *K* and *Rup*, it can be noticed that *K* is characterised by the illustration of sutras as part of interpretation while *Rup* is marked by the presentation of rupas which accidentally helps to illustrate the sutras.

We find that DK does not attempt to illustrate each and every *sūtra* selected from *Ast*, since it is not for the illustration of sutras that rupas are cited, but in order to present a *rūpa* and to point out its *vyutpatti* that a rule is interpreted. Hence we find that many rules like *'vipratiṣedhe param kāryam'* (1-4-2) are not readily provided with their examples.[17] So also DK takes much pains to narrate the *prakriyā* and in this respect we find *K* is lacking comparatively. Further, DK presents the sutras not in their order found in *Ast* but in a different order which suits the presentation of rupas and narration of their *vyutpatti* (derivation). Therefore though in the introductory verses to *K*, the work is claimed to be *vyutpannarūpasiddhi*, it is *Rup* which can be, more properly called *vyutpannarūpasiddhi.'*

Here the remark of Nārāyaṇa Bhaṭṭa is noteworthy. Referring to *K* he says, 'vṛttau cāru na rūpasiddhikathanā' and referring to *Rup* he says, 'rūpāvatāre punaḥ, kaumudyādiṣu cātra sūtramakhilam nāstyeva.'[18] He means that in *K* the narration of the derivation of a *rūpa* is not so meritorious. He does not find fault with *Rup* in this respect. Since the only one drawback in *Rup* pointed out by Nārāyaṇa Bhaṭṭa is that it does not comprehend all the sutras of *Ast*, one can understand that Nārāyaṇa Bhaṭṭa gives recognition to the marvellous presentation of rupas in DK's work.

Rūpāvatāra in comparison with other recasts like Siddhānta Kaumudī

A comparison of *Rup* with the *SK* of BD may seem nothing to an onlooker, since the former is the most primitive form of a recast of *Ast* and the latter is the most developed and systematically furnished form of the same. But to a research student, such a comparison is very necessary, informative and hence unavoidable, since the former is the prototype of the latter. A comparative study of the same with other recasts like *Rūpamālā*, *PK*, *PS* which represent the different stages in the development of the recasts of *Ast* is also worth the effort. But it is the comparative study of *Rup* with *SK* that matters, since the former and the latter represent respectively, the initial and final stages of development of the *prakriyā* style of treatment of *Ast*. Hence, after a comparative study of *Rup* with *K*, we are attempting here a comparative study to *Rup* mainly with *SK* and accidentally with other recasts mentioned above.

The comparative study of *Rup* with *SK* and other recasts is designed here with the purpose of bringing out the extent to which the former has influenced the latter. Hence we are to discuss the same in a manifold manner based on their contents, arrangement, interpretation of sutras and presentation of rupas.

Contents

All the recasts of *Ast* have mainly the same i.e. the sutras of *Ast*, as their contents. But they differ from each other only in the number of sutras taken from *Ast*. DK selects for this work only 2381 sutras out of the nearly 4000 sutras of *Ast*, Vimalasaraswathy has taken about 2000 rules for his *Rupamālā* while Ramachandra has completed his work *PK* taking 2470 rules though the physical dimension of the work is greater than *Rup*. All the sutras of *Ast* are taken for study only in two recasts viz. *PS* of Nārāyaṇa Bhaṭṭa and *SK* of BD.

Arrangement

The sutras of *Ast*, are arranged quite differently in the various recasts of *Ast*. It is to be borne in mind that these different kinds of arrangement based on the subject-wise grouping of the sutras had their origin in *Rup*. In *Rup*, the sutras are dealt with in two separate parts which are subdivided into avataras and paricchedas. *Rūpamālā* of Vimalasaraswathy is a single but short work consisting of ten sections called malas. The *PK* of Ramachandra and *SK* of BD are divided into two parts called *pūrvārdha* and *uttarārdha*. With regard to the contents of these two parts it can be seen that the same is also modelled on the two parts of *Rup* but modified according to the whims and fancies of the authors. *PS* of *Nārāyaṇa Bhaṭṭa* is divided into two parts called *pūrvabhāga* and *uttarabhāga*. But the arrangement of the topics dealt with in these two parts of *PS* is different from that of *Rup* and we find that the *pūrvabhāga* of *PS* consists of 17 sections called khandas and *uttarabhāga* three khandas.[19] Now let us attempt a comparative study of the further subdivision of the two major parts as well as the contents of *Rup* with *SK* and other works.

Pūrvabhāga of Rup/Pūrvārdha of SK

The *pūrvabhāga* of *Rup* is subdivided into 8 avataras viz. *samjñā, samhitā, vibhakti, avyaya, strīpratyaya, kāraka, samāsa* and *taddhita* whereas the *pūrvārdha* of *SK* is subdivided into 42 prạkaranas dealing with 9 topics viz. *samjñā, paribhāṣā, sandhi subanta, avyaya, strīpratyaya, kāraka, samāsa* and *taddhita.*

Rup opens with the section named *samjñāvatāra* and *SK* with the section *samjñāprakaraṇa.* DK does not include all the *samjñā* rules in *samjñāvatāra.*[20] This is due to the fact that the author has given more importance to the *samjñā* rules which are essential for the understanding of the different types of sandhis discussed in the following chapters and hence has included only such samjnasutras in this section. Therefore, he discusses the *prātipadikasamjñā,* only while dealing with the declensions, *parasmaipada, ātmanepada, prathamā, madhyama* and *uttama* samjnas only in the second part of the work dealing with the roots. DK is followed in this matter by later writers of *PK, PS* and *SK* only with a difference that they add some more samjnas like *vṛddhi, guṇa, dhātu, nipāta, upasarga, gati, avasāna, samhita, pada, samyoga, laghu* and *guru* also to this section. This initial section dealing with the samjnas is termed *samjñāmālā* in *Rūpamālā, sandhyupayogisamjñāprakaraṇa* in *PK, samjñākhaṇḍa* in *PS* and *samjñāprakaraṇa* in *SK.* Of these the name *sandhyupayogisamjñāprakaraṇa* given by Ramachandra to this section seems more suitable.

In *PK, PS* and *SK* the first section dealing with samjnas is followed by a section dealing with paribhasas wherein the more important among the sutras in *Ast,* which are in the form of postulates relating to the application of sutras in general and hence called paribhasasutras, are explained. Though such a section is quite relevant in a recast of *Ast,* we do not get in *Rup* a section dealing with paribhasasutras in general. DK can never be accused of the non-composition of the same since he introduces these paribhasasutras whenever their relevance occurs in his work. For example while dealing with the *vidhisūtra 'hrasvasya piti kṛti tuk'* (7-1-71) in the beginning itself of *samhitāvatāra* which follows *samjñāvatāra,* he introduces the two paribhasasutras *'ṣaṣṭhīsthāneyogā'* (1-1-49) and *'ādyantau ṭakitau'* (1-1-46).[21] So also other *paribhāṣā* rules like *'alontyasya'* (1-1-52) *'vipratiṣedhe param kāryam'* (1-4-2) etc. are introduced in his work in places where they are necessary.[22] Moreover the idea of the formation of a section giving preliminary details at the outset of the work, had its origin in *Rup* by means of the formation of *samjñāvatāra* and it only got enhanced by later authors by the formation of an additional *prakaraṇa* concerned with the paribhasasutras. Hence the non-composition of *paribhāṣāprakaraṇa* cannot be regarded as a demerit of *Rup*.

DK names the section dealing with *sandhi* as *samhitāvatāra* and divides the same into six sections as pointed out earlier.[23] But in *SK* just as in *PK*, sandhi is dealt with in a four-fold manner, *acsandhi, halsandhi, visargasandhi* and *svādisandhi*. The formation of four sections dealing with *sandhi* as opposed to the six sections of the same in *Rup* is brought about by incorporating *tuksandhi* in *halsandhi* and *prakṛtibhāvasandhi* in *acsandhi*. In the *sandhikhaṇḍa* of *PS*, after dealing with the rules relating to *tuk* and *suṭ*, *acsandhi, prakṛtibhāvasandhi' halsandhi* and *visargasandhi* and *svādisandhi* are taken up in order by the author.

After dealing with *sandhi*, DK takes up declensions in the next section *vibhaktyavatāra* with the three subdivisions of *ajanta* stems into *pulliṅga, strīliṅga* and *napumsakaliṅga* and with the four sub-divisions of *halanta* stems into *pulliṅga, strīliṅga, napumsakaliṅga* and *aliṅga*. The fourth subdivision viz. *aliṅga*, of *halanta* is peculiar to *Rup*.[24] For, in *PK* declensions are dealt with in a section named *svādiprakriyā* with the three subdivisions of *ajanta* stems and *halanta* stems each into *pulliṅga, strīliṅga* and *napumsakaliṅga*. In SK also, declensions are dealt with in six prakaranas of *ajantapuilliṅga, ajantastrīliṅga, ajantanapumsakaliṅga, halantapulliṅga, halantastrīliṅga* and *halantanapumsakaliṅga*. However BD does not give a common name to these six sections dealing with declensions. In *PS* the section dealing with declensions is termed *subvidhikhaṇḍa'* but this section comes only much later after the 5 khandas named *kṛt, taddhita, samāsa, strīpratyaya* and *subartha* which are dealt in order after *sandhikhaṇḍa*.

The order of the next four sections in *Rup*, i.e. *strīpratyayāvatāra, kārakāvatāra, samāsāvatāra* and *taddhitāvatāra* are followed by *PK* and *SK* with the only difference that in *PK* these sections are named *strīpratyayāprakaraṇa, vibhaktyarthaprakaraṇa, samāsaprakaraṇa* and *taddhitaprakaraṇa* whereas in *SK* they are termed as *strīpratyayaprakaraṇa, kārakaprakaraṇa, samāsaprakaraṇa* and *taddhitaprakaraṇa.*

In the *strīpratyayāvatāra* of *Rup* and *strīpratyayaprakaraṇa* of *PK*, we find that all the feminine suffixes which lead to the formation of stripratyayantarupas are dealt with. In the *strīpratyayakhaṇḍa* of *PS* and *strīpratyayaprakaraṇa* of *SK*, all the rules of *Ast* dealing with feminine suffixes are included.

The section dealing the sense of case endings viz. *sup* suffixes is named as *kārakāvatāra* in *Rup*, as *Vibhaktyartha* in *PK*, *kārakaprakaraṇa* in *SK* and *subarthakhaṇḍa* in *PS*. Of these the title *subartha* in *PS* seems more appropriate since in this section, as pointed out just above, it is the sense of *sup* suffixes that is dealt with. The naming of this section as *vibhaktyartha* in *PK* is over-pervading since *vibhakti* includes not only *sup* suffixes but also *tiṅ suffixes, the sense of which (tiṅ suffixes) is not dealt with here.*[25] So also the name of this section as *kārakāvatāra* in *Rup* or *kārakaprakaraṇa* in *SK* is also defective since the meaning of *sup* suffixes include not only *kāraka*, but also, *prātipadikārtha* and *sambandha* in addition. As these two which are not comprehended by the word *kāraka*, are dealt with in this section, both the names *kārakāvatāra* and *kārakaprakaraṇa* are less comprehensive.

The section dealing with *samāsa* is divided into six by DK. Of these the first four sections deal with the four kinds of samasas viz. *avyayībhāva, tatpuruṣa, bahuvrīhi* and *dvandva* and the latter two named *samāsānta* and *alugādisamāsāśrayavidhi*, deal with the accessories of samasas. But in *PK*, samasas are dealt with in four sections dealing with the four kinds of samasas and those, discussed as the accessories of *samāsa* under the two sections *samāsānta* and *alugādisamāsāśrayavidhi* in *Rup*, are dealt with in the said four sections itself by Ramachandra. In *PS* we find that compounds are dealt with in the *samāsakhaṇḍa* in the order of *avyayībhāva, tatpuruṣa, bahuvrīhi, dvandva* and *aluk*. The samasantas relating to *tatpuruṣa* and *bahuvrihi* are given at the end of the respective sections and general ones under the *aluk* section. In *SK*, we find that samasas are dealt with in several prakaranas like, *avyayībhāvasamāsa, tatpuruṣasamāsa, bahuvrīhisamāsa, dvandvasamāsa, ekaśeṣa, sarvasamāsaśeṣa, sarvasamāsānta, aluksamāsa* and *samāsāśrayavidhi*.

For the *taddhitāvatāra* of *Rup*, DK has selected rules dealing with taddhitas from the fourth and fifth adhyayas of *Ast* concerned with *taddhita* suffixes. DK has arranged them more or less in the same order in which they are found in *Ast*. Also he includes other sutras found necessary from other chapters of *Ast* in this section.[26] In *PK* also the section dealing with taddhitas include sutras selected from fourth and fifth chapters of *Ast* and they are arranged in the same order of *Ast*. The entire *taddhita* section of *Ast* has been divided into 19 prakaranas in *SK*. It is clear that in the *taddhita* section, BD did not face any trouble in placing the sutras in the order of *Ast*, although he does include in it, as in *Rup* sutras found necessary from chapters other than the fourth and fifth chapters of *Ast*. In the *taddhitakhaṇḍa*, of *PS* also, the entire *taddhita* rules are dealt with. The *pūrvabhāga* of *Rup*, as well as *pūrvārdha* of *PK* and *SK* end with the *taddhita* section while in *PS* alone *taddhita* is dealt with much earlier. The order of the various topics discussed in the 17 khandas of *PS* are *saṃjñā, paribhāṣā, sandhi, kṛt, taddhita, samāsa, strīpratyaya, subartha, subvidhi, ātmanepadavibhāga, tiṅ, lārthaviśeṣa, sannanta, yaṅanta, yaṅluk, subdhātu* and *nyāya*. It is clear that the *pūrvabhāga* of *PS* present a striking contrast to the *pūrvabhāga* of *Rup*.

Uttarabhāga of Rup/Uttarārdha of SK

Uttarabhāga of *Rup*, titled as *Dhātupratyayapañcikā* deals with roots and suffixes like *tiṇ, kṛt* etc. added to them. The *uttarārdha* of *PK* and *SK* is also concerned with the same. The topic dealt with in the three khandas coming under the *uttarabhāga* of *PS*, are *dhātu, uṇādi* and *chāndasa*.

In *Rup*, we find that tinantarupas of ten lakaras derived from certain roots coming under the ten ganas and occurring in the sense of *kartṛ, karman, bhāva* and *karmakartṛ*, are dealt with in the two sections called *sārvadhātukapariccheda* and *ārdhadhātukapariccheda*. Here there is the defect that the various rupas in the different lakaras of one and the same root are scattered over the different sub-sections coming under these two major sections.[27] Hence one finds himself at a loss to gather the rupas of one and the saṃe root in all the lakaras, at a time. This inconvenience is avoided in *PK* and *SK* wherein the tinantarupas of roots are dealt with in ten sections of ten ganas and in each section all the tinantarupas of a root in all the lakaras except the Vedic lakara *leṭ* are discussed at a time itself. Thus we find that *PK* and *SK* deviate from *Rup* in the treatment of tinantarupas derived from roots coming under the ten ganas.

The tinantarupas derived from *pratyayānta* roots like *sannanta* are dealt with in separate sections in *Rup*.[28] In *SK* after the first ten sections dealing with tinantas in the order of the ten ganas of roots, *pratyayānta* roots are dealt with in prakaranas concerned with *ṇic, san, yaṅ, yaṅluk, nāmadhātu, kaṇḍvādi*, and *pratyayamālā*.

Another deviation from *Rup* in *PK* and *SK*, is that separate sections viz. *Ātmanepadaprakaraṇa* and *Parasmaipadaprakaraṇa* are formed to deal with *padavyavasthā* (the conditions when roots are to take *parasmaipada* termination or *ātmanepada* termination or both of them). But no such separate section is formed in *Rup*, though certain rules relating to *parasmaipada* and *ātmanepada* are included by DK in the *Sārvadhātukapariccheda* and *Ārdhadhātukapariccheda* itself.[29] So also two separate sections named *Bhāvakarmatiṅprakaraṇa* and *Karmakartṛtiṅprakaraṇa* for dealing with *tiṅ* suffixes occurring in the sense of *bhāva, karma*, and *karmakartṛ* is formed in *PK* and *SK* while this too is also dealt with in the *Sārvadhātukapariccheda* and *Ārdhadhātukapariccheda* itself by DK.

In *Rup*, the section dealing with the varieties of sense conveyed by *tiṅ* suffixes, is named *Tiṅvibhaktyartha* by DK whereas the same is termed by BD as *Lakārārthaprakaraṇa* which comes after *Karmakartṛtiṅprakaraṇa* in *SK*. *Kṛdantāvatāra* dealing with *kṛdanta* stems is one of the major sections in the second part of *Rup* with which the work ends. Though the *uttarārdha* of SK also, ends with the *kṛdantaprakaraṇa* the author appends at the end two more prakaranas viz. *Vaidikasvaraprakriyā* and *Liṅgānuśāsana*.

Finally it is clear from the above that the arrangement of the various topics in the two parts of *PK* and *SK* is modelled on the two parts of *Rup*. It can also be noticed that it is *PS* which among the various later recasts, deviate most from *Rup*. The more and more convenient methods adopted by the authors of these later recasts, seen in the presentation of tinantarupas, the discussion of all the sutras of *Ast*, forming of separate sections for dealing with paribhasas, *padavyavasthā bhāvakarmakarmakartṛprakriyā* etc. undoubtedly bring credit to those authors. But it is to be understood that when one pays homage to these authors for these innovations, DK too is being honoured since he is the discoverer of the idea of reshuffling the sutras of *Ast* which is the basis of all these innovations.

Interpretation of sutras

With regard to the interpretation of rules in *Rup* and later recasts, it deserves mention that in *Rup* a rule is interpreted with a view to help the presentation of a *rūpa* for which the rule is selected. Hence we find that one and the same rule is interpreted twice or thrice in *Rup* so as to help the derivation of rupas cited in different contexts. We get numerous instances of this repeated interpretation of one and the same rule in the *pūrvabhāga* of *Rup* as well as its latter part, *Dpp*.[30] Two examples are given below :

1.	*aco ñṇiti* (7-2-115)	:	In ajantapulliṅga while dealing with the *rūpa sakhāyau* of the '*i*' stem *sakhi* and the *rūpa gauḥ* of the '*o*' stem '*go*.'[31]
2.	*liṅsicāvātmanepade* (1-2-11)	:	While dealing with the rupas upagūhiṣīṣṭa of the root '*guh*' and *mukṣīṣṭa* of the root '*muc*' in the *āśirliṅprakaraṇa* and *abhitta* of the root '*bhid*' in the *luṅprakaraṇa*.[32]

PK is influenced by *Rup* in this respect. There also we get repeated interpretation of a few sutras. They are given below :

1.	adeḥ parasya (1-1-54)	:	In halsandhi and *halantaprakaraṇa*
2.	*anekālśitsarvasya* (1-1-55)	:	In *saṃjñāprakaraṇa* and *ajantaprakaraṇa*
3.	*dhātoḥ* (3-1-91)	:	In the bhvādi section and *kṛdanta* section
4.	*varṣābhvaśca* (6-4-84)	:	In ajantapulliṅgaprakaraṇa and *strīliṅgaprakaraṇa*
5.	*visarjanīyasya saḥ* (8-3-15)	:	In halsandhi and *visargasandhi*
6.	'*kupvoḥ . . .*' (8-3-37)	:	In *halsandhi* and *visargasandhi*

Quite in contrast, the aim of the presentation and derivation of rupas is achieved in *SK* even without repeated interpretation of one and the same rule. When we get repeated interpretation of one and the same rule in *Rup*, and *PK*, a rule is interpreted once only in *SK* and this interpretation satisfies the requirements of other rupas also, cited elsewhere in the text. Once a rule is interpreted in *SK*, it is only referred to in other contexts. For example the rule '*pūrvatrāsiddham*' (8-2-1) is interpreted as 'adhikāroyam tena sapādasaptādhyāyīm prati tripādyasiddhā / tripādyāmapi pūrvam prati param śāstramasiddham syāt' / in the *samjñāvatāra* and it is only referred to in *svādisandhi* while dealing with the *rūpa* '*manoratha*' saying 'iti rephalope prāpte, 'pūrvatrāsiddham' iti ro ri ityasyāsiddhatvāt utvameva, 'manorathaḥ.'[33]

Again with regard to the nature of interpretation of rules we find that the interpretation given in *Rup* is similar to that given in *K*. For example, the rule '*pāghrādhmā* . . . (7-3-78) is interpreted in an elaborate way quite similar to what we get in *K* and it can be found that there is difference only in wording.[34] But the authors of later recasts adhere to the concise nature of interpretation. Hence *PK* interprets the rule as 'paghrādīnām kramāt pibādaya ādeśāḥ syuḥ śiti' and BD interprets in *SK* as 'pādīnām pibādayaḥ syuritsamjñakaśakārādau pratyaye pare.'[35] We meet with numerous other instances where later authors stick to the concise nature of interpretation.[36]

Moreover in *Rup*, even simple rules like '*utsādibhyoñ*' (4-1-86) and '*svasucchaḥ*' (4-1-143), '*śivādibhyoṇ*' (4-1-115) and '*godhāyā ḍhrak*' (4-1-129) are provided with *vṛtti* which gives their meaning fully. Quite differently in *PK* and *SK* we find that such rules, the meaning of which can be understood from the rules themselves are not provided with *vṛtti*. For example, in *PK*, rules like '*utsādibhyoñ,*' '*svasucchaḥ,*' '*śivādibhyoṇ,*' '*duṣkulāḍḍhak*' (4-1-142), '*halasīrāṭṭhak*' (4-3-124), '*somāṭṭyaḥ*' (4-2-30), '*agnerḍhak* (4-2-33), '*pāśādibhyo yaḥ*' (4-2-49), *kramādibhyo vun* (4-2-61), '*rathādyat*' (4-3-121), *khaḥ sarvadhurāt* (4-4-78) and '*śakaṭādaṇ*' (4-4-80) are not provided with *vṛtti*. In *SK* also we find that BD does not give any *vṛtti* to such rules and simply states '*spaṣṭam*' or gives the examples alone. For example :

1. '*utsādibhyoñ*' (4-1-86) : '*autsaḥ*'
2. '*svasucchaḥ*' (4-1-143) : '*svasrīyaḥ*'

3. *'nīcairanudāttaḥ'* (1-2-20) : *spaṣṭam arvāṅ*
4. *'jhalam jhas jhaśi'* (8-4-53) : *:spaṣṭam*
5. *'yuṣmadasmadbhyām' ṅasoś* : spaṣṭam
6. *'godhāyā ḍhrak'* (4-1-129) : *gaudheraḥ*
7. *'kṣatrād ghaḥ* (4-1-138) : *kṣatriyaḥ*

In addition to the practice of giving meaning for each and every *sūtra*, it can also be seen that DK pays attention to give a vivid description of the idea conveyed by the component words *'ādhāra cārtha* etc. of sutras like *'ādhārodhikaraṇam'* (1-4-45) *cārthe dvandvaḥ* (2-2-79) etc.[37] It is also noteworthy that the explanation of four varieties of *cārtha* by DK is very clear and discriminative than that given by BD. He very clearly elucidadates *'cārtha* in which *dvandvasamasa* is enjoined and also gives the following verse which clearly explain *itaretarayoga* which is one among the four varieties of *cārtha* :[38]

itaretarayogastu bhinnasaṅghābhidhāyinām /
pratyekañca samūhosau samūhiṣu samāpyate //

Finally in *Rup* we find that an introduction is given before presenting a rule or starting an *avatāra.*[39] For example he gives the introduction 'katham punaranupadiṣṭā dīrghādayo gṛhyante? savarṇagrahaṇāt / katham? and then only presents the rule *'aṇuditsavarṇasya . . .'* (1-1-69) along with its *vṛtti.*[40] So also at the outset of *strīpratyayāvatāra,* DK says 'atha strīpratyayāntaḥ nirdiśyante / ke punaḥ strīpratyayāḥ? tāp, ḍāp, cāp, ṅīp, ṅīṣ, ṅīn, ūṅ, ti ityete strīpratyayāḥ' / prathamam tāvat ṭāp' and then starts with the *sūtra 'ajādyataṣṭāp'* (4-1-4).[41] But this method of introducing a rule or a *prakaraṇa* is not found followed in later recasts like *PK* or *SK*.

Rupas cited

Rup as well as all the later recasts have given great importance to the presentation of rupas. Hence in all these works many a *'rūpa'* is cited by way of illustration of rules. Generally the rupas cited in *Rup* are not orthodox in character though rarely we meet with instances like 'kṛṣṇāya . . .' and so on which are orthodox in nature.[42] But PK emerges with the characteristic feature that almost all the rupas cited as illustration of the rule are orthodox and related to devas. Following *PK*, *SK* too cites similar type of rupas. For example, while citing the declensional forms of stems ending in vowels DK takes bases like *vṛkṣa*, *kavi*, *kāru*, *jāyā*, etc. But in *PK* and *SK* we get bases like *Rāma*, *Hari*, *Guru*, *Ramā*, etc. which refer to Gods. The rupas given as examples in the *kārakāvatāra* also reveal this fact. A few examples are given below :

	Sutra	*Examples in Rup*	*Examples in PK & SK*
1.	'karmaṇi dvitīyā' (2-3-2),	kaṭam karoti[43]	harim bhajati
2.	'adhiśīṅsthāsām karma' (1-4-146)	grāmamadhiśete adhitiṣṭhati adhyāste vā[44],	adhiśete adhitiṣṭhati adhyāste vā vaikuṇṭham hariḥ
3.	'upanvadhyāṅ vasaḥ (1-4-48)	grāmamupavasati grāmamanuvasati grāmamadhivasati grāmamāvasati[45]	upavasati anuvasati adhivasati āvasati va vaikuṇṭham hariḥ.
4.	'hīne' (1-4-86)	anu śākaṭāyanam vaiyākaraṇāḥ[46]	anu harim surāḥ
5.	'upodhike ca' (1-4-87)	upa śākaṭāyanam vaiyākaraṇāḥ[47]	upa harim surāh

We find that the *PS* of Nārāyaṇabhaṭṭa abounds in illustration. Apart from the general feature of the wealth of examples, under a particular *sūtra* we find in *PS* many more examples than those found in other works. Another feature of the rupas cited is that they are concerned with Lord Kṛṣṇa.

Notes and References

1. *Rup* Part I, pp. 44, 51, 171 and 169 and Part II, p. 196 *'prādaya upasarḡaḥ kriyāyoge, vibhāṣāpaparibahirañcavaḥ pañcamya, hvaḥ samprasāraṇamabhyastasya ca and 'audacca gheḥ'* (*Mbh*, Vol. I, Dvitīyakhaṇḍa, pp. 283, 363, Vol. II, p. 697 and Vol. III, p. 239).
2. Vide Appendix 168 to 211.
3. *Rup* Part I, p. 3.

4. 'igyo yaṇaḥ sthāne bhūto bhāvī vā tasya samprasāraṇamityeṣā samjñā bhavati' (*K* under rule 1-1-45)
'yaṇaḥ sthāne bhūto bhāvī vā ya ik sa samprasāraṇasamjño bhavati' (*Rup* Part I, p. 51)
'adarśanamaśravaṇamanuccāraṇamanupalabdhirab hāvo varṇa-vināśa ityanarthāntaram'/etaiḥ sabdairyorthobhidhīyate tasya lopa itīyam samjñā bhavati/arthasyeyam samjñā na śabdasya/prasaktasyādarśanam lopasamjñām bhavati (*K* under rule 1-1-60)
'varnānāmadarśanam lopasamjnām bhavati/ kimadarśanam adarśanam aśravaṇamanupalabdhirabhāvo varṇavināṣa ityanarthāntaram/etaiḥ śabdaiḥ yorthobhidhīyate tasya arthasya iyam lopasamjñā anena vidhīyate' (*Rup* Part I, p. 2).
5. *Rup* Part I, p. 8.
6. Ibid, p. 6.
7. *Rup* Part I, p. 162 and vide Supra, p. 133.
8. *Rup* PART II, p. 247.
9. *Rup* Part I, p. 226.
10. *Rup* Part I, pp. 291 & 292.
11. 'ciṇa uttarasya pratyayasya lugbhavati' (*K* under rule 6-4-104)
12. 'ciṇa uttarasya tapratyayasya lugbhavati, dvivacanādiṣu sijeva bhavati' (*Rup* Part II, p. 166).
13. 'tṝ, phala, bhaja, trpa ityeteṣāmaṅgānāmata ekārādeśo bhavati abhyāsalopaśca liṭi kṅiti paratasthali ca seṭi' (*K* under rule 6-4-122)
'phaṇādinām saptānām dhātūnāmavarṇasya sthāne vā ekāra ādeśo bhavati abhyāsalopaśca liṭi kṅiti paratasthali ca seti'
14. 'tṝ, phala, bhaja, trapa ityeteṣamataḥ sthāne ekārādeśo bhavati, abhyāsalopaśca kiti liṭi parataḥ thali ca seṭi' (*Rup* Part II, p. 126)
'phaṇa gatau, rājṛ dīptau, ṭubhrājṛ, ṭubhrāśṛ, ṭumlāśṛ dīptau, syamu, svana, dhvana, śabde, ityeteṣām saptānām dhātūnāmavarṇasya sthāne vā ekārādesobhavati, abhyāsalopaśca kiti liṭi parataḥ, thali ca seṭi' (*Rup* Part II, pp. 127 & 128)
15. 'okārāduttarasya yakārasya lopo bhavati gārgyasyācāryasya matena aśi parataḥ' (*K* under 8-3-20)

'okāräduttarayoḥ padāntayoryakāravakārayoḥ lopo bhavatyaśi parataḥ' (*Rup* Part I, p. 25).

16. 'iṣṭupasaṅkhyānavatī śuddhagaṇā vivṛtagūḍhasūtrārthā / vyutpannarūpasiddhirvṛttiriyam kāśikā nāma //
17. *Rup* Part I, p. 27.
18. Vide Supra, p. 38.
19. Vide Supra, p. 22.
20. Vide Supra, p. 48.
21. *Rup* Part I, p. 6.
22. Ibid, pp. 24 & 27.
23. Vide Supra, p. 22.
24. Vide Supra, p. 80.
25. Vide the rule '*vibhaktiśca*' (1-4-104) 'suptiṅau pratyāhārau; supaḥ tiṅaśca trīṇitrīṇi vibhaktisamjñāśca bhavanti' (*Rup* Part I, p. 29).
26. Vide Appendix, pp. 183 to 191.
27. Vide Supra, pp. 40 & 41 and 81 & 82.
28. Vide Supra, pp. 82 & 83.
29. Vide Supra, pp. 82 & 83.
30. Vide Supra, p. 65.
31. *Rup* Part I, pp. 46 & 59.
32. *Rup* Part II, pp. 115, 118 & 144.
33. *SK* Part I, pp. 20, 169 & 170.
34. 'pā ghrā dhmā sthā mnā dāṇ dṛśi arti sarti śada sada ityeteṣām piba jighra dhama tiṣṭha mana yaccha paśya ṛccha dhau sīda sīya ityete ādeśā bhavanti śiti parataḥ' (*K*)

    'pā pāne, ghrā gandhopādāne, dhmā śabdāgnisamyogayoḥ ṣṭhā gatinivṛttau, mnā abhyāse, dāṇ dāne, dṛśir prekṣaṇe, ṛ gatau, sṛ gatau, sadḷ śātane, ṣadḷ viśaraṇagatyavasādaneṣu, ityeteṣām dhātūnām yathāsaṅkhyam piba, jighra, dhama, tiṣṭha, mana, yaccha, paśya, ṛccha, dhau, sīya, sīda, ityete ādeśā bhavanti śitpratyaye parataḥ' (*Rup* Part II, p. 14).
35. *PK* Part II, p. 110 & *SK* Part III, p. 198.
36. Vide Adya Prasada Misra, '*Prakriyākaumudīvimarśaḥ*,' p. 25.
37. Vide Supra, pp. 133, 144 & 145.
38. *Rup* Part I, pp. 186 & 187.

39. Vide Supra, pp. 35 & 36.
40. *Rup* Part I, p. 3.
41. Ibid, p. 132.
42. Vide Supra, p. 133.
43. Ibid, p. 146.
44. Ibid, p. 149.
45. Ibid, p. 149.
46. Ibid, p. 149.
47. Ibid, p. 149.

Chapter IX

Conclusion

It has already been stated that the proclaimed necessity of the subjectwise study of *Ast* was the mother of invention of a recast by *DK*. DK has taken great care to make the work capable of executing the purpose for which it has been given birth to. His daring attempt at the rearrangement of the sutras was in order to meet the changing needs of the hour. With the rising of the vernaculars to the status of spoken language, Sanskrit began to lose its hold on people as a medium of conversation and then came a time when Sanskrit became altogether a thing of acquisition. Of course the system of *Ast* was not defective. Yet DK knew that the age in which he flourished needed a method which could teach Sanskrit language more easily through the method of word formation. Consequently, the rewriting or rearrangement of the sutras of *Ast* became a crying need to render it useful for the purpose of teaching Sanskrit by the use of grammar. Thus the *prakriyā* system of grammar envisaged by him responded well to the need of the hour and we are now to evaluate his work on the basis of this present study. Before attempting the evaluation of the work of DK, one cannot ignore the fact that any initial attempt or creation can have certain drawbacks of its own owing to its inception being the first of its kind and hence while evaluating, it can enjoin the advantage of being given a margin for such drawbacks. It is the result of an evaluation, based on such a scheme of examination, that really matters. *Rup* examined in the above line of evaluation, can be ranked high among the similar attempts even without giving a margin to the drawbacks that characterise a new creation. It is to this conclusion that we arrive at when the evaluation of the same is attempted.

First of all let us examine as to how far the work has succeeded in achieving the purpose of presentation of rupas for which it has been framed. It is the *Rūp* of DK, which for the first time in the history of Paninian grammar has given more stress to the various rupas with which the students of Sanskrit language are concerned. It brings before the student the different kinds of rupas which are necessary for the correct understanding of the Sanskrit Language. As a medicated sweet given to the child, the rupas are readily presented with their grammatical details which are otherwise very difficult to understand directly from *Ast.* In the *vibhaktyavatāra* we find that the various declensional forms of different stems are narrated in detail.[1] So also *samāsāvatāra, taddhitāvatāra, kṛdantāvatāra* etc. bear testimony to the success which he has attained in the presentation of *rūpas.*

It can also be seen that DK not only presents the rupas, but he also draws our attention to the usage of these rupas. For example, in the *vibhaktyavatāra* he first of all deals with the various declensional forms of *vṛkṣaśabda* and then gives the following verse in which the usage of the various declensional forms of *vṛkṣaśabda* is shown.

> vṛkṣastiṣṭhati kānane kusimitā vṛkṣam latā samśritā
> vṛkṣeṇābhihato gajo nipatito vṛkṣāya deyam jalam /
> vṛkṣādānaya mañjarīmabhinavām vṛkṣasya śākhonnatā
> vṛkṣe nīḍamidam kṛtam sakuninā he vṛkṣa kim kampase[2] //

So also in the same context while dealing with the usage of the vocative case forms of *vṛkṣaśabda* he says, 'sambodhanābhivyaktyartham kecit heśabdam, bhos-śabdam, va prayunjate.[3] Similarly he points out the stems ending in certain vowels and consonants as not in vogue.[4]

Again while dealing with tinantarūpas we find that they are dealt with in two major sections vi. *Sārvadhātukapariccheda* and *Ārdhadhātukapariccheda.* Though it is a defect that one cannot at a glance study the rūpas of one and the same root in all the lakaras as they are scattered in the various prakaranas of the *Sārvadhātukapariccheda* and *Ārdhadhātukapariccheda,* one ought to admit the fact that DK is more practical.[5] This is because in the *Sārvadhātukapariccheda,* he deals with tinantarūpas in the four lakaras, *laṭ, laṇ, loṭ* and *vidhiliṅ* and it is only a fact that one can readily converse in Sanskrit language if he has mastered these four lakaras. Thus it can be pointed out that while educating the reader with the rupas of Sanskrit language, DK has shown his originality by initially making him aware of the rupas which are the most necessary ones for achieving mastery over the language.[6]

Further we find that it is in order to achieve the purpose of presentation of rupas that the rules of *Ast* are recast in *Rup* rejecting their order found in Ast. This recasting of the rules of *Ast* is brought about by the subject, wise grouping of the rules of *Ast*. The originality and discriminative power of the author in this regard is wonderfully and explicitly exhibited in this work as in the presentation of apavadasutras and vikalpasutras and so on.[7] The author deserves special applause for framing a recast since it is only on this path discovered and trodden by him first, that his successors could introduce modifications and amenities. Hence the exclusive credit for excavating a new style of treatment of the Paninian rules viz. the subjectwise grouping of them, goes to DK who thus got successors to imitate his new creation.

Now let us turn our attention to the influence exerted by *Rup* on later recasts.[8] It can be said without any doubt that whatever be the merits of later recasts, all those merits had their indebtedness to *Rup*. This is because *Rup* stands out singular by framing a new net work to the rules of *Ast* and their interpretation. DK has appended wherever necessary the vars of KAT, istis of PAT, paribhāṣās, uṇādisūtras, gaṇapāthas and gaṇasūtras.[9] Not only that he has appended them in his work, but he has also made a selection of them. Hence all the vars, istis, paribhasas etc. found in *Mbh* do not get a place in *Rup*. The inclusion of these accessories in a single work, along with the rupas of Sanskrit language and sutras of PAN is the singular achievement of DK. That *PK* or *SK* has got a separate *prakaraṇa* for paribhasas, unadisutras, *padavyavasthā* and *bhāvakarmaprakriyā* is definitely a meritorious feature of the said works. Though *Rup* is lacking in this respect, it deserves mention that the idea for such separate prakaranas had their origin in *Rup*. Hence the credit goes to the authors of later recasts only for enhancing the new style of treatment which had its discovery by DK himself.

Now we turn our attention to view DK as a *vṛttikāra*. There are many vrttis written by the authors like Śvobhūti, Vyāḍi, Kuṇi, etc. But all these works are not now available. The *Kāśikāvṛtti* of Jayāditya and Vāmana is a valuable work written in 7th century

A.D. To quote the words of Winternitz, 'the admittedly best on account of brevity and clarity, commentary par excellence on the sutras of Panini is the Kaśikāvṛtti, the commentary of Jayāditya and Vāmana.'[10] After a careful study of *Rup* we can understand that the work is mainly based on this *K*. Though DK closely follows *K* in the interpretation and illustration of sutras, he has not blindly followed everything found in *K*. The altered version of the verse rudro . . .' with the words *yuvayoḥ* and *āvayoḥ* instead of *yuṣmākam* and *asmākam* found in the same verse in *K* throws light on the originality of the work.[11]

A *vṛtti* does not mean the mere division of the words of sutras.[12] But it is supposed to do something more and should cite examples and counter-examples besides the completion of the original sutras by adding new words to it.[12] We also get the popular verse :

> padacchedaḥ padārthoktiḥ vigraho vākayajojanā /
> pūrvapakṣasamādhānam vyākhyānam pañcalakṣaṇam[13] //

While giving the *vṛtti* of the sutras DK has adopted a style which is simple.[14] There are numerous instances where he gives the *padaccheda*, *padārthokti*, and *vigraha* of the sutras. For *padārthokti* and the like we get various instances in *Rup*. The *vṛtti* of the rule '*tulyāsyaprayatnam savarṇam*' (1-1-9) is a good example of *padārthokti*. To quote the same 'tulyaśabdaḥ sadṛśaparyāyaḥ, tulayā sammitam tulyam; āsyam mukham, āsye bhavam āsyam, talvādisthānam; prayatnah prayatanam; ābhyantaraprayatnaḥ spṛṣṭādirvarṇaguṇaḥ; tulyau āsyaprayatnau yasya varṇasya yena varṇena saha sa samānajātīyam prati savarṇasamjño bhavati / catvāra ābhyantaraprayatnaḥ savarṇasamjñāyāmāśrīyante - spṛṣṭatā, īṣaspṛṣṭatā, vivṛtatā, samvṛtatā ceti/ bāhyaprayatnāstu na tathā / te tu vivāra - samvāra - svāsa - nāda ghoṣa - aghoṣa - alpaprāṇa - mahāprāṇāścetyaṣṭaprakārāḥ āntaratamyaparīkṣopayoginaḥ'[15] / So also in the rule 'ukālojjhrasvadīrghaplutaḥ' (1-2-27) he says, 'u ū ū3 ityevam kālaḥ ūkālaḥ; kālo mātrā; ekamātrikadvimātrikatrimātrikā aco yathākramam hrasvadīrghaplutasamjña bhavanti.'[16] In the rule 'mukhanāsikāvacanonunāsikaḥ' (1-1-8) he explains mukhanāsikā as mukhasahitā nāsikā mukhanāsikā.[17] On the word *yathāsaṅkhya* in the rule 'yathāsahyamanudeśaḥ samānām' (1-3-10) he makes the comment 'saṅkhyāśabdena kramo lakṣyate; samānām amasaṅkhyānām samaparipaṭhitānām uddesināmanudeśinām ca yathākramam uddeśibhiḥ anudeśinaḥ sambadhyante.'[18] In the rule *'arthavadadhāturapratyayaḥ . . .'* (1-2-45) he gives the meaning of the word *artha* as *'abhidheyavacanorthaśabdaḥ.'*[19] Rules are also provided with *pūrvapakṣasamādhānam* and *vākyayojanā.*[20]

Moreover the citation of verses meant for the explanation of sutras, illustration of sutras and the discussion of topics related to the application of sutras is a complementary feature of this work.[21] It has won applause from later authors and has persuaded them to compare other works with *Rup* in this respect.[22]

While assessing the value of *Rup*, we have to turn our attention to its defects and drawbacks also which are already dealt with previously.[23] When we examine them it can be found that most of them are not peculiar to his work alone but a common feature of all recasts of Ast. This is most evident in the rearrangement of the rules of *Ast*. Everyone can suggest one's own method of rearrangement and hence criticism in this regard can never be avoided. Again with regard to the later recasts which steadily strive for a better rearrangement of the rules of *Ast* from the previous recasts, it is likely that shortcomings may exceed in *Rup*. But it can be pointed out that only in comparison with later recasts, the rearrangement of rules in *Rup* becomes less meritorious. Therefore the credit of its first inception by DK empower us to nullify all the defects pointed out in this regard. Again even with regard to *SK* the most popular and well established recast of *Ast*, criticism is found in regard to the reshuffling of the sutras of *Ast*.[24] Again with regard to the presentation of rupas and narration of *prakriyā* for which this recasting of rules is made, we find that *Rup* is more simple and illustrative than SK.[25] Hence one can easily ignore the defects of Rup.

Over and above all it is to be noted that the work is meant for a preliminary study of Paninian grammar with main stress on the rupas and this purpose is more than fully achieved by DK. No doubt his work deserves to be regarded as a preliminary text for the study of grammar, a recognition which it had enjoyed before the advent of *SK* and its abridged editions like *Madhyasiddhāntakaumudī* and *Laghusiddhāntakaumudī*. Hence we have to pay homage to DK, the author of this work by reinstating the status which it once had in our motherland.

Notes and References

1. Vide Supra, pp. 79 & 80.
2. *Rup* Part I, p. 36.
3. Ibid, p. 31.
4. Vide Supra, pp. 79 & 80.
5. Vide Supra, pp. 40 & 41.
6. Vide Mahesh Dutt Sharma, 'Kāśikāvṛttivaiyākaraṇa-siddhāntakaumudyoḥ tulanātmakamadhyanam,' pp. 46 & 47.
7. Vide Supra, pp. 65 & 66.
8. Vide Supra, pp. 148 to 158.
9. Vide Supra, pp. 87 to 94.
10. Vide '*A History of Indian Literature,*' Vol. III, Part II, p. 433.
11. Vide Supra, p. 127.
12. "na kevalam carcāpadāni vyākhyānam' vṛddhiḥ,' āt, aic'iti/ kim tarhị? udāharaṇam pratyudāharaṇam vākyādhyāhāraḥ ityetatsamuditam vyākhyānam bhavati" (*Mbh* Vol. I, Prathamakhaṇḍa, p. 57).
13. Vide Sṛṣṭidhara, *Vivṛti* on *Bhāṣāvṛtti.*
14. Vide Supra, pp. 62 to 66.
15. *Rup* Part I, p. 3.
16. Ibid, p. 3.
17. Ibid, p. 4.
18. Ibid, p. 6.
19. Ibid, p. 23.
20. Vide Supra, pp. 63 & 64 and 66 to 70.
21. Vide Supra, pp. 117 to 136.
22. Vide Supra, p. 117.
23. Vide Supra, pp. 37 to 43.
24. Vide Suryakant Bali '*Bhaṭṭoji Dīkṣita - His Contribution to Sanskrit Grammar,*' pp. 30 to 33.
25. Vide Supra, pp. 141 to 167 & p. 316.

Appendix

1. LIST OF RULES OF AṢṬĀDHYĀYĪ INTERPRETED IN RŪPĀVATĀRA

This list comprehends those rules of *Ast* which are interpreted or the idea of which is referred to in *Rup*. The adhikarasutras found in *Rup* are mentioned in this list only once in accordance with the place where they occur first in this work.

SAMJÑĀVATĀRA (14 rules)

1. halantyam . . . (1-3-3)
2. ādi . . . (1-1--71)
3. tasya...... (1-3--39)
4. adarśanam.. (1-1--60)
5. upadeśe.... (1-3---2)
6. aṇudit..... (1-1--69)
7. taparas.... (1-1--70)
8. tulyā........ (1-1---9)
9. ūkāloj..... (1-2-27)
10. uccair..... (1-2--29)
11. nīcair..... (1-2--30)
12. samāhāra... (1-2--31)
13. mukha...... (1-1---8)
14. a a (8-4--68)

SAMHITĀVATĀRA (113 rules)

Tuksandhi:

15. parah...... (1-4-109)
16. samhitāyam (6-1-72)
17. che ca (6-1--73)
18. ṣaṣṭhī..... (1-1--49)
19. ādyantau... (1-1--46)
20. stoḥ........ (8-4--40)
21. yathā........ (1-3--10)
22. dīrghāt (6-1--75)
23. padāntādvā (6-1--76)
24. āṅmāṅośca (6-1--74)

Svarasandhi:

25. iko yaṇaci (6-1--77)
26. anaci ca (8-4--47)

Rup. Part I, pp. 1 to 8

27. jhalām..... (8-4-53)
28. sthāne..... (1-1--50)
29. halo....... (1-1---7)
30. samyogā.... (8-2--23)
31. ecoyavāyāvaḥ (6-1-78)
32. adeṅ guṇaḥ (1-1---2)
33. ekaḥ.......... (6-1--84)
34. ādguṇaḥ (6-1--87)
35. uraṇraparaḥ (1-1--51)
36. aco.......... (6-4--46)
37. vṛddhirādaic (1-1--1)
38. vṛddhireci (6-1--88)
39. eṅi......... (6-1--94)
40. etyedhat... (6-1--89)
41. upasargād.. (6-1--91)
42. omāṅośca (6-1--95)
43. akaḥ........ (6-1--101)
44. nājhalau (1-1--10)

45. eṅaḥ.......... (6-1-109)
46. lopaḥ........ (8-3--19)
47. pūrvatrā... (8-2---1)
48. sarvatra... (6-1-122)
49. avaṅ....... (6-1-123)
50. alontyasya (1-1--52)
51. anekāl..... (1-1--55)
52. ṅicca (1-1--53)
53. indre ca (6-1-124)

Prakṛtisandhi :

54. acontyādi ṭi (1-1-64)
55. ādyantavad.. (1-1-21)
56. vākyasya... (8-2--82)
57. dūrad...... (8-2--84)
58. pluta...... (6-1-125)
59. īdūded..... (1-1--11)
60. Yena........ (1-1--72)
61. adasomāt... (1-1--12)
62. prāg........ (1-4--56)
63. cādayo...... (1-4--57)
64. nipāta..... (1-1--14)
65. prādayaḥ (1-4--58)
66. ot (1-1--15)

Vyañjanasandhi :

Rep. stoḥ...... (No. 20)

67. śāt (8-4--44)
68. ṣṭunā ṣṭuḥ (8-4--41)
69. na padānta.. (8-4-42)
70. padasya (8-1--16)
71. jhalām..... (8-2--39)

Rup. Part I, pp. 8 to 16

72. yaro........ (8-4--45)
73. jhayo....... (8-4--62)
74. khari ca (8-4--55)
75. śaśchoṭi (8-4--63)
76. udaḥ........ (8-4--61)
77. jharo........ (8-4-65)
78. ṅamo........ (8-3--32)
79. halo........ (8-4--64)
80. naśchavya.. (8-3--7)
81. atrānu..... (8-3---2)
82. anunāsikāt.. (8-3--4)
83. khar........ (8-3--15)
84. visarja.... (8-3--34)
85. naśca (8-3--30)

Rep. khari ca (No. 74)

86. śi tuk (8-3--31)
87. monusvāraḥ (8-3--23)
88. vā padāntasya (8-4-59)
89. torli (8-4--60)

Visarjanīyasandhi :

Rep. visarja... (No. 84)

90. vā śari (8-3--36)
91. kupvoḥ...... (8-3--37)
92. śarpare.... (8-3--35)
93. idud.......... (8-3--41)
94. dvistri.... (8-3--43)

Svādisandhi :

95. arthavad... (1-2--45)
96. pratyayaḥ.. (3-1---1)
97. paraśca (3-1---2)
98. ṅyāp......... (4-1---1)
99. svaujas.... (4-1---2)
100. prāti........ (2-3--46)
101. dvekayor... (1-4--22)
102. supaḥ (1-4-103)
103. suptiṅ.... (1-4--14)
104. tarap...... (1-1--22)
105. gharūpa.... (6-3--43)
106. sasajuṣo ruḥ (8-2-66)

Rep. alontyasya (No. 50)
107. ato ro..... (6-1-113)
108. haśi ca (6-1-114)

Rup. Part I, pp. 16 to 25
109. bho bhago.. (8-3--17)
110. oto gārgya.. (8-3-20)
111. hali........ (8-3--22)
112. svarādi.... (1-1--37)
113. avyayādāp.. (2-4--82)
114. pratyayasya (1-1--61)
115. ro ri (8-3--14)
116. ḍhralope... (6-3-111)
117. svamor..... (7-1--23)
118. pratyaya... (1-1--62)
119. vipratiṣedhe.. (1-4-2)
120. tyadādīnamaḥ (7-2-102)
121. ato gune (6-1--97)
122. tados...... (7-2-106)
123. etattados.. (6-1-132)
124. apadānta... (8-3--55)
125. iṇkoḥ (8-3--57)
126. ādeśa...... (8-3--59)
127. socilope... (6-1-134)

VIBHAKTYAVATĀRA (289 rules)

Ajantapulliṅga :
128. vibhaktiśca (1-4-104)
129. virāmo..... (1-4-110)
130. sarūpāṇām.. (1-2--64)
131. prathama... (6-1-102)
132. nādici (6-1-104)
133. bahuṣu..... (1-4--21)
134. cuṭū (1-3---7)
135. na .... (1-3---4)
136. sam........ (2-3--47)
137. eka........ (2-3--49)
138. eṅhrasvāt.. (6-1--69)
139. kārake (1-4--23)
140. kartur..... (1-4--49)
141. anabhi..... (2-3---1)
142. karmaṇi.... (2-3---2)
143. ami pūrvaḥ (6-1-107)

Rup. Part I, pp. 25 to 31
144. laśakva.... (1-3---8)
145. tasmāccha.. (6-1-103)
146. aṭkupvāṅ... (8-4---2)
147. padāntasya (8-4--37)
148. svatantra.. (1-4--54)
149. sādhaka... (1-4--42)
150. kartṛ........ (2.3--18)
151. yasmāt...... (1-4--13)
152. aṅgasya (6-4---1)
153. ṭāṅasi...... (7-1--12)
154. supi ca (7-3-102)
155. ato bhisa.. (7-1---9)
156. ādeḥ........ (1-1--54)
Rep. anekāl.... (No. 51)
157. bahu........ (7-3-103)
158. karmaṇā... (1-4--32)
159. caturthī... (2-3--13)
160. ṅeryaḥ (7-1--13)
161. sthānivad.. (1-1--56)
Rep. bahu........ (No. 157)
162. dhruvam.... (1-4--24)
163. apādāne.... (2-3--28)
164. ṣaṣṭhī..... (2-3--50)
165. osi ca (7-3-104)
166. hrasva........ (7-1--54)
167. nāmi (6-4---3)
168. ādhāro...... (1-4--45)

169. sapta........ (2-3--36)
170. jarāyā...... (7-2-101)
171. paddanno... (6-1--63)
172. saṅkhyā.... (6-3-110)
173. avyaya..... (5-3--71)
174. sarvādīni.. (1-1--27)
175. jasaśśī.... (7-1--17)
176. sarva...... (7-1--14)
177. ṅasiṅyoḥ... (7-1--15)
178. āmi.......... (7-1--52)
179. pūrva........ (1-1--34)
180. svam........ (1-1--35)
181. antaram.... (1-1--36)
182. pūr̄vadi.... (7-1--16)
183. prathama... (1-1--33)

Rup. Part I, pp. 31 to 41

184. bhūvādayo.. (1-3---1)
185. karmaṇyaṇ (3-2---1)
186. ātonupa.... (3-2---3)
187. ātomanin... (3-2--74)
188. dhātoḥ (3-1--91)
189. kṛdatiṅ (3-1--93)
190. kartari.... (3-4--67)
Rep. pratyaya... (No. 118)
191. kṛt...... (1-2--46)
192. supo...... (2-4--71)
193. suḍ......... (1-1--43)
194. yaci bham (1-4--18)
Rep. aṅgasya (No. 152)
195. bhasya (6-4-129)
196. āto dhātoḥ (6-4-140)
197. jasi ca (7-3-109)
198. iko guṇa... (1-1---3)
199. hrasvasya.. (7-3-108)
200. śeṣo........ (1-4---7)
201. āṅo........ (7-3-120)
202. gheṛṅiti (7-3-111)
203. ṅasi........ (6-1-110)
204. acca gheḥ (7-3-119)
205. anaṅ sau (7-1--93)
206. alontyāt... (1-1--65)
207. sarvanāma.. (6-4---8)
208. apṛkta...... (1-2--41)
209. hal.......... (6-1--68)
210. nalopaḥ.... (8-2---7)
211. sakhyur.... (7-1--92)
212. aco ññiti (7-2-115)
213. khyatyat... (6-1-112)
214. aut (7-3-118)
215. ṭeḥ (6-4-143)
216. patiḥ........ (1-4---8)
Rep. tyad........ (No. 120)
217. trestrayaḥ (7-1--53)
218. kimaḥ...... (5-2--41)
Rep. ṭeḥ (No. 215)
219. taddhitāḥ (4-1--76)
220. bahugaṇa... (1-1--23)
221. dati ca (1-1--25)
222. ṣaḍbhyoluk (7-1--22)
223. na lumatā.. (1-1--63)
224. ṣaḍ........ (7-1--55)
225. ṇo naḥ (6-1--65)

Rup. Part I, pp. 41 to 49

226. aciśnu...... (6-4--77)
227. eranekāco.. (6-4--82)
228. ṅerām....... (7-3-116)
229. dīrghāt.... (6-1-105)
230. ambārtha... (7-3-107)
231. yū........... (1-4---3)
232. āṇnadyāḥ... (7-3-112)

233. āṭaśca (6-1--90)
234. ādeca..... (6-1--45)
Rep. prādayaḥ (No. 65)
235. upasargāḥ.. (1-4--59)
236. gatiśca (1-4--60)
237. te prāg.... (1-4--80)
Rep. avyayādāp.. (No. 113)
238. igyaṇaḥ.... (1-1--45)
239. sampra...... (6-1-108)
240. halaḥ (6-4---2)
241. na bhū...... (6-4--85)
242. tṛjvad...... (7-1--95)
243. ṛduśanas... (7-1--94)
244. aptṛntṛc... (6-4--11)
245. ṛto ṅi..... (7-3-110)
246. vibhāṣā.... (7-1--97)
247. ṛta ut (6-1-111)
248. rāt sasya (8-2--24)
249. oḥ supi (6-4-83)
250. bhuvaḥ..... (3-2-179)
251. varṣā...... (6-4--84)
Rep. sarvanāma.. (No. 207)
252. nṛ ca (6-4---6)
253. ādirñi...... (1-3---5)
254. ṇvultṛcau (3-1-133)
255. goto ṇit (7-1--90)
Rep. aco ñṇiti (No. 212)
256. automśasoḥ (6-1--93)
257. rāyo hali (7-2--85)

Ajantastrīliṅga :

258. striyām (4-1---3)
259. ajādyataṣ.. (4-1---4)
260. auṅa āpaḥ (7-1--18)
261. sambuddh... (7-3-106)

Rup. Part I, pp. 49 to 61

262. āṅi cāpaḥ (7-3-105)
263. yāḍāpaḥ (7-3-113)
264. ṣidbhid.... (3-3-104)
Rep. jarāyā...... (No. 170)
265. sarva........ (7-3-114)
266. vibhāṣā.... (7-3-115)
267. vibhāṣā.... (1-1--28)
268. vraśca..... (8-2--36)
269. ṅiti........ (1-4---6)
Rep. āṇnadyāḥ (No. 232)
Rep. āṭaśca (No. 233)
270. idudbhyām.. (7-3-117)
271. tri........ (7-2--99)
272. ṛnnebhyo... (4-1---5)
273. na ṣaṭ..... (4-1--10)
274. aci ra ṛtaḥ (7-2-100)
275. na tisṛ.... (6-4---4)
Rep. ṛnnebhyo... (No. 272)
Rep. dīrghāt.... (No. 229)
Rep. Yū.......... (No. 231)
Rep. ambārtha... (No. 230)
276. ugitaśca (4-1---6)
277. ācchī...... (7-1-80)
278. antādivacca (6-1--85)
279. midaco...... (1-1--47)
280. śapśyanor.. (7-1--81)
281. striyām ca (7-1--96)
282. sakhyaśis... (4-1--62)
283. tiḍḍhāṇañ.. (4-1--15)
284. yasyeti ca (6-4-148)
285. striyāḥ (6-4--79)
286. vāmśasoḥ (6-4--80)
287. neyaṅuvaṅ.. (1-4---4)
288. vāmi (1-4---5)
289. ekāj........ (8-4--12)

Ajantanapumsakaliṅga :

Rep. svamor...... (No. 117)
290. atom (7-1--24)
291. napumsaka.. (7-1--19)
292. jaśśasośśiḥ (7-1--20)
293. śi sarva... (1-1--42)

Rup. Part I, pp. 61 to 73

294. napumsaka.. (7-1--72)
295. aḍḍatarā... (7-1--25)
296. vāvasāne (8-4--56)
297. sānta...... (6-4--10)
298. alloponaḥ (6-4-134)
299. hrasvo...... (1-2--47)
300. ikoci...... (7-1--73)
301. asthi...... (7-1--75)
Rep. alloponaḥ (No. 298)
302. vibhāṣā..... (6-4-136)
303. tṛtīyādi... (7-1--74)
304. na ṅi...... (8-2---8)
305. eca ig..... (1-1--48)

Halantapulliṅga :

306. ho ṭhaḥ (8-2--31)
307. dāder........ (8-2--32)
308. ekāco...... (8-2--37)
309. svādi...... (1-4---7)
310. ākaḍārād... (1-4---1)
311. vā druha... (8-2--33)
312. catur...... (7-1--98)
313. sāvanaḍuhaḥ (7-1--82)
314. am........... (7-1--99)
315. vasu........ (8-2--72)
Rep. igyaṇaḥ...... (No. 238)
316. vāha ūṭh (6-4-133)
Rep. sampra...... (No. 239)
317. diva out (7-1--84)
318. diva ut (6-1-131)
319. raṣabhyām.. (8-4---1)
320. rossupi (8-2--69)
321. śaroci (8-4--49)
322. mono dhātoḥ (8-2--64)
323. kimaḥ kaḥ (7-2-103)
324. idamo maḥ (7-2-108)
325. idoy pumsi (7-2-111)
326. daśca (7-2-109)
327. anāpyakaḥ (7-2-112)
328. hali lopaḥ (7-2-113)
Rep. ādyantavad.. (No. 55)
329. nedamadas.. (7-1--11)

Rup. Part I, pp. 73 to 90

330. dvitīyā..... (2-4--34)
331. ṅṇoḥ kuk... (8-3--28)
Rep. na ṅi......... (No. 304)
332. nalopas..... (8-2---2)
333. inhan....... (6-4--12)
334. sau ca (6-4--13)
335. ho hanter.. (7-3--54)
336. hanterat... (8-4--22)
337. na samyog.. (6-4-137)
338. śvayuva.... (6-4-133)
339. na sampra.. (6-1--37)
340. maghavā.... (6-4-128)
341. ugitacām... (7-1--70)
342. arvaṇa..... (6-4-127)
343. naścāpadā.. (8-3--24)
344. anusvāra... (8-4--58)
345. sṇāntā ṣat (1-1--24)
346. nopadhāyāḥ (6-4---7)
347. aṣṭana...... (7-2--84)
348. aṣṭābhya... (7-1--21)
349. pathi...... (7-1--85)

350. itotsarva.. (7-1--86)
351. tho nthaḥ (7-1--87)
352. bhasya..... (7-1--88)
353. co kuḥ...... (8-2--30)
354. yujer...... (7-1--71)
355. kvin....... (8-2--62)
356. mo rāji.... (8-3--25)
357. visvasya... (6-3-128)
358. pādaḥ pat (6-4-130)
359. acaḥ (6-4-138)
360. cau (6-3-138)
361. uda īt (6-4-139)
Rep. ādeḥ........ (No. 156)
362. tirasas.... (6-3--94)
363. samaḥ samī (6-3--93)
364. sahasya.... (6-3--95)
365. viṣvag..... (6-3--92)
366. aniditām... (6-4--24)
367. nāñjeḥ..... (6-4--30)
Rep. ṅṇoḥ kuk.... (No. 331)
368. atvasanta... (6-4-14)
Rep. sānta........ (No. 297)
369. nābhyasta... (7-1-78)
370. jakṣi...... (6-1---6)
371. naśervā (8-2--63)

Rup. Part I, pp. 91 to 107

372. ḍassi dhut (7-3--29)
373. vasos........ (6-4-131)
374. rvor........ (8-2--76)
375. num.......... (8-3--58)
376. pumsosuṅ (7-1--89)
377. adasa au... (7-2-107)
378. adasoser... (8-2--80)
379. eta īd..... (8-2--81)
380. na mu ne (8-2--3)

Halantastrīliṅga :

381. naho dhaḥ (8-2--34)
Rep. rvor......... (No. 374)
382. yassau...... (7-2-110)
383. manaḥ (4-1--11)
384. apo bhi (7-4--48)

Halantanapumsakaliṅga :

385. ahan (8-2--68)
386. rosupi (8-2--69)
387. vā napum... (7-1--79)

Aliṅga :

388. ṅe.......... (7-1--28)
389. maparyant.. (7-2--91)
390. tvāhau sau (7-2--94)
391. śeṣe lopaḥ (7-2--90)
392. yuvāvau.... (7-2--92)
393. prathamā... (7-2-88)
394. yūyavayau.. (7-2--93)
395. tvamāveka.. (7-2--97)
396. dvitīyā.... (7-2--87)
397. śaso na (7-1--29)
398. yoci (7-2--89)
399. yuṣmad...... (7-2--86)
400. tubhya...... (7-2--95)
401. bhyaso...... (7-1--30)
402. ekavacana.. (7-1--32)
403. pañcamyā at (7-1--31)
404. tavamamau (7-2--96)
405. yuṣmad...... (7-1--27)
406. sāma ākam (7-1--33)
Rep. padasya (No. 70)
407. padāt (8-1--17)
408. yuṣmad...... (8-1--20)
409. bahu....... (8-1--21)
410. temayā...... (8-1--22)

411. tvāmau...... (8-1--23)

Rup. Part I, pp. 108 to 126

412. na cavāhā.. (8-1--24)
413. paśyā........ (8-1--25)
414. sāmantri... (2-3--48)
415. āmantri...... (8-1--72)
416. nāmantri... (8-1--73)

AVYAYĀVATĀRA (2 rules)

Rep. svarādi.... (No. 112)
Rep. avyayād.... (No. 113)
Rep. Prāg... (No. 62)

417. aca........... (7-4--47)
418. upasargād.. (8-4--14)

STRĪPRATYAYĀVATĀRA (64 rules)

Rep. ajādyataṣ.. (No. 259)
Rep. manaḥ (No. 383)

419. ano bahu... (4-1--12)
420. ḍābubhā.... (4-1--13)
421. ana.......... (4-1--28)
422. yaṅaścāp... (4-1--74)
423. āvatyācca (4-1--75)

Rep. ṛnnebhyo... (No. 272)
Rep. ugitaśca (No. 276)

424. vano ra ca (4-1---7)
425. pādo........ (4-1---8)

Rep. idud.......... (No. 93)

426. tābṛci...... (4-1--99)

Rep. na............... (No. 273)
Rep.ṭiḍḍhāṇañ.. (No. 283)

427. careṣṭaḥ (3-2--16)
428. strībhyo... (4-1-120)

Rep. karmaṇyaṇ (No. 185)

429. tasyedam (4-3-120)
430. utsādibhyo.. (4-1-86)
431. pramāṇe.... (5-2--37)
432. saṇkhyāyā.. (5-2--42)
433. tena.......... (4-4---2)
434. lāvaṇāṭṭhañ (4-4--52)
435. tyadādiṣu.. (3-2--60)
436. iṇṇaśaji... (3-2-163)
437. āḍhya...... (3-2--56)
438. yañaśca (4-1--16)
439. gargā...... (4-1-105)
440. hala........ (6-4-150)
441. prācām...... (4-1--17)
442. sarvatra... (4-1--18)
443. kauravya... (4-1--19)
444. vayasi...... (4-1--20)
445. dvigoḥ...... (4-1--21)

***Rup.* Part I, pp. 126 to 137**

446. aparimāṇa.. (4-1--22)
447. kāṇḍāntāt.. (4-1--23)
448. puruṣāt.... (4-1--24)
449. antarvat... (4-1--32)
450. patyurno... (4-1--33)
451. udhasonaṅ (5-4-131)
452. bahuvrīher.. (4-4-25)
453. saṅkhyā..... (4-1--26)
454. dāma.......... (4-1--27)
455. varṇād........ (4-1--39)
456. anyato ṅīṣ (4-1--40)
457. ṣid............... (4-1--41)
458. jalpa........ (3-2-155)
459. śilpini....... (3-1-145)
460. jānapada.... (4-1--42)
461. śoṇāt...... (4-1--43)
462. voto......... (4-1--44)

463. bahvādi...... (4-1--45)
464. pumyogād.... (4-1--48)
465. indra........ (4-1--49)
466. krītāt...... (4-1--50)
467. svāṅgā... (4-1--54)
468. nāsiko... (4-1--55)
469. na kroḍā.. (4-1-56)
470. sahanañ... (4-1--57)
471. nakha.... (4-1--58)
472. pūrva.... (8-4---3)
473. jāter.... (4-1--63)
474. pāka...... (4-1--64)
475. ito........ (4-1--65)
476. śārṅga... (4-1--73)
477. ūṅutaḥ (4-1--66)

Rep. antādi... (No. 278)

478. bāhvantāt.. (4-1-67)
479. paṅgośca (4-1--68)
480. ūruttara.. (4-1-69)
481. samhita.. (4-1--70)
482. yūnastiḥ (4-1-77)

Rep. taddhitāḥ (No. 219)

KĀRAKĀVATĀRA (81 rules)

Rep. kṛt...... (No. 191)

Rep. sam....... (No. 136)

Rup. Part I, pp. 137 to 144

Rep. karmaṇi.... (No. 142)

Rep. kartur...... (No. 140)

483. uparya...... (8-1---7)
484. antarā..... (2-3---4)
485. karma........ (2-3---8)
486. kālā........ (2-3---5)
487. tathā........ (1-4--50)
488. akathitañca (1-4--51)
489. gati......... (1-4-52)
490. hṛkror...... (1-4--53)
491. upān........ (1-4--48)
492. adhi........ (1-4--46)
493. abhi........ (1-4--47)
494. karma...... (1-4--83)
495. anur...... (1-4--84)
496. tṛtīyārthe (1-4--85)
497. hīne (1-4--86)
498. upodhike (1-4--87)
499. abhirabhāge (1-4-91)
500. lakṣaṇe.... (1-4--90)
501. gatyartha.. (2-3--12)

Rep. Kartṛ...... (No. 150)

Rep. svatantraḥ.. (No. 148)

Rep. sādhaka.... (No. 149)

502. divah...... (1-4--43)
503. apavarge... (2-3---6)
504. sahayukte.. (2-3--19)
505. yenā....... (2-3--20)
506. itham...... (2-3--21)
507. samjñonya.. (2-3--22)
508. hetau (2-3-23)
509. akartha.... (2-3--24)
510. tat....... (1-4--55)
511. vibhāṣā.... (2-3--25)
512. ṣaṣṭhī...... (2-3--26)
513. sarva........ (2-3--27)

Rep. caturthī... (No. 159)

Rep. karmaṇā.... (No. 158)

514. rucyarthā.. (1-4--33)
515. ślāgha..... (1-4--34)
516. dhārer..... (1-4--35)
517. spṛher...... (1-4--36)
518. krudha...... (1-4--37)

519. krudha...... (1-4--38)
520. rādhī....... (1-4--39)
521. pratyāṅ.... (1-4--40)

Rup. **Part I, pp. 146 to 155**

522. anu......... (1-4--41)
523. pari........ (1-4--44)
524. kriyā...... (2-3--14)
525. tumarthā... (2-3--15)
526. nāma........ (2-3--16)
527. manya...... (2-3--17)
Rep. apādāne.... (No. 163)
Rep. dhruvam.... (No. 162)
528. bhītrā..... (1-4--25)
529. parājer.... (1-4--26)
530. vāraṇā...... (1-4--27)
531. anthardhau.. (1-4-28)
532. ākhyāto...... (1-4--29)
533. janikartuḥ.. (1-4-30)
534. bhuvaḥ........ (1-4-31)
535. anyārād...... (2-3-29)
536. ṣaṣṭhya...... (2-3--30)
537. enapā...... (2-3--31)
538. pṛthag...... (2-3--32)
539. dūrāntikā.. (2-3--34)
540. dūrāntikā.. (2-3--35)
541. pañcamī.... (2-3--42)
Rep. ṣaṣṭhī śeṣe (No 164)
542. jño......... (2-3--51)
543. adhīgartha.. (2-3-52)
544. kṛñaḥ........ (2-3-53)
545. āśiṣi...... (2-3--55)
546. jāsini..... (2-3--56)
547. kartṛ........ (2-3--65)
548. ubhaya...... (2-3--66)
549. kṛtyānām... (2-3--70)
550. tulyārthai.. (2-3-72)
551. caturthī... (2-3--73)
552. na lokā.... (2-3--69)
553. ktasya...... (2-3--67)
554. adhikaraṇa.. (2-3-68)
Rep. sapta........ (No. 169)
Rep. ādhāro.... (No. 168)
555. yasya........ (2-3--37)
556. saṣṭhī...... (2-3--38)
557. svāmī...... (2-3--39)
558. yataśca.... (2-3--41)

Rup. **Part I, pp. 155 to 164**

559. sādhu...... (2-3--43)
560. prasito.... (2-3--44)
561. nakṣatre... (2-3--45)
562. nakṣatrena.. (4-2--3)
563. lubaviśese (4-2--4)

SAMĀSĀVATĀRA
(286 rules)

Avyayībhāva :

564. samarthaḥ.. (2-1---1)
565. prāk........ (2-1---3)
566. avyayībhāvaḥ (2-1--5)
567. avyayam..... (2-1--6)
568. prathamā... (1-2--43)
569. upasarjanam.. (2-2-30)
Rep. supo........ (No. 192)
570. avyayī...... (1-1--41)
Rep. avyayādāp... (No. 113)
571. nāvyayī..... (2-4--83)
572. tṛtīyā...... (2-4--84)
573. samāsāntāḥ (5-4--68)
574. avyayī...... (5-4-107)

575. anaśca (5-4-108)
576. nadī........ (5-4-110)
577. avyayī...... (2-4--18)
578. napum...... (5-4-109)
579. jhayaḥ (5-4-111)
580. yathā...... (2-1---7)
581. avyayī...... (6-3--81)
582. pra........ (8-4---5)
583. gireśca.... (5-4-112)
584. yāvad...... (2-1---8)
585. sup........ (2-1---9)
586. akṣa........ (2-1--10)
587. apa........ (2-1--12)
588. āṅ........ (2-1--13)
589. lakṣaṇenā.. (2-1--14)
590. tiṣṭhad.... (2-1--17)
591. pāre...... (2-1--18)
592. saṅkhyā.... (2-1--19)
593. nadībhiśca (2-1--20)

Tatpuruṣa :

594. vibhāṣā.... (2-1--16)
595. tatpuruṣaḥ (2-1--22)
596. dvitīyā.... (2-1--24)
597. kālāḥ.... (2-1--28)
598. atyanta.... (2-1--29)
599. tṛtīyā..... (2-1--30)

Rup. **Part I, pp. 164 to 172**

600. pūrva...... (2-1--31)
601. kartṛ...... (2-1--32)
602. annena.... (2-1--34)
603. caturthī... (2-1--36)
604. pañcamī.... (2-1--37)
605. apetā...... (2-1--38)
606. stokā..... (2-1--39)
607. saṣṭhī..... (2-2---8)
608. yājakā..... (2-2---9)
609. kartari ca (2-2--16)
610. na.......... (2-2--10)
611. pūraṇa.... (2-2-11)
612. karmaṇi ca (2-2--14)
613. tṛja...... (2-2--15)

Rep. kartari ca (No. 609)

614. pūrva...... (2-2---1)
615. ardham..... (2-2---2)
616. eka........ (1-2--44)
617. rājadanta.. (2-2---31)
618. saptamī.... (2-1--40)
619. siddha..... (2-1--41)
620. dhvāṅ..... (2-1--42)
621. kṛtyairṛṇe (2-1--43)
622. ktenā...... (2-1--45)
623. taddhitā... (2-1--51)
624. saṅkhyā.... (2-1--52)
625. dvigu...... (2-4--11)
626. sa napum... (2-4--17)
627. viśeṣaṇam.. (2-1--57)
628. tatpuruṣaḥ.. (1-2-42)
629. striyāḥ...... (6-3-34)
630. vṛndāraka... (2-1-62)
631. pumvat...... (6-3-42)
632. na.......... (6-3--37)
633. upamānāni.. (2-1--55)
634. upamitam... (2-1--56)
635. kṛtya...... (2-1--68)
636. kim kṣepe (2-1--64)
637. mayūra..... (2-1--72)
638. nañaḥ (2-2---6)
639. alug........ (6-3---1)
640. nalopo nañaḥ (6-3-73)

Rup. Part I, pp. 172 to 180

641. tasmād..... (6-3--74)
642. nabhrāṇ.... (6-3--75)
643. ekādi...... (6-3--76)
644. nago........ (6-3--77)
645. kugati..... (2-2--18)
646. gostriyor.. (1-2--48)
647. upapadamatiṅ (2-2-19)

Bahuvrīhi :

648. anekam...... (2-2-24)
649. saptamī..... (2-2-35)
650. niṣṭhā (2-2--36)

Rep. na........ (No. 632)

651. samjñā..... (6-3--38)
652. svāṅga..... (6-3--40)
653. jāteśca.... (6-3--41)
654. vṛddhi..... (6-3--39)

Rep. anekam..... (No. 648)

655. saṅkhyāyā.. (2-2--25)
656. diṅ........ (2-2--26)
657. tatra..... (2-2--27)
658. tena...... (2-2--28)
659. vopa...... (6-3--82)
660. vāhitā...... (2-2--37)
661. amūrdha.... (6-3--12)
662. ānmahata... (6-3--46)

Dvandvaḥ :

663. cārthe.... (2-2--29)
664. dvandve ghi (2-2--32)
665. ajādyadantam (2-2-33)
666. alpāctaram (2-2-34)
667. vibhāṣā..... (2-4-12)

Rep. sa napum.... (No. 626)

668. para........ (2-4--26)
669. pūrvavad... (2-4--27)
670. rātrāhnāḥ.. (2-4--29)
671. dvandvaśca.. (2-4--2)
672. jāti........ (2-4--6)
673. kṣudra........ (2-4--8)
674. yeṣāñca...... (2-4--9)
675. śūdrāṇām.... (2-4--10)
676. viprati.... (2-4---13)
677. na dadhi... (2-4--14)

Rup. Part I, pp. 180 to 190

678. ānaṅṛto.... (6-3--25)
679. devadā...... (6-3--26)

Rep. sarūpāṇām.. (No. 130)

680. pumānstriyā (1-2--67)
681. bhrātṛ..... (1-2--68)
682. pitā mātrā (1-2--70)
683. mātara..... (6-3--32)
684. śvaśura.... (1-2--71)
685. tyadādīni.. (1-2--72)

Samāsānta :

Rep. samāsāntāḥ (No. 573)

686. ṛk.......... (5-4--74)
687. dvyantar... (6-3--97)
688. udanordeśe (6-3--98)
689. upasargād.. (5-4--85)
690. nastaddhite (5-4--144)
691. ac.......... (5-4--75)
692. avasam.... (5-4--79)
693. brahma..... (5-4--78)
694. tatpuruṣa.. (5-4--86)
695. ahas........ (5-4--87)
696. upasargācca (5-4-119)
697. upasargād.. (8-4--28)
698. añnāsikā... (5-4-118)
699. rājāhas.... (5-4--91)

700. ahnohna.... (5-4--88)
701. ahnodantād (8-4---7)
702. na.......... (5-4--89)
703. uttamaika.. (5-4-90)
704. kumahad.... (5-4-105)
705. nāvo dvigoḥ (5-4--99)
706. ardhācca (5-4-100)
707. dvitri...... (5-4-102)
708. gor.......... (5-4--92)
709. ano........ (5-4--94)
710. nañas.... (5-4--71)
711. na pūjanāt (5-4--69)
712. kimaḥ kṣepe (5-4--70)
Rep. ūdhasonaṅ (No. 451)
713. dhanuṣaśca (5-4-132)
714. vā........ (5-4-133)
715. jāyāyā niṅ (5-4-134)
716. suhṛd...... (5-4-150)
717. vayasi...... (5-4-141)

Rup. **Part I, pp. 190 to 196**

718. striyām.... (5-4-143)
719. vibhāṣā.... (5-4-144)
720. agrānta.... (5-4-145)
721. uraḥ........ (5-4-151)
722. sopadādau (8-3--38)
723. inastriyām (5-4-152)
724. nadyṛtaśca (5-4-153)
725. ke ṇaḥ (7-4--13)
726. na kapi (7-4--14)
727. śeṣād...... (5-4-154)
728. āpo........ (7-4--15)
729. īyasaśca (5-4-156)
730. gandha..... (5-4-156)
731. alpā........ (5-4-136)
732. upamānācca (5-4-137)
733. prasam..... (5-4-129)
734. urdhvād.... (5-4-130)
735. pādasya.... (5-4-138)
736. saṅkhyā.... (5-4-140)
737. kakudasya.. (5-4-146)
738. udvibhyam.. (5-4-148)
739. pūrṇād..... (5-4-149)
740. bahu........ (5-4--73)
741. ti.......... (6-4-142)
742. bahu...... (5-4-113)
743. anguler.... (5-4-114)
744. dvitri..... (5-4-115)
745. ap pūraṇī.. (5-4-166)
746. antar...... (5-4-117)
747. nañdus..... (5-4-121)
748. nityam...... (5-4-122)
749. dharmād.... (5-4-124)
750. ic karma... (5-4-127)
751. anyeṣām.... (6-3-137)
752. dvandvā.... (5-4-106)

ALUGĀDISAMĀSĀŚRAYA -VIDHI

Rep. alug...... (No. 639)
753. stokālpa... (2-3--33)
Rep. dūrā........ (No. 540)
Rep. stokā..... (No. 606)
754. pañcamyāḥ... (6-3---2)
755. ojas....... (6-3---3)
756. manasaḥ.... (6-3---4)
757. ājñāyayini.. (6-3--5)

Rup. **Part I, pp. 196 to 202**

758. ātmanaśca.. (6-3---6)
759. vaiyākaraṇā.. (6-3-7)

760. parasya ca (6-3-8)
761. samjñāyām (2-1--44)
762. haladantāt.. (6-3--9)
763. gavi........ (8-3--95)
764. madhyād.... (6-3--11)
Rep. amūrdha.... (No. 661)
765. bandhe..... (6-3--13)
766. tarpuruṣe.. (6-3--14)
767. vibhāṣā.... (6-3--16)
768. ghakāla.... (6-3--17)
769. śaya...... (6-3-18)
770. nensiddha.. (6-3--19)
771. sthe ca (6-3--20)
772. ṣaṣṭhyā.... (6-3--21)
773. putre...... (6-3--22)
774. rto........ (6-3--23)
775. vibhāṣā.... (6-3--24)
776. mātṛ........ (8-3--34)
777. mātuḥ........ (8-3--85)
Rep. ānaṅṛto.... (No. 678)
Rep. devatā...... (No. 679)
778. īdagne...... (6-3--27)
779. agnestut... (8-3--82)
Rep. gharūpa.... (No. 105)
780. nadyāḥ..... (6-3--44)
781. ugitaśca (6-3--45)
782. dvyaṣṭana.. (6-3--47)
783. trestrayaḥ (6-3--48)
784. iko.......... (6-3--61)
785. eka.......... (6-3--62)
786. ṅyāpo...... (6-3--63)
787. iṣṭa........ (6-3--65)
788. hṛdayasya.. (6-3--50)
789. vā śoka.... (6-3--51)
790. pādasya.... (6-3--52)
791. pad......... (6-3--53)
792. himakāṣī... (6-3-54)
793. udakasyo... (6-3--57)
794. peṣam........ (6-3--58)
795. eka.......... (6-3--59)
796. manthau.... (6-3--60)
797. arurdviṣad.. (6-3-67)

Rup. **Part I, pp. 203 to 210**

798. ica.......... (6-3--68)
799. vācam...... (6-3--69)
800. kāre...... (6-3--70)
801. rātreh...... (6-3--72)
802. jyotir...... (6-3--85)
803. caraṇe...... (6-3--86)
804. tīrthe ye (6-3-87)
805. vibhāṣodare (6-3--88)
806. dṛgdrśa.... (6-3--89)
807. idam...... (6-3--90)
808. ā sarva.... (6-3--91)
809. samāse...... (8-3--80)
810. jyotir...... (8-3-83)
811. aṣaṭhya.... (6-3--99)
812. arthe...... (6-3-100)
813. koḥ kat.... (6-3-101)
814. ratha...... (6-3-102)
815. kā pathya.. (6-3-104)
816. īṣadarthe.. (6-3-105)
817. vibhāṣā.... (6-3-106)
818. kavañcoṣṇe (6-3-107)
819. pṛoṣodarā.. (6-3-109)
820. karṇe......... (6-3-115)
821. nahi...... (6-3-106)
822. vana........ (6-3-117)
823. vale........ (6-3-118)

824. matau...... (6-3-119)
825. śarādī...... (6-3-120)
826. upasarga... (6-3-122)
827. ikaḥkāśe (6-3-123)
828. aṣṭanaḥ..... (6-3-125)
Rep. viśvasya... (No. 357)
829. nare........ (6-3-129)
830. mitre...... (6-3-130)
831. sarvasya.. (8-1---1)
832. nitya...... (8-1---4)
Rep. uparya.... (No. 483)
833. vākyāder.. (8-1---8)
834. ekam........ (8-1---9)
835. ābādhe ca (8-1--10)
836. karma...... (8-1--11)
837. prakāre.... (8-1--12)
838. akṛcchre... (8-1--13)
839. yathāsve... (8-1--14)
840. dvandvam... (8-1--15)
841. kustumburū.. (6-1-143)

Rup. **Part I, pp. 210 to 217**

842. aparasparāḥ (6-1-144)
843. goṣpadam... (6-1-145)
844. āspadam.... (6-1-146)
845. āścarya.... (6-1-147)
846. varcaske... (6-1-148)
847. praskaṇva... (6-1-153)
848. maskara.... (6-1-154)
849. pāraskara.. (6-1-157)

TADDHITĀVATĀRA (554 rules)

850. samarthaḥ... (4-1-82)
851. prāg........ (4-1--83)
852. tasya...... (4-1--92)
853. taddhite... (7-2-117)
854. orguṇaḥ (6-4-146)
855. apatyam.... (4-1-162)
856. eko gotre (4-1--93)
857. jīvati...... (4-1-163)
858 gotrād...... (4-1--94)
859. ata iñ (4-1--95)
860. yañiñośca (4-1-101)
861. kiti ca (7-2-118)
862. āyan........ (7-1---2)
Rep. yasyeti ca (No. 284)
Rep. gargādi...... (No. 439)
863. yañañośca (2-4--64)
Rep. yañaśca (No. 438)
Rep. prācām...... (No. 441)
864. aśva....... (4-1--84)
865. ditya......... (4-1--85)
Rep. halo........ (No. 79)
866. māturut.... (4-1-115)
867. kanyāyāḥ... (4-1-116)
Rep. utsādibhyoñ (No. 430)
868. strī........ (4-1--87)
869. sudhātur... (4-1--97)
870. śivādibhyoṇ (4-1-112)
871. ṛṣyandhaka.. (4-1-114)
872. agastya.... (2-4--70)
873. svasuśchaḥ (4-1-143)
Rep. strībhyo.... (No. 428)
874. itaścāniñaḥ (4-1-122)
875. atri........ (2-4--65)
876. śubhrādi... (4-1-123)

Rup. **Part I, pp. 217 to 225**

877. ṭhe lopo... (6-4-147)
878. kalyāṇyā... (4-1-126)

879. hṛdbhaga... (7-3--19)
880. kulṭāyā vā (4-1-127)
881. caṭakāyā... (4-1-128)
882. godhāyā.... (4-1-129)
883. lopo........ (6-1--66)
884. ārag........ (4-1-130)
885. kṣudrābhyo.. (4-1-131)
886. pitṛ........ (4-1-132)
887. ḍhaki lopaḥ (4-1-133)
888. mātṛ........ (4-1-134)
Rep. svasuśchaḥ (No. 873)
889. bhrātur.... (4-1-144)
890. vyan sapatne (4-1-145)
891. rāja........ (4-1-137)
892. kṣatrādghaḥ (4-1-138)
893. kulāt khaḥ (4-1-139)
894. manor...... (4-1-161)
895. kurvādi.... (4-1-151)
896. tikādi..... (4-1-154)
897. aṇo........ (4-1-156)
898. janapada... (4-1-168)
899. sālveya.... (4-1-169)
900. dvyañ...... (4-1-170)
901. vṛddhir.... (1-1--73)
902. vṛddhet.... (4-1-171)
903. kuru........ (4-1-172)
904. te tadrājāḥ (4-1-174)
905. tadrāja.... (2-4--62)
906. kambojālluk (4-1-175)
907. striyām.... (4-1-176)
908. tena........ (4-2---1)
909. lākṣā........ (4-2---2)
910. ṭhasyekaḥ (7-3--50)
Rep. nakṣatreṇa.. (No. 562)
Rep. lubaviśeṣe (No. 563)
911. drṣṭam..... (4-2---7)
912. parivṛto... (4-2-10)
913. tatro...... (4-2--14)
(*Rup* Part I pp.225 to 231)
914. sthaṇḍilā (4-2--15)
915. samskṛtam.. (4-2--16)
916. sāsmin..... (4-2--21)
917. sāsya...... (4-2--24)
918. kasyet (4-2--25)
919. śukrāt ghan (4-2--26)
920. apo....... (4-2--27)
921. cha ca (4-2--28)
922. mahendrād.. (4-2--29)
923. somāṭṭyaṇ (4-2--30)
924. vāyvṛtu.... (4-2--31)
Rep. orguṇaḥ (No. 854)
925. vānto..... (6-1--79)
926. rīṅ ṛtaḥ (7-4--27)
927. dyāvā..... (4-2--32)
928. agnerḍhak (4-2--33)
929. idvṛddhau (6-3--28)
930. devatā.... (7-3--21)
931. nendrasya.. (7-3--22)
932. dīrghācca (7-3--23)
933. mahārāja... (4-2--35)
934. tasya..... (4-2--37)
935. brāhmaṇa... (4-2--42)
936. bikṣādi.... (4-2--38)
937. inaṇyanapatye (6-4-124)
938. grāma...... (4-2--43)
939. acitta..... (4-2--47)
Rep. ṭhasyekaḥ (No. 910)
940. isus...... (7-3--51)
941. gotro..... (4-2--39)
942. kedārād.... (4-2--40)

943. yuvoranākau (7-1--1)
944. ṭhañ....... (4-2--41)
945. keśā....... (4-2--48)
946. pāśā....... (4-2--49)
947. khala...... (4-2--50)
948. initra..... (4-2--51)
949. viṣayo..... (4-2--52)
950. sosyādi.... (4-2--55)
951. saṅgrāme... (4-2--56)
952. tadasyām... (4-2--57)
953. ghañas...... (4-2--58)
954. tadadhīte.. (4-2--59)
955. na yvābhyām.. (7-3-3)
(*Rup* Part I, pp. 231 to 237)
956. dvigor..... (4-1--88)
957. kratūk..... (4-2--60)
958. kramā...... (4-2--61)
959. anu....... (4-2--62)
960. proktālluk (4-2--64)
961. sutrācca... (4-2--65)
962. chando..... (4-2--66)
963. tadasmin... (4-2--67)
964. tena....... (4-2--68)
965. tasya...... (4-2--69)
966. adūra...... (4-2--70)
967. janapade... (4-2--81)
968. lupi....... (1-2--51)
969. śarkarāyā.. (4-2--83)
970. nadyām..... (4-2--85)
971. naḍa....... (4-2--88)
972. utkarādi... (4-2--90)
973. śeṣe (4-2--92)
974. rāṣṭhrā..... (4-2--93)
975. gramād..... (4-2--94)
976. kartryādi.. (4-2--95)
977. nadyādi.... (4-2--97)
978. kula..... (4-2--96)
979. dakṣiṇā.... (4-2--98)
980. dyu....... (4-2-101)
981. avyayāttyap (4-2-104)
982. vṛddhācchaḥ (4-2-114)
983. tyadādīni.. (1-1--74)
984. bhavata.... (4-2-115)
985. siti ca (1-4--16)
986. iñaśca (4-2-112)
987. kāśyādi.... (4-2-116)
988. araṇyān.... (4-2-129)
989. gahādi..... (4-2-138)
990. rājñaḥ..... (4-2-140)
991. parvatācca (4-2-143)
992. yuṣmad.... (4 3---1)
993. tasmin..... (4-3---2)
994. tavaka..... (4-3---3)
995. pratyayo... (7-2--98)
996. madhyanmaḥ (4-3---8)
997. kālāṭṭhañ (4-3--11)
(*Rup* Part I, pp. 237 to 244)
998. ahnaṣ...... (6-4-145)
999. śvasastuṭ.. (4-3--15)
1000. dvārā...... (7-3---4)
1001. sandhi.... (4-3--16)
1002. prāvṛṣa.... (4-3--17)
1003. varṣā...... (4-3--18)
1004. sarvatrāṇ.. (4-3--22)
1005. sāyam...... (4-3--23)
1006. tatra jātaḥ (4-3--25)
1007. prāvṛṣa.... (4-3--26)
1008. sraviṣṭhā.. (4-3--34)
1009. luk........ (1-2--49)
1010. nakṣatre... (4-3--37)

1011. aci śīrṣaḥ (6-1--62)
1012. tatra...... (4-3--53)
1013. digādi..... (4-3--54)
1014. pathaḥ..... (4-3--29)
1015. śarīrā..... (4-3--55)
1016. dṛti...... (4-3--56)
1017. grīvā...... (4-3--57)
1018. gambhīrā... (4-3--58)
1019. antaḥ...... (4-3--60)
Rep. anaśca (No. 575)
1020. anu........ (7-3--20)
1021. jihvā...... (4-3--62)
1022. vargāntācca (4-3--63)
1023. aśabde...... (4-3--64)
1024. karṇa..... (4-3--65)
1025. tasya...... (4-3--66)
1026. tata....... (4-3--74)
1027. ṭhagāyā.... (4-3--75)
1028. vidyā...... (4-3--77)
1029. ṝtaṣṭhañ (4-3--78)
1030. pituryacca (4-3--79)
Rep. rīṅ ṛtaḥ (No. 926)
1031. prabhavati (4-3--83)
1032. tạd........ (4-3--85)
1033. abhi....... (4-3--86)
1034. adhi....... (4-3--87)
1035. śiśu....... (4-3--88)
1036. sosya...... (4-3--89)
1037. abhi....... (4-3--90)
(*Rup* Part I, pp. 244 to 250)
1038. bhaktiḥ (4-3--95)
1039. tena....... (4-3-101)
1040. kalāpinoṇ (4-3-108)
Rep. iñaśca (No. 986)
Rep. proktālluk (No. 960)
1041. tittiri.... (4-3-102)
1042. kāśyapa.... (4-3-103)
1043. kalāpi..... (4-3-104)
1044. pūrāṇa..... (4-3-105)
1045. pārāśarya.. (4-3-110)
1046. tenaikadik (4-3-112)
1047. upajñāte (4-3-115)
1048. kṛte grandhe (4-3-116)
1049. samjñāyām (4-3-117)
1050. kulālādi... (4-3-118)
Rep. tasyedam (No. 429)
1051. rathādyat (4-3-121)
1052. tasya...... (4-3-134)
1053. an (6-4-167)
1054. trapu...... (4-3-138)
1055. avayave ca (4-3-135)
1056. mayaḍ...... (4-3-143)
1057. gośca...... (4-3-145)
1058. gopayasor.. (4-3-160)
1059. phale luk (4-3-163)
1060. plakṣādi... (4-3-164)
1061. jambvā vā (4-3-165)
1062. orañ (4-3-139)
1063. lup ca (4-3-166)
1064. lupi....... (1-2--51)
1065. prāg....... (4-4---1)
1066. svāgatā.... (7-3---7)
Rep. tena....... (No. 433)
1067. samskṛtam (4-4---3)
1068. iṇaṣṣaḥ (8-3--39)
1069. tarati (4-4---5)
1070. naudyaca... (4-4---7)
1071. carati..... (4-4---8)
1072. vetanā..... (4-4--12)
1073. vasna...... (4-4--13)

1074. āyudhāccha.. (4-4--14)
1075. haratyut... (4-4--15)
(*Rup* Part I, pp. 250 to 257)
1076. aṇ......... (4-4--18)
1077. nirvṛtte... (4-4--19)
1078. trer....... (4-4--20)
1079. samsṛṣṭe (4-4--22)
1080. curṇādiniḥ (4-4--23)
1081. lavaṇālluk (4-4--24)
1082. mudgādaṇ (4-4--25)
1083. vyañja..... (4-4--26)
1084. ojas....... (4-4--27)
1085. tat........ (4-4--28)
1086. pari....... (4-4--29)
1087. prayacch... (4-4--30)
1088. uñchati (4-4--32)
1089. rakṣati (4-4--33)
1090. śabda...... (4-4--34)
1091. pakṣi...... (4-4--35)
1092. pari....... (4-4--36)
1093. mātho...... (4-4--37)
1094. padottara.. (4-4--39)
1095. prati...... (4-4--40)
1096. dharmam.... (4-4--41)
1097. prati...... (4-4--42)
1098. samavāyān.. (4-4--43)
1099. pariṣado... (4-4--44)
1100. senāyā vā (4-4--45)
1101. tasya....... (4-4--27)
1102. aṇ......... (4-4--48)
1103. tadasya.... (4-4--51)
1104. śilpam..... (4-4--55)
1105. praharaṇam (4-4--47)
1106. asti....... (4-4--60)
1107. śīlam (4-4--61)
1108. chātrā..... (4-4--62)
1109. hitam...... (4-4--65)
1110. tadasmai... (4-4--66)
1111. tatra...... (4-4--69)
Rep. dvārā...... (No. 1000)
1112. agrā...... (4-4--70)
1113. kaṭhinā.... (4-4--72)
1114. nikaṭe...... (4-4--73)
1115. prāg....... (4-4--75)
1116. tadvahati.. (4-4--76)
(*Rup* Part I, pp. 257 to 262)
1117. dhuro...... (4-4--77)
1118. na bhakur.. (8-2--79)
1119. khas....... (4-4--78)
1120. ekadhurā... (4-4--79)
1121. śakaṭādaṇ (4-4--80)
1122. hala........ (4-4--81)
1123. vidhya..... (4-4--83)
1124. dhana...... (4-4--84)
1125. vaśam gataḥ (4-4--86)
1126. padam...... (4-4--87)
1127. mūlam...... (4-4--88)
1128. gṛha....... (4-4--90)
1129. nauvayor... (4-4--91)
1130. dharma..... (4-4--92)
1131. chandaso... (4-4--93)
1132. urasoṇ ca (4-4--94)
1133. hṛdayasya.. (4-4--95)
1134. tatra...... (4-4--98)
1135. ye........ (6-4-168)
1136. bhaktāṇṇaḥ (4-4-100)
1137. pariṣado... (4-4-101)
1138. pratijñā... (4-4--99)
1139. pathya..... (4-4-104)
1140. sabhāyā yaḥ (4-4-105)

1141. samāna..... (4-4-107)
1142. sodarādyaḥ (4-4-109)
1143. prāk krītāt.. (5-1-1)
1144. tasmai....... (5-1--5)
1145. śarīrā....... (5-1-6)
1146. khala....... (5-1-7)
1147. ātman...... (5-1---9)
1148. ātmā....... (6-4-169)
1149. sarva...... (5-1--10)
1150. tadartham.. (5-1--12)
1151. tadasya.... (5-1--16)
1152. prāg....... (5-1--18)
1153. ārhād...... (5-1--19)
1154. śatācca.... (5-1--21)
1155. tena...... (5-1--37)
1156. saṅkhyāyā.. (5-1--22)
1157. tasya...... (5-1--38)
1158. sarva...... (5-1--41)
(*Rup* Part I, pp. 262 to 267)
1159. tasyeśvaraḥ (5-1--42)
1160. loka....... (5-1--44)
1161. tasya vāpaḥ (5-1--45)
1162. tadasmin... (5-1--47)
1163. tad....... (5-1--50)
1164. sam....... (5-1--52)
1165. sosyām..... (5-1--56)
1166. tadasya.... (5-1--57)
1167. tadarhati (5-1--63)
1168. daṇḍādi.... (5-1--66)
1169. chedā...... (5-1--64)
1170. śīrṣa...... (5-1--65)
1171. pārāyaṇa... (5-1--72)
1172. samśayam... (5-1--73)
1173. yojanam.. (5-1--74)
1174. pathaḥ..... (5-1--75)
1175. pantho..... (5-1--76)
1176. uttara...... (5-1--77)
1177. kalāt (5-1--78)
1178. tena...... (5-1--79)
1179. tam...... (5-1--80)
1180. tena....... (5-1--93)
1181. tadasya.... (5-1--91)
1182. tasya...... (5-1--95)
1183. tatra...... (5-1--96)
1184. sampādini.. (5-1--99)
1185. tasmai..... (5-1-101)
1186. samaya..... (5-1-104)
1187. prayojanam (5-1-109)
1188. tena....... (5-1-115)
1189. tatra...... (5-1-116)
1190. tadarham (5-1-117)
1191. tasya...... (5-1-119)
1192. ā ca tvāt (5-1-120)
1193. pṛthvā..... (5-1-122)
1194. ṭeḥ (6-4-155)
1195. ra ṛto..... (6-4-161)
1196. varṇa...... (5-1-123)
1197. guṇa...... (5-1-124)
1198. stenād..... (5-1-125)
1199. sakhyuryaḥ (5-1-126)
1200. kapi....... (5-1-127)
(*Rup* Part I, pp. 267 to 274)
1201. patyanta... (5-1-128)
1202. hāyanā..... (5-1-130)
1203. igantācca.. (5-1-131)
1204. yopadhād.. (5-1-132)
1205. dvandva.... (5-1-133)
1206. brahmaṇa... (5-1-136)
1207. dhānyānām.. (5-2---1)
1208. vrīhi...... (5-2---2)

1209. yava.......	(5-2---3)	1238. vatorithuk	(5-2--53)
1210. vibhāṣā....	(5-2---4)	(*Rup* Part I, pp. 274 to 282)	
1211. tata......	(5-2---7)	1239. dvestīyaḥ	(5-2--54)
1212. āprapadam..	(5-2---8)	1240. tres.......	(5-2--55)
1213. anupada....	(5-2---9)	1241. vimśat.....	(5-2--56)
1214. adhvano....	(5-2--16)	1242. nityam.....	(5-2--57)
1215. ātmā.......	(6-4-169)	1243. ṣaṣṭyā.....	(5-2--58)
1216. sāpta......	(5-2--22)	1244. tatra......	(5-2--63)
1217. tasya......	(5-2--24)	1245. ākarṣādi...	(5-2--64)
1218. pakṣāt tiḥ	(5-2--25)	1246. dhana......	(5-2--65)
1219. tena.......	(5-2--26)	1247. svāṅge.....	(5-2--66)
1220. haiyaṅga...	(5-2--23)	1248. tadasyā....	(5-2--94)
1221. veḥ........	(5-2--28)	1249. mād.......	(8-2---9)
1222. sam........	(5-2--29)	1250. tasau.....	(1-4--19)
1223. upā........	(5-2--34)	1251. prāṇi.....	(5-2--96)
1224. karmaṇi....	(5-2--35)	1252. siddhmā....	(5-2--97)
1225. tadasya....	(5-2--36)	1253. vatsā.....	(5-2--98)
Rep. pramāṇe...	(No. 431)	1254. phenād.....	(5-2--99)
1226. puruṣa.....	(5-2--38)	1255. lomādi.....	(5-2-100)
Rep. inaṇy......	(No. 937)	1256. prajñā.....	(5-2-101)
1227. yattad.....	(5-2--39)	1257. tapas.....	(5-2-102)
Rep. ā sarva....	(No. 808)	1258. aṇ ca	(5-2-103)
1228. kimidam....	(5-2--40)	1259. sikatā.....	(5-2-104)
Rep. idam......	(No. 807)	1260. deśe.......	(5-2-105)
Rep. kimaḥ......	(No. 218)	1261. danta......	(5-2-106)
Rep. saṅkhyāyā..	(No. 432)	1262. ūṣa........	(5-2-107)
1229. dvitri.....	(5-2--43)	1263. keśād......	(5-2-109)
1230. ubhād......	(5-2--44)	1264. rajaḥ.....	(5-2-112)
1231. tadasmin...	(5-2--45)	1265. danta......	(5-2-113)
1232. śadanta....	(5-2--46)	1266. jyotsnā....	(5-2-114)
1233. saṅkhyāyā..	(5-2--47)	1267. ata........	(5-2-115)
1234. tasya.......	(5-2--48)	1268. vrīhyādi...	(5-2-116)
1235. nāntād.....	(5-2--49)	1269. tundādi....	(5-2-117)
1236. ṣaṭkati....	(5-2--51)	1270. ekago.....	(5-2-118)
1237. bahu......	(5-2--52)	1271. śata.....	(5-2-119)

1272. rūpād...... (5-2-120)
1273. asmāya..... (5-2-121)
1274. jhayaḥ (8-2--10)
1275. vāco gminiḥ (5-2-124)
1276. ālaj...... (5-2-125)
1277. arśa...... (5-2-127)
1278. svāmin.... (5-2-126)
1279. vātā...... (5-2-129)
1280. hastā...... (5-2-133)
(*Rup* Part I, pp. 282 to 288)
1281. tundi...... (5-2-139)
1282. aham...... (5-2-140)
1283. prāg....... (5-3---1)
1284. kim....... (5-3---2)
1285. ku tihoḥ (7-2-104)
1286. taddhita... (1-1--38)
1287. idama iś (5-3---3)
1288. etadoś (5-3---5)
1289. tasilādi... (6-3--35)
1290. pañcamyā... (5-3---7)
1291. paryapi.... (5-3---9)
1292. saptamyā... (5-3--10)
1293. kimot (5-3--12)
1294. kvāti (7-2-105)
1295. itarā...... (5-3--14)
1296. idamo haḥ (5-3--11)
1297. sarvai..... (5-3--15)
1298. sarvasya... (5-3---6)
1299. idamorhil (5-3--16)
1300. etaitau.... (5-3---4)
1301. adhunā..... (5-3--17)
1302. dāmīñca (5-3--18)
1303. tadc....... (5-3--19)
1304. anadya..... (5-3--21)
1305. sadyaḥ..... (5-3--22)
1306. prakāra.... (5-3--23)
1307. idam....... (5-3--24)
1308. kimaśca (5-3--25)
1309. dik....... (5-3--27)
1310. pūrvā...... (5-3--39)
1311. astāti ca (5-3--40)
1312. vibhāṣā.... (5-3--41)
1313. dakṣiṇo.... (5-3--28)
1314. uttarā..... (5-3--34)
1315. enabanya... (5-3--35)
1316. vibhāṣā.... (5-3--29)
1317. añcerluk (5-3--30)
1318. uparyupa... (5-3--31)
1319. paścāt (5-3--32)
1320. dakṣiṇādāc (5-3--36)
1321. āhi ca dūre (5-3--37)
1322. uttarācca (5-3--38)
1323. pūrvā...... (5-3--39)
1324. saṅkhyāyā.. (5-3--42)
1325. adhikaraṇa.. (5-3--43)
1326. ekāddho...... (5-3--44)
(*Rup* Part I, pp. 288 to 294)
1327. dvi....... (5-3--45)
1328. edhācca (5-3--46)
1329. yāpye...... (5-3--47)
1330. ekād...... (5-3--52)
1331. bhūta...... (5-3--53)
1332. saṣṭyā..... (5-3--54)
1333. ātiśāyane.. (5-3--55)
1334. tiṅaśca (5-3--56)
Rep. tarap...... (No. 104)
1335. kimettiṅ... (5-4--11)
1336. dvivacana.. (5-3--57)
1337. ajādi..... (5-3--58)
Rep. gharūpa.... (No. 105)

1338. praśasya... (5-3--60)
1339. prakṛ...... (6-4-163)
1340. jya ca (5-3--61)
1341. jyādād..... (6-4-160)
1342. vṛddhasya ca (5-3--62)
1343. antika...... (5-3--63)
1344. yuvā........ (5-3--64)
1345. sthūla...... (6-4-156)
1346. vinmator... (5-3--65)
Rep. ra ṛto..... (No. 1195)
1347. priya..... (6-4-157)
1348. bahor..... (6-4-158)
1349. iṣṭhasya... (6-4-159)
1350. praśam.... (5-3--66)
1351. īṣad...... (5-3--67)
1352. vibhāṣā.... (5 3--68)
1353. prakāra.... (5-3--69)
1354. prāgivāt kaḥ (5-3--70)
Rep. avyaya...... (No. 173)
1355. ajñāte (5-3--73)
1356. kutsite (5-3--74)
1357. anukampāyām (5-3--76)
1358. alpe (5-3--85)
1359. hrasve (5-3--86)
1360. pratyaya... (7-3--44)
1361. na yāsayoḥ (7-3--45)
1362. udīcām..... (7-3--46)
1363. bhastrai... (7-3--47)
1364. abhāṣita... (7-3--48)
(*Rup* Part I, pp. 295 to 302)
1365. ādācāryāṇām (7-3--49)
Rep. na kapi (No. 726)
Rep. āpo........ (No. 728)
1366. kimyat..... (5-3--92)
1367. vā........ (5-3--93)
1368. katara..... (2-1--63)
1369. ekācca..... (5-3--94)
1370. avakṣepaṇe.. (5-3--95)
1371. ive........ (5-3--96)
1372. saṅkhyāyāḥ.. (5-4-17)
1373. dvitri...... (5-4-18)
1374. ekasya..... (5-4--19)
1375. vibhāṣā.... (5-4--20)
1376. tat........ (5-4--21)
1377. ananta..... (5-4--23)
1378. pāda....... (5-4--25)
1379. atitherñyaḥ (5-4--26)
1380. yāva....... (5-4--29)
1381. vinayādi... (5-4--34)
1382. tadyuktat.. (5-4--36)
1383. prajñā..... (5-4--38)
1384. mṛdastikan (5-4--39)
1385. sasnau..... (5-4--40)
1386. bahva...... (5-4--42)
1387. saṅkhyai... (5-4--43)
1388. prati...... (5-4--44)
1389. apādāne.... (5-4--45)
1390. abhūta..... (5-4--50)
1391. asya cvau ca (7-4--32)
1392. arurmana.... (5-4--51)
1393. cvau ca (7-4--26)
1394. vibhāṣā.... (5-4--52)
1395. tadadhīna.. (5-4--54)
1396. deye trā ca (5-4--55)
1397. avyaktā.... (5-4--57)
1398. sapatra.... (5-4--61)
1399. sukha...... (5-4--63)
1400. dukhāt...... (5-4--64)
1401. śūlāt pāke (5-4--65)
1402. satyād.... (5-4--66)

1403. madrāt.... (5-4--67)
(*Rup* Part I, pp. 302 to 308)

DHĀTUPRATYAYAPAÑCIKĀ

anubandhādi (4 rules) :

1404. tiptas..... (3-4--78)
1405. laḥ........ (1-4--99)
1406. taṅānāv.... (1-4-100)
1407. laḥ........ (3-4--69)

SĀRVADHĀTUKAPARICCHEDA (263 rules)

Rep. bhūvā...... (No. 184)
1408. vartamāne.. (3-2-123)
1409. lasya (3-4--77)
Rep. tiptas..... (No. 1404)
1410. śeṣāt...... (1-3--78)
1411. tiṅas...... (1-4-101)
1412. śeṣe....... (1-1-108)
1413. tānyeka.... (1-4-102)
Rep. dvekayor... (No. 101)
1414. tiṅśit..... (3-4-113)
1415. kartari.... (3-1--68)
1416. sārva...... (7-3--84)
Rep. bahuṣu..... (No. 133)
1417. jhontaḥ (7-1---3)
Rep. ato guṇe (No. 121)
1418. yuṣmad..... (1-4-105)
1419. asmad...... (1-4-107)
1420. ato dīrgho.. (7-3-101)
1421. anudātta... (1-3--12)
Rep. aco....... (No. 54)
1422. ṭita....... (3-4--79)
1423. sārva..... (1-2---4)
1424. āto ṅitaḥ (7-2--81)
Rep. lopo....... (No. 883)
1425. thāsasse (3-4--80)
Rep. ādirñi...... (No. 253)
1426. svarita.... (1-3--72)
1427. viparā..... (1-3--19)
1428. dhātvādeḥ.. (6-1--64)
Rep. ṇo naḥ (No. 225)
Rep. upasargāḥ.. (No. 235)
Rep. gatiśca (No. 236)
Rep. te prāg.... (No. 237)
Rep. upasargād.. (No. 418)
1429. nisam...... (1-3--30)
(*Rup* Part II, pp. 1 to 11)
1430. spardhā.... (1-3--31)
1431. idito...... (7-1--58)
1432. puganta.... (7-3--86)
1433. krīḍo...... (1-3--21)
1434. ūdupadhā... (6-4--89)
1435. kṛpo ro laḥ (8-2--18)
1436. radhi...... (7-1--61)
1437. ṣṭivu...... (7-3--75)
1438. anupasargā.. (1-3--43)
1439. kramaḥ..... (7-3--76)
1440. āṅa........ (1-3--40)
1441. propā...... (1-3--42)
1442. iṣugami.... (7-3--77)
1443. pāghrā..... (7-3--78)
1444. śadeśśitaḥ (1-3--60)
1445. sadirapratеḥ (8-3--66)
1446. damśa...... (6-4--25)
1447. upasargād.. (8-3--65)
1448. rañjeśca (6-4--26)
1449. gupū...... (3-1--28)
1450. sanādyantā.. (3-1--32)
1451. ārdha...... (3-4-114)
Rep. puganta.... (No. 1432)

1452. āyādaya.... (3-1--31)
1453. ṛterīyaṅ (3-1--29)
1454. kamerṇiṅ (3-1--30)
1455. ata....... (7-2-116)
1456. adi....... (2-4--72)
Rep. sārva...... (No. 1423)
1457. kṅiti ca (1-1---5)
1458. śīṅah (7-4--21)
1459. ātma....... (7-1---5)
1460. śīṅo ruṭ (7-1--6)
1461. bruva īṭ (7-3--93)
1462. bruvaḥ..... (3-4--84)
1463. āhasthaḥ (8-2--35)
1464. anudātto... (6-4--37)
1465. gama...... (6-4--98)
Rep. ho hanter.. (No. 335)
1466. acaḥ....... (1-1--57)
(*Rup* Part II, p. 11 to 18)
1467. vamorvā.... (8-4--23)
1468. āṅo....... (1-3--28)
1469. ṣadoḥ...... (8-2--41)
1470. jhaṣa...... (8-2--40)
Rep. ekāco...... (No. 308)
1471. nergada.... (8-4--17)
1472. ḍho ḍhe.... (8-3--13)
1473. sko....... (8-2--29)
1474. īḍajanor... (7-2--78)
1475. īśasse (7-2--77)
1476. dhi ca (8-2--25)
1477. vā nimsa... (8-4--33)
1478. uto........ (7-3--89)
1479. ūrṇoter.... (7-3--90)
1480. iṇo yaṇ (6-4--81)
1481. vida...... (3-4--83)
1482. samo...... (1-3--29)
1483. vetter..... (7-1---7)
1484. śnasor..... (6-4-111)
1485. tāsastyor.. (7-4--50)
1486. kartari.... (1-3--14)
1487. upasarga... (8-3--87)
1488. sāt........ (8-3-111)
1489. ha eti (7-4--52)
1490. mṛjer...... (7-2-114)
1491. rudādi..... (7-2--76)
1492. aniteḥ (8-4--19)
1493. jakṣi...... (6-1---6)
1494. adabhyastāt (7-1---4)
1495. iddaridra.. (6-4-114)
1496. śnā........ (6-4-112)
1497. śāsa...... (6-4--34)
1498. śāsi...... (8-3--60)
1499. grahi..... (6-1--16)
1500. juhotyādi.. (2-4--75)
1501. ekāco..... (6-1---1)
1502. ajāder..... (6-1---2)
1503. ślau (6-1--10)
1504. pūrvo..... (6-1---4)
1505. kuho ścuḥ..... (7-4---62)
1506. abhyāse.... (8-4--54)
1507. ubhe....... (6-1---5)
(*Rup* Part II, pp. 18 to 26)
1508. husnu...... (6-4--87)
1509. bhṛñāmit (7-4--76)
1510. īhalyaghoḥ (6-4-113)
1511. hrasvaḥ (7-4--59)
1512. dādhā...... (1-1--20)
1513. dadhas..... (8-2--38)
1514. bhiyo..... (6-4-115)
1515. halādi...... (7-4--60)
1516. āṅo........ (1-3--20)

1517. ṇijām...... (7-4--75)
1518. jahāteśca (6-4--116)
1519. arti....... (7-4--77)
1520. abhyāsa.... (6-4--78)
1521. udoṣṭhya... (7-1-102)
1522. hali ca (8-2--77)
1523. urat (7-4--66)
1524. divādi..... (3-1--69)
Rep. hali ca (No. 1522)
Rep. dhātvādeḥ (No. 1428)
1525. pari...... (8-3--70)
1526. vā bhrāśa.. (3-1--70)
1527. otaḥ śyani (7-3--71)
1528. jñā....... (7-3--79)
1529. parermṛṣaḥ (1-3--82)
Rep. aniditām... (No. 366)
1530. śamām...... (7-3--74)
1531. yaso...... (3-1--71)
1532. samyasaśca (3-1--72)
1533. mider...... (7-3--82)
1534. svādi...... (3-1--73)
1535. lopaścā.... (6-4-107)
1536. hinu....... (8-4--15)
1537. śruvaḥ..... (1-3--29)
Rep. samo...... (No. 1482)
Rep. aniditam... (No. 366)
1538. akṣo....... (3-1--75)
1539. tanūkaraṇe (3-1--76)
1540. mriyater... (1-3-61)
1541. riṅ........ (7-4--28)
1542. avātgraḥ (1-3--51)
1543. aci....... (8-2--21)
1544. samaḥ...... (1-3--52)
(*Rup* Part II, pp. 26 to 37)
1545. nerviśaḥ (1-3--17)
1546. śe........ (7-1--59)
1547. rudhādi.... (3-1--78)
Rep. śnasor..... (No. 1484)
Rep. jharo..... (No. 77)
1548. bhujonavane (1-3--66)
1549. propā...... (1-3--64)
1550. śnānnalopaḥ (6-4--23)
1551. tṛṇaha im (7-3--92)
1552. tanādi..... (3-1--79)
1553. tanādi..... (2-4--79)
1554. ata ut..... (6-4-110)
Rep. na....... (No. 1118)
1555. nityam.... (6-4-108)
1556. anuparā.... (1-3--79)
1557. dhinvi..... (3-1---8)
1558. ato lopaḥ (6-4--48)
1559. kryādi..... (3-1--81)
1560. pari...... (1-3--18)
Rep. grahi...... (No. 1499)
Rep. hinu...... (No. 1536)
1561. pvādīnām... (7-3--80)
Rep. halaḥ (No. 240)
Rep. jñājanorjñā (No. 1528)
1562. samprati... (1-3--46)
1563. anupasargād.. (1-3-76)
1564. stambhu...... (3-1-82)
1565. satyā........ (3-1--25)
Rep. sanādyantā.. (No. 1450)
1566. ṇicaśca (1-3--74)
Rep. ata....... (No. 1455)
1567. mitām...... (6-4--92)
1568. arti....... (7-3--36)
1569. upadhāyāśca (7-1-101)
1570. upadhāyām ca (8-2--78)
1571. gṛdhi....... (1-3--69)

Rep. gupū......	(No. 1449)	1600. suṭkāt....	(6-1-135)
Rep. āyādaya.....	(No. 1452)	1601. ṛtaśca.....	(7-2--43)
1572. līlor......	(7-3--39)	1602. gunorti....	(7-4--29)
1573. vibhāṣā....	(6-1--51)	1603. aḍābhyāsa..	(6-1-136)
1574. līyaḥ......	(1-3--70)	1604. loṭ ca	(3-3-162)
Rep. acaḥ......	(No. 1466)	1605. āśiṣi......	(3-3-173)
(*Rup* Part II, pp. 38 to 49)		1606. eruḥ	(3-4--86)
1575. bhūte	(3-2--84)	1607. tuhyoḥ.....	(7-1--35)
1576. anadyatane..	(3-2-111)	1608. loṭo laṅvat	(3-4--85)
1577. luṅlaṅ.....	(6-4--71)	1609. serhyapicca	(3-4--87)
1578. itaśca	(3-4-100)	1610. ato heḥ	(6-4-105)
1579. tasthas....	(3-4-101)	1611. merniḥ	(3-4--89)
Rep. saṃyogā....	(No. 30)	1612. āḍutta.....	(3-4--92)
1580. nityam.....	(3-4--99)	1613. āmetaḥ	(3-4--90)
1581. āḍajādīnām	(6-4--72)	1614. savābhyām..	(3-4--91)
Rep. āṭaśca	(No. 233)	1615. eta ai	(3-4--93)
1582. adas........	(7-3-100)	1616. sammānano..	(1-3--36)
1583. dviṣaśca	(3-4-112)	(*Rup* Part II, pp. 51 to 76)	
1584. guṇo.......	(7-3--91)	1617. kartṛsthe..	(1-3--37)
1585. asiddhavad..	(6-4-22)	1618. vyāṅ.......	(1-3--83)
1586. laṅa.......	(3-4-111)	1619. upācca	(1-3--84)
1587. usyapadā...	(6-1--96)	1620. vibhāṣā....	(1-3--85)
1588. sija.......	(3-4-109)	1621. vṛtti......	(1-3--38)
1589. daśca	(8-2--75)	1622. upaparā....	(1-3--39)
Rep. vetter.....	(No. 1483)	1623. veḥ........	(1-3--41)
1590. asti.......	(7-3--96)	1624. samava.....	(1-3--22)
1591. rudaśca....	(7-3--98)	1625. prakāśana..	(1-3--23)
1592. aḍgārgya...	(7-3--99)	1626. udo	(1-3--24)
1593. jāgro......	(7-3--85)	1627. upān.......	(1-3--25)
1594. tipya......	(8-2--73)	1628. akarma.....	(1-3--26)
1595. sipi.......	(8-2--74)	1629. udaścara...	(1-3--53)
1596. yīvarṇa....	(7-4--53)	1630. sama.......	(1-3--54)
1597. nābhyasta..	(7-3--87)	1631. dāṇaśca....	(1-3--55)
1598. savādīnām..	(8-3--71)	1632. upādyamaḥ..	(1-3--56)
1599. sam........	(6-1-137)	1633. bhāsano....	(1-3--47)

1634. vyaktā..... (1-3--48)
1635. hujhal..... (6-4-101)
1636. hanterjaḥ (6-4--36)
1637. vidām...... (3-1--41)
1638. ghvasor.... (6-4-119)
1639. śā hau (6-4--35)
1640. ā ca hau (6-4-117)
1641. utaśca..... (6-4-106)
1642. halaśśna... (3-1--83)
1643. vidhi...... (3-3-161)
1644. yāsuṭ...... (3-4-103)
1645. liṅa....... (7-2--79)
1646. ato yeyaḥ (7-2--80)
1647. jherjus (3-4-108)
1648. liṅas...... (3-4-102)
1649. jhasya..... (3-4-105)
1650. iṭot (3-4-106)
Rep. usyapadā... (No. 1587)
1651. lopo yi (6-4-118)
1652. ye ca (6-4-109)
Rep. laḥ........ (No. 1407)
1653. bhāva...... (1-3--13)
1654. sārva...... (3-1--67)
Rep. ādeca....... (No. 234)
1655. vaci....... (6-1--15)
(*Rup* Part II, pp. 77 to 101)
1656. ārdhadhātuke (6-4-46)
Rep. ato lopaḥ (No. 1558)
1657. ayaṅ........ (7-4--22)
1658. bruvo...... (2-4--53)
1659. akṛt....... (7-4--25)
1660. ghumā...... (6-4--66)
1661. tanoter.... (6-4--44)
Rep. guṇorti... (No. 1602)
1662. ṇeraniṭi (6-4--51)
1663. ye vibhāṣā (6-4--43)
1664. asterbhūḥ (2-4--52)
1665. cakṣiṅaḥ... (2-4--54)
1666. ajer....... (2-4--56)
1667. upasargād.. (7-4--23)
1668. karmavat... (3-1--87)
1669. na duha.... (3-1--89)
1670. kuṣi....... (3-1--90)

ĀRDHADHĀTUKAPARIC-CHEDA (194 rules)

1671. kidāśiṣi (3-4-104)
1672. liṅāśiṣi (3-4-116)
1673. ārdha...... (7-2--35)
1674. suṭ tithoḥ (3-4-107)
1675. ekāca...... (7-2--10)
1676. iṇaḥ....... (8-3--78)
1677. vibhāṣeṭaḥ (8-3--79)
1678. svarati.... (7-2--44)
1679. liṅsicā.... (1-2--11)
1680. snukramor.. (7-2--36)
1681. erliṅi (6-4--67)
1682. vānyasya... (6-4--68)
1683. hano...... (2-4--42)
1684. vibhāṣorṇoḥ (1-2---3)
1685. eterliṅi (7-4--24)
Rep. naho dhaḥ (No. 381)
1686. uśca (1-2--12)
Rep. liṅsicā... (No. 1679)
1687. liṅsicor... (7-2--42)
1688. vṝtō vā (7-2--38)
1689. na liṅi (7-2--39)
1690. graho...... (7-2--37)
Rep. ṛtaśca.... (No. 1601)
1691. parokṣe liṭ (3-2-115)
(*Rup* Part II, pp. 101 to 119)

1692. liṭ ca (3-4-115)
1693. parasmai... (3-4--82)
1694. indhi...... (1-2---6)
1695. bhuvo...... (6-4--88)
1696. liṭi...... (6-1---8)
Rep. pūrvo...... (No. 1504)
1697. bhavateraḥ (7-4--73)
1698. hrasvam laghu (1-4-10)
1699. dīrghañca (1-4--12)
1700. ijādeśca... (3-1--36)
1701. āmaḥ (2-4--81)
1702. kṛnmejantaḥ (1-1--39)
1703. kṛñcā...... (3-1--40)
1704. ām........ (1-3--63)
1705. liṭasta.... (3-4--81)
1706. asamyogā... (1-2---5)
1707. dvirvacaneci (1-1-59)
1708. ata ādeḥ (7-4--70)
1709. ṛcchatyṝtām (7-4--11)
1710. tasmānnuḍ.. (7-4--71)
1711. iḍa........ (7-2--66)
1712. sṝdṝprām... (7-4--12)
1713. dayāyāsaśca (3-1--37)
1714. upasarga... (8-2--19)
1715. uṣavida.... (3-1--38)
1716. ata eka.... (6-4-120)
1717. kṛsṛbhṛ.... (7-2--13)
1718. acasthāsvat.. (7-2--61)
1719. upadeśe..... (7-2--62)
1720. ṛto........ (7-2--61)
1721. thali..... (6-4-121)
1722. ṇaluttamo.. (7-1--91)
1723. tṝphala.... (6-4-122)
1724. rādho...... (6-4-123)
1725. vā jṝ...... (6-4-124)
1726. phaṇañca... (6-4-125)
1727. na śasa.... (6-4-126)
1728. na vyo..... (6-1--46)
1729. liṭya...... (6-1--17)
Rep. iḍa........ (No. 1711)
1730. sanliṭorjeḥ (7-3--57)
1731. liṭya...... (2-4--39)
(*Rup* Part II, pp. 119 to 129)
Rep. śāsi....... (No. 1498)
1732. sahi....... (6-3-112)
1733. veño vayiḥ (2-4--41)
1734. liṭi vayo.. (6-1--38)
1735. vaścā....... (6-1--39)
1736. veñaḥ (6-1--40)
1737. āta au..... (7-1--34)
1738. āto lopa... (6-4--64)
1739. abhyasta... (6-1--33)
1740. vibhāṣā.... (6-1--30)
1741. bhrasjo.... (6-4--47)
1742. dyuti...... (7-4--67)
1743. vyatho liṭi (7-4--68)
Rep. gamahana... (No. 1465)
1744. abhyāsācca (7-3--55)
1745. vā liṭi (2-4--55)
1746. dīrgha..... (7-4--69)
1747. gāṅ liṭi (2-4--49)
1748. śarpūrvāḥ.. (7-4--61)
Rep. uṣavida.... (No. 1715)
Rep. asterbhūḥ (No. 1664)
1749. bhīhrī..... (3-1--39)
1750. dīṅo...... (6-4--63)
1751. dayater.... (7-4---9)
1752. radhādi.... (7-2--45)
1753. anudātta... (6-1--59)
1754. masji,...... (7-1--60)

1755. vibhāṣā.... (7-2--65)
1756. srji....... (6-1--58)
1757. ṛtaśca..... (7-4--10)
1758. aśnoteśca (7-4--72)
1759. vibhāṣā.... (7-3--58)
1760. kās........ (3-1--35)
Rep. āyādaya.... (No. 1452)
1761. ayāmantā... (6-4--55)
1762. luṅ (3-2-110)
1763. māṅi luṅ (3-3-175)
1764. smottare... (3-3-176)
1765. cli luṅi (3-1--43)
1766. clessic (3-1--44)
1767. gātisthā... (2-4--77)
1768. bhū....... (7-3--88)
(*Rup* Part II, pp. 130 to 142)
Rep. dhi ca (No. 1476)
1769. na māṅ yoge (6-4--74)
1770. vada...... (7-2---3)
Rep. asti...... (No. 1590)
1771. jhalo...... (8-2--26)
1772. sassyā..... (7-4--49)
Rep. sahi....... (No. 1732)
Rep. liṅsicā.... (No. 1679)
1773. irito vā (3-1--57)
1774. neṭi (7-2---4)
1775. iṭa īṭi (8-2--28)
1776. puṣādi..... (3-1--55)
1777. ato....... (7-2---7)
1778. dīdhī....... (1-1---6)
1779. yama (5-2--73)
1780. śala...... (3-1--45)
1781. ksasyāci (7-3--72)
Rep. irito vā (No. 1773)
1782. ṛdṛśoṅi.... (7-4--16)
1783. na dṛśaḥ (3-1--47)
Rep. srji....... (No. 1756)
1784. śliṣa...... (3-1--46)
Rep. puṣādi..... (No. 1776)
1785. asyatesthuk (7-4--17)
1786. asyati..... (3-1--52)
1787. dyudbhyo... (1-3--91)
1788. luṅsanor... (2-4--37)
Rep. asyati..... (No. 1786)
1789. vaca um (7-4--20)
1790. pataḥ pum (7-4--19)
1791. lipi........ (3-1--53)
1792. ātmanepade.. (3-1--54)
1793. sarti...... (3-1--56)
Rep. ṛdrśoṅi..... (No. 1782)
Rep. śāsa....... (No. 1497)
1794. jṛstanbhu.. (3-1--58)
1795. sici....... (7-2---1)
1796. stanbheḥ (8-3--67)
1797. prāksitād.. (8-3--63)
1798. śvayateraḥ (7-4--18)
1799. hmyanta.... (7-2---5)
1800. vā gamaḥ (1-2--13)
(*Rup* Part II, pp. 143 to 154)
1801. hrasvād .... (8-2--27)
1802. luṅi ca (2-4--43)
1803. ātmane .... (2-4--44)
1804. hanassic (1-2--14)
1805. yamo (1-2--15)
1806. samudāṅ ... (1-3--75)
1807. vibhāṣa ... (1-2--16)
1808. iṇo gā luṅi (2-4--45)
1809. ātaḥ ... (3-4-110)
1810. vibhāṣā ... (2-4--50)
1811. gāṅ ... (1-2---1)

1812. vija iṭ (1-2---2)
Rep. vibhāṣorṇoḥ (No. 1684)
1813. ūrṇoter . . . (7-2---6)
Rep. ato . . . (No. 1777)
1814. Lugvā . . . (7-3--73)
Rep. ksasyāci (No. 1781)
1815. atolrāntasya (7-2--2)
Rep. dādhā . . . . (No. 1512)
1816. vibhāṣā . . . (2-4--78)
1817. vibhāṣā . . . (3-1--49)
1818. caṅi (6-1--11)
Rep. śvayateraḥ (No. 1798)
1819. sthā . . . . (1-2--17)
1820. añceḥ . . . . . (7-2--71)
1821. stu . . . (7-2--72)
Rep. uśca (No. 1686)
Rep. irito vā (No. 1773)
Rep. ιanādi . . . . . . (No. 1553)
Rep. liṅsicor . . . (No. 1687)
Rep. vṛtō vā (N0. 1688)
1822. sici ca . . . . . . (7-2--40)
Rep. ṛtaśca . . . (No. 1601)
1823. nonayati (3-1--51)
Rep. jāgro . . . . (No. 1593)
1824. ciṇ te . . . . (3-1--60)
1825. ciṇo luk (6-4-104)
1826. dīpa . . . . (3-1--61)
1827. jani . . . . (7-3--35)
1828. ṅiśri . . . (3-1--48)
1829. ṇau . . . (7-4---1)
Rep. caṅi (No. 1818)
1830. sanval . . . . . (7-4--93)
1831. sanyataḥ (7-4--79)
(*Rup* Part II, pp. 154 to 167)
1832. dīrgho . . . (7-4--94)
Rep. ṇeraniṭi (No. 1662)
1833. nandrās . . . . (6-1---3)
1834. anadyadane . . . (3-3--15)
1835. syatāsi . . . . . (3-1--33)
1836. luṭaḥ . . . (2-4--85)
1837. ri ca (7-4--51)
Rep. tāsastyor . . (No. 1485)
Rep. dhi ca (No. 1476)
Rep. ha eti (No. 1489)
1838. tīṣa . . . . . (7-2--48)
1839. soḍhaḥ (8-3-115)
Rep. nergada . . . (No. 1471)
Rep. bhrasjo . . . (No. 1741)
Rep. masji . . . (No. 1754)
Rep. ṣṛji . . . (No. 1756)
Rep. anudātta . . . (No. 1753)
Rep. svarati . . . (No. 1678)
Rep. radhādi . . . (No. 1752)
Rep. vādruha . . . (No. 311)
1840. luṭi ca . . . (1-3--93)
Rep. kṛpo ro laḥ (No. 1435)
1841. tāsi . . . . (7-2--60)
Rep. graho . . . . (No. 1690)
1842. liṅ . . . . (3-3-139)
1843. hetu . . . . (3-3-156)
1844. bhūte ca (3-3-140)
1845. gameriṭ . . . . (7-2---58)
1846. navṛdbhya . . . (7-2--59)
1847. vṛdbhya . . . . (1-3--92)
Rep. sassyā . . . . (No. 1772)
1848. sesici . . . (7-2--57)
1849. ṛddhanoḥ . . . (7-2--70)
1850. lṛt śeṣe ca (3-3--13)
Rep. sesici . . . . . (No. 1848)
Rep. gameriṭ . . . . (No. 1845)

Rep. vṛdbhya . . . . (No. 1847)
Rep. na vṛdbhya . . (No. 1846)
Rep. luṭi ca . . . . (No. 1840)
Rep. tāsi ca . . . . (No. 1841)
1851. syasic . . . . (6-4--62)
1852. āto yuk . . . . (7-3--33)
(*Rup* Part II, pp. 167 to 177)
1853. ciṇ . . . . . . (6-4--93)
Rep. vibhāṣā . . . (No. 1759)
1854. ciṇ . . . (3-1--66)
Rep. ciṇo . . . (No. 1825)
Rep. sassyā . . . (No. 1772)
Rep. sthā . . . (No. 1819)
1855. nodātto . . . . (7-3--34)
1856. bhañjeśca (6-4--33)
Rep. radhi . . . . (No. 1436)
1857. rabher . . . . (7-1--63)
1858. labheśca (7-1--64)
1859. vibhāṣā . . . . (7-1--69)
Rep. karmavat . . . (No. 1668)
1860. acaḥ . . . (3-1--62)
1861. duhaśca (3-1--63)
1862. na rudhaḥ (3-1--64)
1863. tapo . . . . (3-1--65)
1864. tapas . . . . (3-1--88)

SANNANTAPARICCHEDA
(34 rules)

1865. guptij . . . . . (3-1---5)
1866. sanyaṅoḥ (6-1---9)
1867. mān . . . . . (3-1---6)
Rep. sanyataḥ (No. 1831)
1868. dhātoḥ . . . (3-1---7)
1869. sani . . . (7-2--12)
1870. iko jhal (1-2---9)
Rep. ato lopaḥ (No. 1558)
Rep. ajāder . . . . (No. 1502)
1871. pūrvavat . . . (1-3--62)
Rep. sassyā . . . . (No. 1772)
Rep. gameriṭ . . . . (No. 1845)
1872. sani ca (2-4--47)
1873. iṅaśca (2-4--48)
1874. ajjhana . . . . (6-4--16)
Rep. abhyāsācca (No. 1744)
1875. sanīvanta . . (7-2--49)
1876. janasana . . . (6-4--42)
1877. smipūṅ . . . . . (7-2--74)
1878. oḥ puyaṇ . . . (7-4--80)
1879. kiraśca . . . . (7-2--75)
1880. rudavida . . . (1-2---8)
1881. halantācca (1-2--10)
(*Rup* Part II, pp. 177 to 193)
1882. ralo . . . . . (1-2--26)
Rep. dyuti . . . (No. 1742)
Rep. na . . . (No. 1846)
Rep. vṛdbhya . . . (No. 1847)
Rep. sesici . . . (No. 1848)
Rep. nandrās . . . . (No. 1833)
Rep. ajjhana . . . . (No. 1874)
1883. sani . . . . . . (7-4--54)
1884. atra . . . . . . (7-4--58)
1885. āpjñap . . . . . . (7-4--55)
1886. danbha . . . . . . (7-4--56)
1887. muco . . . . . . (7-4--57)
1888. jñā . . . . . . (1-3--57)
1889. apahnave . . . (1-3--44)
1890. nānor. . . . . (1-3--58)
1891. pratyāṅ . . . . (1-3-59)
Rep. abhyasta . . . (No. 1739)
1892. heracaṅi (7-3--56)
Rep. sanīvanta . . . (No. 1875)

1893. cchvośśūḍ .. (6-4--19)
Rep. bhrasjo .... (No. 1741)
1894. stauti .... (8-3--61)
1895. tanoter .... (6-4--17)
Rep. stauti ... (No. 1894)
1896. sunoteḥ .... (8-3-117)
1897. ṝta .... (7-1-100)
1898. iṭ sani .... (7-2--41)
Rep. vṝto vā (No. 1688)

YAṆPARICCHEDA (28 rules)

1899. dhāto ..... (3-1--22)
1900. guṇo ..... (7-4--82)
1901. dīrgho ..... (7-4--83)
1902. nugato ..... (7-4--85)
1903. yaṅi ca (7-4--30)
1904. nityam ..... (3-1--23)
Rep. nugato ..... (No. 1902)
1905. lupa ..... (3-1--24)
1906. cara ..... (7-4--87)
1907. utpara ..... (7-4--88)
1908. japa ..... (7-4--86)
1909. gro yaṅi (8-2--20)
Rep. dīrgho ... (No. 1901)
(*Rup* Part II, pp. 193 to 203)
1910. yasya ..... (6-4--49)
1911. na dhātu ... (1-1---4)
1912. nīg ...... (7-4--84)
1913. svapi ...... (6-1--19)
1914. na vaśaḥ (6-1--20)
1915. cāyaḥ kī (6-1--21)
1916. liṅyaṅośca (6-1--29)
Rep. vibhāṣā .... (No. 1740)
Rep. ye ..... (No. 1663)
Rep. nugato ..... (No. 1902)
Rep. ayaṅ ...... (No. 1657)
1917. ī ghrā ... (7-4--31)
Rep. heracaṅi (No. 1892)
1918. rīg ...... (7-4--90)
1919. na kava .... (7-4--63)
Rep. rīṅṛtaḥ (No. 926)
1920. sicoyaṅi (8-3-112)

YAṆLUKPARICCHEDA (4 rules)

1921. yaṅoci ca (2-4--74)
1922. yaṅo vā (7-3--94)
Rep. indhi ..... (No. 1694)
Rep. nīg ...... (No. 1912)
1923. ṛtaśca ... (7-4--92)
1924. rugrikau ... (7-4--91)

HETUMANNIC (39 rules)

1925. ḥetumati ca (3-1--26)
Rep. oḥ puyaṇ ... (No. 1878)
1926. śāchā ...... (7-3--27)
1927. hvas ...... (6-1--32)
1928. lopaḥ ...... (7-4--4)
1929. vo ...... (7-3--38)
Rep. līlor ..... (No. 1572)
1930. bhiyo ..... (7-3--40)
1931. bhīsmi .... (1-3--68)
1932. nityam .... (6-1--57)
1933. sphāyo vaḥ (7-3--41)
1934. śader ..... (7-3--42)
1935. ruhaḥ ..... (7-3--43)
Rep. arti ..... (No. 1568)
1936. cisphuror... (6-1--54)
1937. krīṅ ...... (6-1--48)
1938. sidhyater .. (6-1--49)
1939. mīnāti ..... (6-1--50)

Rep. vibhāṣā . . . . (No. 1573)
(*Rup* Part II, pp. 203 to 215)
1940. prajane . . . (6-1--55)
1941. hanasto . . . (7-3--32)
1942. nāg . . . (7-4--2)
1943. doṣo ṇau (6-4--90)
1944. vā citta . . . (6-4--91)
Rep. mitām . . . (No. 1567)
1945. atsmṛ . . . (7-4--95)
1946. nau gami . . . (2-4--46)
Rep. gṛdhi . . . . (No. 1571)
Rep. liyaḥ . . . (No. 1574)
1947. mithyo . . . . . (1-3--71)
1948. budha . . . (1-3--86)
1949. aṇāvakarma . . . (1-3-87)
1950. nigaraṇa . . . (1-3--87)
Rep. aṇāvakarma . (No. 1949)
1951. na pādam . . . (1-3--89)
1952. sravati . . . . (7-4--81)
1953. ṇau ca . . . . . (6-1--31)
Rep. hvas . . . . (No. 1927)
1954. vibhāṣā . . . . (7-4--96)
1955. ī ca gaṇaḥ (7-4--97)
Rep. nāg . . . . . (No. 1942)
1956. ṇau ca . . . . . (2-4--51)
1957. bhrāja . . . . (7-4---3)
1958. tiṣṭha . . . . (7-4---5)
1959. jighra . . . (7-4---6)
Rep. upadhāyā . . . (No. 1569)
1960. urṛt (7-4--7)
Rep. ra ṛto . . . . (No. 1195)
Rep. sthūla . . . . (No. 1345)
Rep. priya . . . (No. 1347)
Rep. prakṛtyai . . . (No. 1339)
Rep. iṣṭhasya . . . (No. 1349)
Rep. praśasya . . . (No. 1338)
Rep. jya ca (No. 1340)
Rep. vṛddhasya . . (No. 1342)
Rep. antika . . . . (No. 1343)
Rep. yuvā . . . . (No. 1344)
Rep. vinmator . . . (No. 1346)
1961. puccha . . . . (3-1--20)
1962. muṇḍa . . . . (3-1--21)
1963. striyām . . . (3-3--94)
(*Rup* Part II, pp. 216 to 227)

PRATYAYAMĀLĀPARICC -HEDA

Rep. yasya halaḥ (No. 1910)
Rep. ṇeraniṭi (No. 1662)

SUBDHĀTUPARICCHEDA (21 rules)

1964. supa . . . (3-1---8)
1965. kyaci ca (7-4--33)
1966. naḥ kye (1-4--15)
1967. aśva . . . . (7-1---51)
Rep. akṛt . . . . . (No. 1659)
Rep. rīṅṛtaḥ (No. 926)
Rep. vānto . . . . . (No. 925)
Rep. pratyayo . . . (No. 995)
1968. kyasya . . . . (6-4--50)
1969. kāmyacca (3-1---9)
1970. upamānād . . . (3-1--10)
1971. kartuḥ . . . . . (3-1--11)
1972. kyaṅ . . . . . (6-3--36)
1973. bhṛśādi . . . . (3-1--12)
1974. lohitādi . . . (3-1--13)
1975. vā kyaṣaḥ (1-3--90)
Rep. avyaktā . . . . (No. 1397)
1976. tasya . . . . . (8-1---2)
1977. nityam . . . . . (6-1-100)

1978. namo .... (3-1-19)
1979. kaṣṭāya ... (3-1--14)
1980. karmaṇo .... (3-1--15)
1981. bāṣpo ...... (3-1--16)
1982. śabda ..... (3-1--17)
1983. sukhādi .... (3-1--18)
Rep. satyā .... (No. 1565)
1984. kāṇḍvādi ... (3-1--27)

TIṆVIBHAKTYARTHA (22 rules)

Rep. luṅ (No. 1762)
Rep.anadyatane (No. 1576)
1985. abhijñā .... (3-2-112)
1986. na yadi. (3-2-113)
1987. vibhāṣā .... (3-2-114)
Rep. parokṣe .... (No. 1691)
1988. haśaśvator ... (3-2-116)
1989. prasne .... (3-2-117)
1990. laṭsme (3-2-118)
1991. aparokṣe ca (3-2-119)
(*Rup* Part II, pp. 227 to 237)
1992. nanu ..... (3-2-120)
1993. nanvor ..... (3-2-121)
1994. puri luṅ ... (3-2-122)
Rep. vartamāne ...(No. 1408)
1995. yāvat ... (3-3---4)
1996. vibhāṣā ... (3-3--5)
1997. kim. .... (3-3---6)
1998. lipsya .... (3-3---7)
1999. loḍartha ... (3-3---8)
2000. liṅ ... (3-3---9)
2001. vartamāna ... (3-3-131)
2002. āśamsāyām ...(3-3-132)
2003. kṣipra ... (3-3-133)
2004. āśamsā ... (3-3-134)
2005. nānādya .... (3-3-135)
2006. bhaviṣyati .. (3-3-136)

K'ṚDANTĀVATĀRA (375 rules)

Rep. dhātoḥ (No. 188)
Rep. kṛdatiṅ (No. 189)
2007. vāsarūpo ... (3-1--94)
2008. laṭas .... (3-2-124)
2009. āne muk (7-2--82)
2010. īdāsaḥ (7-2--83)
Rep. nābhyastā ... (No. 369)
Rep. vā ... (No. 387)
Rep. otaḥ śyani (No. 1527)
Rep. śamām ... (No. 1530)
Rep. pāghrā ... (No. 1443)
2011. sambodha ... (3-2-125)
2012. lakṣaṇa ... (3-2-126)
2013. tausat (3-2-127)
2014. pūṅ ..... (3-2-128)
2015. tācchīlya ... (3-2-129)
2016. iṅ ..... (3-2-130)
2017. dviṣo ..... (3-2-131)
2018. lṛṭassadvā (3-3--14)
2019. kvasuśca (3-2-107)
2020. vasvekāj ... (7-2--67)
2021. vibhāṣā .... (7-2--68)
2022. mvośca (8-2--65)
2023. dāśvān ..... (6-1--12)
(*Rup* Part II, pp. 237 to 246)
2024. bhāṣayām ... (3-2-108)
2025. upeyivān ... (3-2-109)
2026. kṛtyāḥ ... (3-1--95)
2027. tayoreva ... (3-4--70)
Rep. vāsarūpe ... (No. 2007)
2028. kṛtyallyuṭo ... (3-3-113)

2029. tavyat . . . (3-1--96)
2030. arhe . . . (3-3-169)
2031. aco yat (3-1--97)
2032. īdyati (6-4--65)
2033. dhātos. . . . . (6-1--80)
2034. ṛhalorṇyat (3-1-124)
2035. cajoḥ . . . . . (7-3--52)
2036. na kvādeḥ (7-3--59)
2037. aji . . . (7-3--60)
2038. ṇya . . . (7-3--65)
2039. yaja . . . (7-3--66)
2040. vaco . . . (7-3--67)
2041. proyojya . . . (7-3--68)
2042. bhojyam . . . . (7-3-69)
2043. orāvaśyake (3-1-125)
2044. porad . . . . . (3-1--98)
2045. śakisahośca (3-1--99)
2046. gadamada . . . (3-1-100)
2047. avadya . . . . . (3-1-101)
2048. vahyam . . . . . (3-1-102)
2049. aryaḥ . . . . . (3-1-103)
2050. upasaryā . . . (3-1-104)
2051. ajaryam . . . . (3-1-105)
2052. vadassupi . . . (3-1-106)
2053. bhuvo . . . . . (3-1-107)
2054. hanasta ca (3-1-108)
2055. etistu . . . . (3-1-109)
2056. hrasvasya . . . (6-1-71)
2057. ṛdupadhā . . . (3-1-110)
2058. ī ca khanaḥ (3-1-111)
2059. bhṛño . . . . . (3-1-112)
2060. mṛjer . . . . . (3-1-113)
2061. rāja . . . . . (3-1-114)
2062. bhidyo . . . . . (3-1-115)
2063. puṣya . . . . . (3-1-116)
2064. vipūya . . . . . (3-1-117)
(*Rup* Part II, pp. 246 to 252)
2065. padāsvairi . . . (3-1-119)
2066. vibhāṣā . . . . . (3-1-120)
2067. yugyañca . . . (3-1-121)
2068. amāvāsyad . . . (3-1-122)
2069. āsu . . . (3-1-126)
2070. praṇāyyo . . . (3-1-128)
Rep. kartari . . . (No. 190)
Rep. ṇvultṛcau (No. 254)
Rep. yuvoranākau (No. 943)
Rep. pratyaya . . . (No. 1360)
Rep. gāṅ . . . . (No. 1811)
Rep. vija iṭ (No. 1812)
Rep. vibhāṣorṇoḥ (No. 1684)
Rep. hanasto . . . . (No. 1941)
Rep. āto yuk . . . . (No. 1852)
Rep. nodātto . . . . . (No. 1855)
Rep. jani . . . . . (No. 1827)
Rep. radhi . . . (No. 1436)
Rep. radhādi . . . . (No. 1752)
2071. neṭyaliṭi . . . (7-1--62)
Rep. masji . . . . . (No. 1754)
Rep. rabher . . . (No. 1857)
Rep. labheśca (No. 1858)
Rep. tīṣa . . . (No. 1838)
2072. niraḥ kuṣaḥ (7-2--46)
Rep. kṛtya . . . . . (No. 2028)
2073. nandi . . . . . (3-1-134)
2074. igupadha . . . (3-1-135)
2075. ātaścopa . . . (3-1-136)
2076. pāghrā . . . . (3-1-137)
2077. anupasargā . . . (3-1-138)
2078. dadāti . . . . . (3-1-139)
2079. jvaliti . . . . (3-1-140)

2080. śyād . . . . . (3-1-141)	2110. stamba . . . (3-2--24)
2081. dunyor . . . (3-1-142)	2111. harater . . . (3-2--25)
2082. vibhāṣā . . . (3-1-143)	2112. phale . . . (3-2--26)
2083. gehe kaḥ (3-1-144)	2113. ejeḥ khaś (3-2--28)
Rep. śilpini . . . . (No. 459)	Rep. arur . . . (No. 797)
2084. gasthakan (3-1-146)	2114. khityana . . . (6-3--66)
2085. ṇyut ca (3-1-147)	2115. nasikā . . . (3-2--29)
2086. haśca . . . . . (3-1-148)	2116. nāḍī . . . (3-2--30)
2087. prusṛ . . . . . (3-1-149)	2117. udikūle . . . (3-2--31)
2088. aśiṣi ca (3-1-150)	2118. vahābhre . . . (3-2--32)
(*Rup* Part II, pp. 252 to 259)	2119. parimāṇe . . . (3-2--33)
Rep. karmaṇyaṇ (No. 185)	2120. mitanakhe ca (3-2-34)
2089. hvāvāmaśca (3-2---2)	2121. vidhvaruṣo . . . (3-2-35)
Rep. ātonu . . . . . (No. 186)	2122. asūrya . . . . . (3-2--36)
2090. supi sthaḥ (3-2---4)	2123. ugram . . . (3-2--37)
2091. ambāmba . . . (8-3--97)	2124. priya . . . (3-2--38)
2092. tunda . . . (3-2---5)	2125. dviṣat . . . (3-2--39)
2093. predājñaḥ (3-2---6)	2126. khaci . . . (6-4--94)
2094. sami khyaḥ (3-2---7)	(*Rup* Part II, pp. 259 to 266)
2095. gāpoṣṭak (3-2---8)	2127. vāci . . . (3-2--40)
2096. harater . . . . (3-2---9)	2128. pūssarva . . . (3-2--41)
2097. vayasi ca (3-2--10)	2129. sarvakūlā . . . (3-2--42)
2098. āṅi . . . (3-2--11)	2130. mekharti . . . (3-2--43)
2099. arhaḥ (3-2--12)	2131. kṣema . . . (3-2--44)
2100. stamba . . . (3-2--13)	2132. āśite . . . (3-2--45)
2101. śami . . . (3-2--14)	2133. samjñāyām . . . (3-2--46)
2102. adhikaraṇe . . . (3-2-15)	2134. gamaśca (3-2--47)
Rep. careṣṭaḥ (No. 427)	2135. antā . . . (3-2--48)
2103. bhikṣā . . . (3-2--17)	2136. āśiṣi hanaḥ (3-2--49)
2104. purograto . . . (3-2--18)	2137. apekleśa . . . (3-2--50)
2105. pūrve . . . (3-2--19)	2138. kumāra . . . (3-2--51)
2106. kṛño . . . (3-2--20)	2139. lakṣaṇe . . . (3-2--52)
2107. divā . . . (3-2--21)	2140. amanuṣya . . . (3-2--53)
2108. karmaṇi . . . (3-2--22)	2141. śaktau . . . (3-2--54)
2109. na śabda . . . (3-2--23)	2142. pāṇi . . . (3-2--55)

Rep. āḍhya . . . (No. 437)
2143. kartari . . . (3-2--57)
2144. spṛśo . . . (3-2--58)
2145. ṛtvig . . . (3-2--59)
Rep. tyadādiṣu . . . (No. 435)
Rep. pratyayo . . . (No. 995)
2146. satsū . . . (3-2--61)
2147. bhajo . . . (3-2--62)
2148. chandasi . . . (3-2--63)
2149. adonanne (3-2--68)
2150. kravye ca (3-2--69)
2151. duhaḥ . . . (3-2--70)
Rep. ātomanin . . . (No. 187)
2152. anyebhyo . . . (3-2--75)
2153. neḍvaśi . . . (7-2---8)
2154. viḍvanor . . . (6-4--41)
2155. kvip ca (3-2--76)
Rep. chvośśūḍ . . . (No. 1893)
2156. rāllopaḥ (6-4--21)
2157. anunāsika . . . (6-4--15)
Rep. mo no. . . . (No. 322)
2158. supyajā . . . (3-2--78)
2159. kartaryupa . . . (3-2-79)
2160. vrate (3-2--80)
2161. bahulam . . . (3-2--81)
2162. prāti . . . (8-4--11)
(*Rup* Part II, pp. 266 to 273)
2163. manaḥ (3-2--82)
2164. atmamāne . . . (3-2--83)
2165. brahma . . . (3-2--87)
2166. sukarma . . . (3-2--89)
2167. some suñaḥ (3-2--90)
2168. agnau ceḥ (3-2--91)
2169. karmaṇi . . . (3-2--93)
2170. drśeḥ . . . (3-2--94)
2171. rājani . . . (3-2--95)
2172. sahe ca (3-2--96)
2173. suyajor . . . . (3-2-103)
2174. saptamyām . . . (3-2--97)
2175. pañcamyām . . . (3-2-98)
2176. upasarge . . . (3-2--99)
2177. anau . . . (3-2-100)
2178. anyeṣvapi . . . (3-2-101)
2179. ktaktavatū . . . (1-1-26)
2180. niṣṭhā . . . (3-2-102)
2181. niṣṭhāyām . . . (6-4--52)
2182. śvīdito . . . (7-2--14)
2183. oditaśca (8-2--45)
2184. yasya . . . (7-2--15)
2185. āditaśca (7-2--16)
2186. radābhyām . . . (8-2-42)
2187. samyogā . . . (8-2--43)
2188. lvādi . . . (8-2--44)
2189. kṣiyo . . . (8-2--46)
2190. niṣṭhāyām . . . (6-4--60)
2191. śyosparśe (8-2--47)
2192. drava . . . (6-1--24)
2193. prateśca (6-1--25)
2194. vibhāṣā . . . (6-1--26)
2195. śuṣaḥ kaḥ (8-2--51)
2196. paco vaḥ (8-2--52)
2197. kṣāyo maḥ (8-2--53)
2198. prastyo . . . (8-2--54)
2199. anupa . . . (8-2--55)
2200. ti ca (7-4--89)
2201. nuda . . . (8-2-56)
2202. na dhyā . . . (8-2--57)
2203. divo . . . (8-2--49)
2204. nirvāṇo . . . (8-2--50)
Rep. jana . . . (No. 1876)

2205. sphāyaḥ . . . (6-1--22)
(*Rub* Part II, pp. 273 to 278)
2206. pyāyaḥ pī (6-1--28)
2207. vasati . . . (7-2--52)
2208. anjeḥ . . . (7-2--53)
2209. niṣṭhā . . . (1-2--19)
2210. vibhāṣā . . . (7-2--17)
2211. udupadhāt . . . (1-2--21)
2212. pūṇ ktvā ca (1-2--22)
2213. pūṅaśca (7-2--51)
2214. dṛḍhah . . . (7-2--20)
2215. prabhau . . . (7-2--21)
2216. kṛcchṛ . . . (7-2--22)
2217. ghuṣi . . . (7-2--23)
2218. arde . . . (7-2--24)
2219. abheścā . . . (7-2--25)
2220. vādānta . . . (7-2--27)
2221. ruṣyama . . . (7-2--28)
2222. hṛṣerlomasu . . . (7-2--29)
2223. apacitaśca . . . (7-2--30)
2224. ado . . . (2-4--36)
2225. dyati . . . (7-4--40)
2226. śā chor . . . (7-4--41)
2227. dadhāterhiḥ . . . (7-4--42)
2228. do dadghoḥ . . . (7-4--46)
Rep. aca . . . (No. 417)
2229. dasti . . . (6-3-124)
Rep. tayoreva . . . (No. 2027)
2230. ādikarmaṇi . . . (3-4-71)
2231. gatyarthā . . . (3-4--72)
2232. kto . . . (3-4--76)
2233. ñītaḥ ktaḥ . . . (3-2-187)
2234. mati . . . (3-2-188)
2235. ktena . . . (2-2--12)
2236. napumsake . . . (3-3-114)
2237. ākves . . . (3-2-134)
2238. tṛn (3-2-135)
2239. alaṅkrñ . . . (3-2-136)
2240. bhuvaśca . . . (3-2-138)
2241. glāji . . . (3-2-139)
Rep. kṅiti ca . . . (No. 1457)
2242. trasi . . . (3-2-140)
2243. śamitya . . . (3-2-141)
2244. sampṛcā . . . (3-2-142)
2245. vau kaṣa . . . (3-2-143)
2246. prelapa . . . (3-2-145)
(*Rup* Part II, pp. 278 to 286)
2247. minda . . . (3-2-146)
2248. devi . . . (3-2-147)
2249. calana . . . (3-2-148)
2250. anudāttet . . . (3-2-149)
2251. ju . . . (3-2-150)
2252. krudha . . . (3-2-151)
2253. na yaḥ (3-2-152)
2254. sūda . . . (3-2-153)
2255. laṣa . . . (3-2-154)
Rep. jalpa . . . (No. 458)
2256. prajoriniḥ . . . (3-2-156)
2257. jidṛkṣi . . . (3-2-157)
2258. spṛhi . . . (3-2-158)
2259. sṛdha . . . (3-2-160)
2260. bhañja . . . (3-2-161)
2261. vidi . . . (3-2-162)
Rep. iṇṇaśiji . . . (No. 436)
2262. gatvaraśca (3-2-164)
2263. jagarūkaḥ (3-2-165)
2264. yajajapa . . . (3-2-166)
2265. nami . . . (3-2-167)
2266. sanāśamsa . . . (3-2-168)
2267. sṝvandyor . . . (3-2-173)

2268. bhiyaḥ . . . (3-2-174)
2269. stheśa . . . (3-2-175)
2270. yaśca . . . (3-2-176)
2271. bhrāja . . . (3-2-177)
2272. anye . . . (3-2-178)
2273. dhaḥ . . . (3-2-181)
2274. dāmnī . . . (3-2-182)
2275. hala . . . (3-2-183)
2276. arti . . . (3-2-184)
2277. puvas . . . (3-2-185)
2278. uṇādayo . . . (3-3---1)
2279. tumun . . . (3-3--10)
2280. bhāva . . . (3-3--11)
2281. aṇ . . . (3-3--12)
2282. pada . . . (3-3--16)
2283. sṛ sthire (3-3--17)
2284. bhāve (3-3--18)
2285. akartari . . . (3-3--19)
2286. iṅaśca (3-3--21)
2287. upasarge . . . (3-3--22)
2288. sami . . . (3-3--23)
(*Rup* Part II, 286 to 291)
2289. śriṇī . . . (3-3--24)
2290. vau kṣu . . . (3-3--25)
2291. avodor . . . (3-3--26)
2292. pre . . . (3-3--27)
2293. nirabhyoḥ . . . (3-3--28)
2294. unyorgraḥ . . . (3-3--29)
2295. parau . . . (3-3--55)
2296. erac (3-3--56)
2297. ṝdorap (3-3--57)
2298. graha . . . (3-3--58)
2299. ḍvitaḥ . . . (3-3--88)
2300. ktrer . . . (4-4--20)
2301. ṭvitothuc (3-3--89)
2302. yaja . . . (3-3--90)
2303. svapo nan . . . (3-3--91)
2304. upasarge . . . (3-3--92)
2305. karmaṇya . . . (3-3--93)
2306. karma . . . (3-3--43)
2307. ṇacastriyām . . . (5-4--14)
2308. abhividhau . . . (3-3-44)
2309. aṇinuṇaḥ (5-4--15)
Rep. striyam . . . (No. 1963)
2310. titu (7-2---9)
2311. sthā . . . (3-3--95)
2312. vraja . . . (3-3--98)
2313. samjñāyām . . . (3-3--99)
2314. krñaḥ . . . (3-3-100)
2315. icchā (3-3-101)
2316. a pratyayāt (3-3-102)
2317. gurośca . . . . (3-3-103)
Rep. ṣid . . . (No. 264)
2318. cinti . . . (3-3-105)
2319. ātaścopa . . . (3-3-106)
2320. ṇyāsa . . . (3-3-107)
2321. rogā . . . (3-3-108)
2322. samjñāyām . . . (3-3-109)
2323. vibhāṣā . . . (3-3-110)
2324. paryāya . . . (3-3-111)
2325. ākrośe . . . (3-3-112)
Rep. kṛtya . . . . . (No. 2028)
2326. lyuṭ ca . . . (3-3-115)
2327. karaṇā . . . (3-3-117)
(*Rup* Part, II pp. 291 to 298)
2328. pumsi . . . (3-3-118)
2329. cchāder . . . (6-4--96)
2330. avetṛ . . . (3-3-120)
2331. halaśca (3-3-121)
2332. upasarga . . . (6-3-122)

2333. adhyāya . . . (3-3-122)
2334. īṣad . . . (3-3-126)
2335. kartṛ . . . (3-3-127)
2336. āto yuc . . . (3-3-128)
2337. alam . . . (3-4--18)
2338. ktvātosun . . . (1-1--40)
2339. udīcām . . . (3-4--19)
2340. samāna . . . (3-4--21)
2341. na ktvā . . . (1-2--18)
2342. udito . . . (7-2--56)
Rep. ralo . . . (No. 1882)
2343. nopadhāt . . . (1-2--23)
2344. vañci . . . (1-2--24)
2345. tṛṣi . . . (1-2--25)
2346. mṛda . . . (1-2---7)
2347. ktvi . . . (6-4--31)
2348. jānta . . . (6-4--32)
2349. krama . . . (6-4--18)
2350. kliśaḥ (7-2--50)
Rep. pūṅaśca . . . (No. 2213)
Rep. vasati . . . (No. 2207)
Rep. anjeḥ . . . (No. 2208)
2351. lubho . . . (7-2--54)
2352. jṝvṛ . . . (7-2--55)
2353. jahāteśca . . . (7-4--43)
2354. samasenañ . . . (7-1--37)
2355. vā lyapi . . . (6-4--38)
Rep. mīnāti . . . (No. 1939)
Rep. vibhāṣā . . . (No. 1573)
2356. na lyapi . . . (6-4--69)

2357. mayater . . . (6-4--70)
Rep. ado . . . (No. 2224)
2358. lyapi . . . (6-4--56)
2359. vibhāṣāpaḥ (6-4--57)
2360. kṣiyaḥ (6-4--59)
2361. ābhikṣṇye . . . (3-4--22)
Rep. nitya . . . (No. 832)
(*Rup* Part II, 298 to 303)
2362. vibhāṣā . . . (3-4--24)
2363. karma . . . (3-4--25)
2364. svādumi . . . (3-4--26)
2365. anyathaivam . . . (3-4-27)
2366. karmaṇi . . . (3-4--29)
2367. yāvati . . . (3-4--30)
2368. carmodara . . . (3-4--31)
2369. celeknopeḥ . . . (3-4--33)
2370. nimūla . . . (3-4--34)
2371. śuṣka . . . (3-4--35)
2372. samūlaā . . . (3-4--36)
2373. karaṇe . . . (3-4--37)
2374. snehane . . . (3-4--38)
2375. haste . . . (3-4--39)
2376. svepuṣaḥ (3-4--40)
2377. adhi . . . (3-4--41)
2378. kartror . . . (3-4--43)
2379. ūrdhve . . . (3-4--44)
2380. upamāne . . . (3-4--45)
2381. kaṣādiṣu . . . (3-4--46)
(*Rup* Part II, pp. 304 to 306)

2. LIST OF RULES OF AṢṬĀDHYĀYĪ REFERRED TO IN RŪPĀVATĀRA

Rup Part I

1.	svam rūpam . . .	(1-1--68)	p. 2
2.	vyorlaghu . . .	(8-3--18)	p. 12
3.	prakṛtyā .. .	(6-1--115)	p. 13
4.	matuvaso .. .	(8-3---1)	p. 19
5.	pumaḥ .. .	(8-3---6)	p. 19
6.	he mapare vā .. .	(8-3--26)	p. 20
7.	ṇyakṣatriyā .. .	(2-4--58)	pp. 26 & 221
8.	saheḥ sāḍaḥ .. .	(8-3--56)	p. 28
9.	na bhāpū .. .	(8-4--34)	p. 32
10.	ājjaserasuk	(7-1--50)	p. 38
11.	vibhāṣā jasi	(1-1--32)	pp. 39 & 41
12.	vijupe .. .	(3-2--73)	p. 42
13.	samprasāra .. .	(6-3-139)	p. 51
14.	chanda .. .	(6-4---5)	p. 57
15.	kaḍārāḥ .. .	(2-2--38)	p. 84
16.	aṣṭano .. .	(6-1-172)	p. 97
17.	anudāttam .. .	(8-1--18)	p. 126
18.	noṅdhātvoḥ .. .	(6-1-175)	p. 143
19.	vrddho yūnā .. .	(1-2--65)	p. 151
20.	subāmantrite .. .	(2-1--2)	p. 165
21.	saha supā .. .	(2-1--4)	p. 165
22.	diksaṅkhye .. .	(2-1--50)	p. 177
23.	na samjñāyām .. .	(5-4-155)	p.198
24.	gotre .. .	(4-1--98)	p. 221
25.	naḍādibhyah .. .	(4-1--99)	p. 221
26.	yaskādibhyo .. .	(2-4--63)	pp. 221 & 222
27.	dvyacaḥ	(4-1-121)	p. 225
28.	avyayī .. .	(4-3--59)	p. 246
29.	turiṣṭhe .. .	(6-4-154)	pp. 273 & 296
30.	yāthā .. .	(5-2---6)	p. 275
31.	anugvalam .. .	(5-2--15)	p. 276
32.	goṣadā .. .	(5-2--62)	p. 283

33.	vā ha ca . . .	(5-3--13)	p. 290
34.	māna . . .	(5-3--51)	p. 295
35.	upottamam . . .	(6-1-217)	p. 300

Rup Part II

36.	anudattau . . .	(3-1--4)	p. 2
37.	liṭaḥ kānajvā	(3-2-106)	p. 3 & 245
38.	leṭoḍāṭau . . .	(3-4--94)	p. 3
39.	na rapara . . .	(8-3-110)	p. 23
40.	itaśca lopaḥ . . .	(3-4--97)	p. 51
41.	sa uttamasya	(3-4--98)	p. 51
42.	samyoge guru	(1-4--11)	p. 120
43.	mantre . . .	(2-4--80)	p. 120
44.	kṛño dvitīyā . . .	(5-4-58)	p. 121
45.	bhavisyati . . .	(3-3--3)	p. 168
46.	bahulam . . .	(2-4--73)	p. 206
47.	yato nāvaḥ	(6-1-213)	p. 248
48.	pratyapi . . .	(3-1-118)	p. 252
49.	varṣa . . .	(3-4--32)	p. 305

Select Bibliography

I. Original works in Sanskrit

Aṣṭādhyāyī — of Pāṇini, Venkateswar Steam Press, Bombay, Samvat, 1966.

Aṣṭādhyāyīsūtrapāṭha — of Pāṇini, edited with vartikas and ganas by S. Chandrasekhara Sastrigal, Trichirapoly, 1912.

Bhāṣāvṛtti — of Puruṣottamadeva, edited by Srish Chandra Chakravarty, Varendra Research Society, Rajashahi, 1918.

Dhātupradīpa — of Maitreya Raksita, edited by Srish Chandra Chakravarty, Varendra Research Society, Rajashahi, 1919.

Durghaṭavṛtti — of Śaraṇadeva, edited by T. Ganapathy Sastry, T.S.S. 6 Second Edition, 1942.

Kāśikā — of Jayāditya and Vāmana, edited with Hindi Commentary by Sri Narayana Misra, Chowkhamba Sanskrit Series Office, Varanasi Part I, 1969 & Part II, 1972.

Kāśikāvivaraṇapañcikā — of Jinendrabuddhi, edited by Srish Chandra Chakravarti, Varendra Research Society, Rajashahi, in 3 Vols., Vol. I, 1913-16, Vol. II, 1919, & Vol III, 1925.

Mādhavīyadhātuvṛtti — of Sāyaṇa, edited by Ananta Sastri Phadke and Sadasiva Sarma Sastry, Chowkhamba Sanskrit Series Office, Benares, 1934.

Mahābhāṣya — of Patañjali with the commentaries *Pradīpa* of Kaiyaṭa and *Udyota* of Nāgeśabhaṭṭa in 3

Vols. Motilal Banarsidass, Delhi, 1967.

Nirukta of Yāska edited with Hindi Translation by Uma Shankar Sharma 'Rishi,' Chowkhamba Vidyabhavan, Varanasi, Vol. I, Third Edition, 1977.

Padamañjarī of Haradatta, edited by Damodar Sastri (Reprinted from the Pandit), 2 Vols., Benares, 1895.

Pāṇinīyaśikṣā edited with English translation and notes by Manomohan Ghosh, University of Calcutta, 1938.

Paribhāṣenduśekhara of Nageśabhaṭṭa, edited by K.V. Abhyankar, Bhandarkar Oriental Research Institute, Part II, Poona, 1962.

Prakriyākaumudī of Rāmacandra with the commentary *Prasāda* of Viṭṭhala, edited by K.P. Trivedi, Part I, 1925, Part II, 1931, Bombay Sanskrit and Prakrit Series Nos. 78, 82.

Prakriyāsarvasva of Nārāyaṇabhaṭṭa, edited by K. Sambasiva Sastri, Part I, TSS 106, 1931 & Part II, T.S.S. 139, 1938, Part III (Taddhita), edited by V.A. Ramaswami Sastri, T.S.S. 153, 1948. Part IV edited by Suranad Kunjan Pillai, T.S.S. 174, 1958.

Uṇādi, edited by T.R. Chintamani, Madras University Sanskrit Series, No. 7, Part II, 1933.

Prauḍhamanoramā of Bhaṭṭoji Dīkṣita, edited by Pandit Sadashiva Sharma

Shastri, Chowkamba Sanskrit Series, Benares, 1934.

Rūpamālā — of Vimalasaraswathy, edited by Muralidharamisra, Head of the Dept. of Vyakarana, Varanaseyasamskrtavisvavidyalaya, Samvat 2026.

Rūpāvatāra — of Dharmakirti edited by M. Rangacharya, 2 Parts, Part I, Madras, Part II, Bangalore, 1927.

Śabdakaustubha — of Bhaṭṭoji Dīkṣita, Chowkhamba Sanskrit Series, Benares, Part I, 1933, Part II, 1929.

Siddhāntakaumudī — of Bhaṭṭoji Dīkṣita with the commentary *Bālamanoramā* of Vasudeva Dīkṣita and Tattvabodhinī of Jñānendrasarasvaty, edited by Giridharasarma and Paramesvaranandasarma, in 4 Vols. Motilal Banarsidass, 1965.

Uṇādikośa — of Mahadeva Vedantin edited with the Unadisutras by K. Kunjunni Raja, University of Madras, 1956.

Uṇādikośa — of Dayananda Sarasvaty edited by Yudhishtira Mimamsaka, Dharmartha Trust, Karnal.

Vākyapadīya — of Bhartrhari edited by K.V. Abhyankar and V.P. Limaye, University of Poona, 1965.

II. Modern Works

(a) English

Abhyankar, K.V. — *A Dictionary of Sanskrit Grammar*, Gaekwad Oriental Series, 134, 1961.

Agrawala, V.S. — India as Known to Panini, Second edition, Benares, 1963.

Allen, W.S.	*Phonetics in Ancient India*, London, Oriental Series No. 1, 1961.
Aufrecht	*Catalogus catalogorum*, Second edition, 1962.
Avanindrakumar	*Archaic words in Panini's Aṣṭādhyāyī*, Parimal Publications, Delhi, 1981.
Bali Suryakant	*Bhaṭṭoji Dīkṣita His Contribution to Sanskrit Grammar*, Munshiram Manoharlal Publishers Pvt. Ltd., New Delhi, 1976.
Bandhu, Vishwa and Deo Munishwar	*New Vartikas to Panini's Grammar*, Published by Visvesvarananda Institute, Hoshiarpur, India, 1972.
Belvalkar, S.K.	*Systems of Sanskrit Grammar* Bharatiya Vidya Prakashan, Delhi Second Revised edition 1976.
Bhattacharya, Bishnupada	*A Study in Language and Meaning*, Calcutta, 1962.
Burrow, T.	*The Sanskrit Language*, London, 1955.
Cardona, George	*Panini - A Survey of Research*, Motilal Banarasidass, Delhi, First Indian Reprint, 1980.
Chatterji, Kshitis Chandra	*Technical Terms and Technique of Sanskrit Grammar*, Part I, Calcutta, 1948.
Devasthali, G.V.	*Anubandhas of Panini*, Published by University of Poona, 1967.
Dvivedi, H.P.	*Studies in Panini* (Technical Terms of the Aṣṭādhyāyī), Inter India Publications, Delhi, 1978.
Faddegon, Barend	*Studies in Panini's Grammar* (Reprint), Amsterdam, 1963.
Ghosh Batakrishna	*Pali Literature and Language* of Geiger Wilhelm (English Trans-

lation), published by Calcutta University, 1943.

Gode, P.K. — *Studies in Indian Literary History*, Poona, Vol. III, 1961.

Goldstucker, T. — *Panini - His Place in Sanskrit Literature* (Reprint), Chowkhamba Sanskrit Studies, 1965.

Iyer S. Venkitasubramonia — *Narayanabhatta's Prakriyāsarvasva* - A Critical Study, Kerala University, Dept. Publication No. 1, Trivandrum, 1972.

Joshi, Venkatesh Shastri — *Problems in Sanskrit Grammar*, published by Dasteane Ramachandra & Co., Pune, 1980.

Kielhorn F. — *Katyayana and Patanjali - Their Relation to Each Other and to Panini*, Varanasi, 1963.

Kielhorn F. — *Paribhāṣenduśekhara* of Nāgeśabhaṭṭa (English Translation), Bhandarkar Oriental Research Institute, Second Edition, Part II, Poona, 1960.

Kiparsky, Paul — *Panini as a Variationist*, published by the University of Poona, 1979.

Misra, Vidya Nivas — *The Descriptive Technique of Panini*, published by Mouton & Co., The Hague, Paris, 1966.

Mahavir — *Panini as Grammarian*, Bharatiya Vidya Prakashan, Delhi, 1978.

Raja K. Kunjunni — *Indian Theories of Meaning*, Madras, 1963.

——————— — The Contribution of Kerala to Sanskrit Literature, Madras, 1958.

Sarma, K. Madhavakrishna — *Panini, Katyayana and Patanjali*, Shri Lal Bahadur Shastry Rashtriya Sanskrit Vidyapeeth, Delhi, 1968.

Sastry, P.V. Naganatha

	Vaiyakarana Siddhānta Kaumudī, (An analysis in English), Vol. I, Motilal Banarsidass, Delhi, 1974.
Staal, J.F.	*A Reader on Sanskrit Grammarians*, Cambridge, England, 1972.
Sen, Sunitkumar	*Panini ca*, Calcutta Sanskrit College Research Series, Calcutta, 1970.
Varma, Siddheswar	*Critical Studies in the Phonetic Observations of Sanskrit Grammarians* (Reprint), Delhi, 1961.
Vasu, Srisa Chandra	*The Siddhānta Kaumudī of Bhaṭṭoji Dīkṣita*, Vol. I & II (edited and translated into English), Motilal Banarsidass, Delhi, 1962..
________________	*The Aṣṭādhyāyī of Panini* (edited and translated into English), Motilal Banarsidass, Delhi, (Reprint) 1980.
Whitney, W.D.	*Sanskrit Grammar*, 4th Edition, Boston, 1913.

(b) Sanskrit

Dwivedi Janaki Prasada	*Kātantra-Vyākaraṇa-Vimarśaḥ* Sampurnananda Sanskrit Visvavidyalaya, Varanasi, 1975.
Misra, Adya Prasada	*Prakriyākaumudīvimarśaḥ*, published by the Research Institute, Varanasi, 1966.
Pandeya Ramajna	*Vyākaraṇadarśanabhūmikā*, The Superintendent, Printing and Stationary, Allahabad, U.P., 1954.
Sharma, Mahesh Dutt	*Kāśikāvṛtivaiyākaraṇasiddhānta-kaumudyoḥ tulanātmakamadhyayanam*, University of Poona. 1974.
Tripathi, Tirth Raj	*Padamanjaryāḥ Paryālocanam*, published by Bhavana Prakash, New Delhi, 1981.

(c) Hindi

Bhattacarya, Ramasankara	*Paniniy Vyakaran ka Anusilan,* Indological Book House, Varanasi, 1966.
Mimamsaka, Yudhisthira	*Samskrt Vyakaran Sastr Ka Ithihas* Bharatiya Pracya Vidya Pratisthan, Ajmere, Part I, Second Edition, Samvat 2020, Part II, Samvat 2019.
Misra, Remakanta	*Vyakarana Sastr Ka Samksipta Itihas* Chowkhamba Vidya Bhavan, Varanasi, 1966.
Sastri, Kapila Dev	*Samskrt Vyakaran mem Ganapath Ki parampara aur Acary Panini,* Bhartiya Pracya Vidya Pratisthan, Ajmere, Sam 2018.
Sastry Nemichandr	*Acary Hemachandr our unka Sabdanusasan,* Chowkhamba Vidyabhavan, Varanasi, 1963.
Varma, Satyakama	*Samskrt Vyakaran Ka udbhav Our Vikas,* Motilal Banarsidass, Delhi, 1971.
Vedalankar, Raghuvir	*Kasika Ka Samalocanatmak Adhyayan,* Nag Publishers, Delhi, 1977.

(d) Malayalam

Iyer, Ullur S. Paramesvara	*Kerala Sahitya Caritam,* Vol. II, Kerala University Publication, 1962.
Varma, Vatakkumkur Rajaraja	*Keraliya Samskrta Sahitya Caritram,* Vol. III, Mangalodayam, Trichur, 1950.

III. Manuscripts

Rūpāvatāra Mss. No. 368 Mss. of *Nīvi* on the first part of *Rup* (Nos. 526 A, 527 of	Manuscripts Library, Government Sanskrit College, Tripunithura, Kerala.

T.C. Vol. III & 726 of T.P. Vol. III).	Oriental Research and Manuscripts Library, Kariavattom, Trivandrum.
Mss. of *Nīvi* on the second part of *Rūpāvatāra* (Nos. 528, 529 of T.C. Vol. III & 730 of T.P. Vol. III.	
Tatvārthadīpika Mss. Nos. 802 T.P. Vol. III & 525 T.C. Vol. III)	Oriental Research and Manuscripts Library, Kariavattom, Trivandrum.

IV. Journals and Articles

Abhyankar, K.V.	Euphonic Combination of Ṛ and Ḷ with R and L *Indian Linguistics*, Vol. 26, 1966.
Chatterjee, Kshitis Chandra	'How Panini has been misunderstood' *Indian Linguistics*, Vol. 17, 1957.
Iyer, K.A. Subramania	'The Point of View of the Vaiyakaranas,' *The Journal of Oriental Research*, Vol. XVIII, Part II, 1951.
Iyer, S. Venkitasubramonia	'The Difference between Bhaṭṭoji Dīkṣita and Nārāyaṇa Bhaṭṭa with regard to certain phonetic observations,' *Vishveshvaranand Indolological Journal*, Vol. VIII, 1970.
Kielhorn, F.	'Some devices of Indian Grammarians,' *Indian Antiquary*, Vol. XV, 1886 'Notes on the Mahabhasya,' *Indian Antiquary*, Vol. XVI, 1887 'Notes on the Mahabhasya,' *Indian Antiquary*, Vol. V, 1876.
Sastry, K.A. Nilakantha	'A Note on the Rupavatara,' *Journal of Oriental Research Institute*, Madras, July-September 1934.
Wikremsinghe	'The Several Pali and Sinhalese authors known as Dharmakirti,' *Journal of Royal Asiatic Society*, 1896.